Wealth Management in Any Market

Timeless Strategies for Building Financial Security

BISHARA A. BAHBAH

WILEY

John Wiley & Sons, Inc.

Published by John Wiley & Sons, Inc., Hoboken, New Jersey.
Published simultaneously in Canada.

For general information on our other products and services or for technical support,
please contact our Customer Care Department within the United States at (800)
762–2974, outside the United States at (317) 572–3993 or fax (317) 572–4002.

Wiley also publishes its books in a variety of electronic formats. Some content that
appears in print may not be available in electronic books. For more information about
Wiley products, visit our Web site at www.wiley.com.

Library of Congress Cataloging-in-Publication Data:

Bahbah, Bishara A., 1958–
    Wealth management in any market: timeless strategies for building financial
security / Bishara A. Bahbah.
        p.   cm.
    Includes bibliographical references and index.
    ISBN 978-0-470-40528-4 (cloth)
    1. Finance, Personal.   2. Investments.   I. Title.
    HG179.B266 2009
    332.024'01—dc22

                                                                        2008038665

Printed in the United States of America.

10   9   8   7   6   5   4   3   2   1

I am an American by choice, not by birth.

I dedicate this book to the country that has provided me with unlimited opportunities and the prospect of wealth.

This book is a humble attempt to give back to the country and its people that have given me the most prized of all gifts—education, freedom, physical, and financial security—and the ability to work hard and be rewarded accordingly.

Contents

Foreword

Wealth management is a lifelong journey. Like any journey, it helps to know where you want to go and how you want to get there. The route taken will differ for each individual.

It cannot be said often enough: The better and the earlier you plan, the easier it will likely be to reach your financial destination and to secure your future and those of your loved ones. If the journey was a cross-country family vacation, it might be helpful to know the following: what vehicle to use, what roadways to take, and what time to start, rest, or continue, based on the weather forecast, what your average speed will likely be, and what traffic conditions you are likely to face. The same can be said about wealth management. It is equally important to know what vehicle to use and what investments to consider, based on your goals, personal preferences, family dynamics, risk tolerance, and time horizon, as well as possible tax and estate planning ramifications.

As hard as Americans physically work to earn and make money, few people invest the time to develop a wealth management plan that includes a comprehensive financial plan. Such a plan should be in writing and coordinated among a wealth management team that includes an estate planning attorney, a CPA, an insurance agent, a trust officer, and a wealth manager who is also a financial advisor. The team and the plan will allow individuals to have the proper legal framework and the diversified investment vehicles to help achieve one's goals. The financial plan should be comprehensive in nature, aimed at ensuring that all assets are working for the investor in an efficient, risk-adjusted manner. It should be monitored and reviewed on an ongoing basis. The process can seem daunting, considering the myriad of theories on asset allocation, unknown financial outcomes, the complexity of financial vehicles available, and tax and legal structures that tend to change over time. Nobody said it would be easy, but it just got easier.

Dr. Bishara A. Bahbah's book, *Wealth Management in Any Market: Timeless Strategies for Building Financial Security*, successfully navigates individuals through the arduous process of establishing a comprehensive wealth management plan. Investors at all levels—whether they are starting out the long journey of building financial security, are currently accumulating wealth, or are in the wealth distribution phase of their lives—should benefit tremendously from the comprehensiveness and in-depth research and analysis, backed by facts and figures, found in the book.

Depending on your stage in the wealth life cycle, you will find the book as a whole extremely valuable. Some might find certain chapters more relevant and of exceptional benefit to their particular situations. If retirement planning is on your mind—as it should be—you will find strategies and data that will help you build and achieve retirement security. If you are a professional—a physician, lawyer, or businessperson—historically subject to lawsuits more than most, the chapter on asset protection strategies will provide you with unique insights geared to educate you and help you to protect your hard-earned current and future wealth. Irrespective of your level of wealth, you will find the book informative, easy to read and understand, and quite practical.

I have witnessed the author, Bishara A. Bahbah, over the past ten years develop and implement a holistic approach to financial wealth management that is detailed in this book. I know the motivation for this book came from his personal experience in helping individuals and institutions meet their needs. As a practitioner in the wealth management field with an impressive academic background, Dr. Bahbah is unique among his peer of authors who write about financial and wealth management issues. His insights are not just based on study and research but also emanate from years of being a hands-on wealth advisor. Those who have adopted his approach of comprehensive wealth management have found themselves better served by using his timeless strategies for building financial security.

This book is an invaluable resource on wealth management. It discusses what roads to consider and the many pitfalls to avoid. I know that investors, individuals, and institutions at varying levels of wealth, and irrespective of what stage they are at in the lifelong wealth planning cycle, can greatly benefit from the knowledge and insight exhibited in this must-read book.

Enjoy!

Richard Golod
Director of Global Investment Strategies
Van Kampen Investments

Preface

I could not have written this book at a more tumultuous time in the financial markets since the era of the Great Depression. The bursting of the housing bubble, which affected just about every homeowner in the United States; the subprime lending crisis; the ensuing credit crunch and illiquidity in the financial markets; the unprecedented volatility in commodity prices, especially oil and gold, leading to fears of inflation; the collapse of a major brokerage firm, Bear Stearns Cos., and its fire sale to JP Morgan at $2 a share (subsequently raised to $10 a share, forced by market pressure) from $159 a share a year earlier; the bankruptcy of Lehman Brothers, the absorption of Merrill Lynch by Bank of America; the failure of traditional banks; the Federal Reserve's extraordinary interventions, including the fastest and steepest lowering of prime rates in the span of a few short months, to shore up confidence and provide liquidity—all these developments combined contributed to a tsunami of upheaval in the financial markets not only in the United States but also throughout the world. In fact, 2008 emerged as the year that rewrote the book, at least since the Great Depression, with regard to the structure of the financial industry in the United States for years to come.

Despite all this gloom and doom, history has demonstrated time and time again that following these epic-style crises—whether engendered by the Great Depression, wars (World War II, the Korean War, the Vietnam War, the war in Afghanistan against the Soviets, the first Gulf War, and the U.S. invasion of Iraq), the assassination or resignation of presidents, extraordinary inflation over an extended period of time, the Cold War, and the bursting of the technology bubble—the markets recover. The latest housing, credit, and financial crises will be no exception.

These violent and unsettling episodes, however, force us to reevaluate our views on money and investing, help us learn from the mistakes and the excesses of the past, and force us to emerge stronger and wiser. This is not to say that the future will not hold in store for the next generations other types of "unprecedented" financial crises. Such is the course of history.

Reality, however, paints a different and brighter picture. Admittedly, we have not had time to assess the extent of the damage of the most recent crises. We do know that in the last quarter of 2007, U.S. household wealth fell by $533 billion; nevertheless, U.S. household wealth still stood at a staggering $57,718 billion at the end of 2007.[1] As of the latter part of 2007, about $27,500 billion was in liquid net worth (cash, mutual funds, bond etc.), while household debt stood at about $13,000 billion—not a bad balance sheet. And, up until the recent financial crises, liquid net worth has gone up about $700 billion year-over-year.[2]

Notwithstanding all the negative news emanating from the most recent crises, we are living in a financial era characterized by the following:

- An explosion of wealth followed by a sudden and sharp implosion following the financial crisis that began in late 2007
- Concentrated wealth in the hands of a lucky few
- An increased demand for wealth management

Consider the following data from recent studies by CEG Worldwide, Capgemini Consulting, and Merrill Lynch, among other sources:[3]

- The number of U.S. individuals with investable assets of $1 million or more jumped from 2.0 million in 2002 to 3.1 million in 2007 (1 percent of the U.S. population). Some 460 Americans are billionaires—the largest number of billionaires in the world.[4]
- There are 1.1 million families worldwide with a net worth of at least $10 million. It is estimated that, collectively, these families control some $91.7 trillion in assets (2004). By 2008, the number of these families was expected to increase to 1.9 million—a jump of 74 percent—while cumulative wealth is expected to increase to $154.4 trillion. However, no one is able to assess or numerically measure, at this point, the devastating effects of the turmoil in the financial markets which began in last quarter of 2007.
- The world's 1,100 richest people have almost twice the assets of the poorest 2.5 billion. The United States is still home to the world's truly rich.[5]
- One percent of Americans own 50 percent of U.S. household wealth.[6]
- 1.2 million U.S. households have a net worth of at least $5 million, not counting the family's primary residence. There are approximately 110 million households in the United States.[7]
- There are approximately 916,000 families worth $20 million or more, commanding $112.6 trillion—these are the exceptionally wealthy.[8]

CEG Worldwide divides affluent individuals into four levels:

1. The **mass affluent** with investable assets between $100,000 and $1.0 million
2. The **affluent** with investable assets between $1 million and $5 million
3. The **super affluent** with investable assets between $5 million and $25 million
4. The **ultra affluent** with investable assets of more than $25 million[9]

The largest number of affluent individuals are those whose ages range from 55 to 65 (44.5 percent). Those under 55 represent 31.0 percent, while 65 or older represent 24.5 percent.[10] Among the affluent, 67.8 percent are males, while 32.2 percent are females.[11]

Do not quit your job or hope for a lottery ticket to become wealthy.

The main source of wealth among affluent individuals is:

- Their jobs (44.9 percent)
- Their retirement account rollovers (16.4 percent), clearly job-related as well
- Equity in privately held corporations (21.3 percent)
- Inheritance (9.4 percent)
- The sale of a company (8.1 percent)[12]

Do investors want to work with financial advisors? A vast majority (90.2 percent) of affluent individuals want to work with financial advisors.[13] 42.1 percent have one advisor, 43.7 percent have two advisors, and 14.2 percent have three or more advisors. The tendency is that those with more assets want to deal with more than one advisor[14]—an issue and a concern addressed in Chapter 10 of the book.[15]

Only 13 percent of affluent clients leave their advisors because of the poor performance of their portfolios, while 87 percent state as the main reason for switching advisors is what they perceive as the poor service relationship.[16]

The affluent individual is concerned about three major issues:

1. Taking care of his/her heirs
2. Having enough medical insurance
3. Having a secure retirement[17]

Investors want to deal with wealth managers. The increasing complexity of the evolving financial systems, which extend beyond providing investment advice, is leading clients, people just like you, to prefer the wealth management approach to deal with their financial and other wealth-related issues. A study by CEG's Russ Alan Prince of "middle-class millionaires," those between $500,000 and $5.0 million in liquid assets, has revealed that 77.1 percent prefer working with wealth managers, compared to 18.8 percent that prefer working with a financial advisor or planner, and a mere 4.1 percent that prefer an investment advisor or planner.[18] The more assets individuals have, the more they prefer to work with wealth managers.

As the research in this book reveals, wealth management is complex and entails dealing not only with the ingredients of a successful investment strategy. Wealth management deals with estate planning issues, with learning to save and manage debt, utilizing insurance to mitigate potential liabilities, saving for a comfortable retirement, maximizing the use of gifting, tax planning, and tax-saving strategies, learning how to protect your assets, and selecting a competent wealth management team.

These complex issues are viewed by the wealthy and the not-so-wealthy individuals as too specialized to be managed by one expert. You need a wealth management team, led by an experienced wealth manager who understands these issues, works with tax, trust, and estate planning experts, but is capable, at the same time, of managing and acting as the quarterback of the entire wealth management team and process.

Even though 46.3 percent of advisors identified themselves as wealth managers while others identified themselves according to their investment orientation—financial advisor, investment advisor, financial planner—CEG Worldwide found that only 6.6 percent of advisors are actually wealth managers, while the remaining 93.4 percent were investment-oriented advisors.[19]

What do affluent individuals want from their wealth management team? They want help and guidance with the following:

- Asset allocation, 56.7 percent
- Financial and estate planning, 41.2 percent
- Tax planning, 23.5 percent
- Managing their managers, 1.5 percent want a manager of managers
- Protecting their wealth, 1.0 percent[20]

The twenty-first century has ushered in a new and unchartered era in the investment and wealth management world. We now live in a more complex world, thanks largely to the leaps in advancement in technology; an interconnected global financial, political, and economic system; more complex legal and financial systems; the advancement in science that has extended our life expectancy by decades beyond what it used to be less than 100 years ago, which, in turn, has forced us to either save more to pay for our longer years in retirement or work many years beyond the normal retirement age; and the spiraling cost of health care, which we need more of as we age and live longer. All these and other factors are forcing us to take a new look at how we manage not only our finances, but also our overall wealth being.

This book is a humble attempt to help you, the reader, to better manage your life and future financial security through the prism of wealth management. You do not have to be wealthy or affluent to benefit from learning about the basic principles of wealth management. Wealth, measured by the amount of money that you currently have, is deceptive and misleading. You need to know the basics of wealth management, because if you are a typical American, you continually strive to improve yourself, and the lives of your children and your grandchildren. And, living in this great land of opportunity, wealth is awaiting anyone who works hard and is determined to succeed.

Prepare yourself. Learn. And, enjoy reading this book and using it as a reference or a guide for comprehending the basics of wealth management in the twenty-first century.

Author's Note

The year 2008 has been described as one of the most volatile and challenging years for investors in financial market history. It was a year that also rewrote global financial history. The year was described as the year of the Great Meltdown, the worst year since the Great Depression, the year of panic, the year of terror on Wall Street, and a year of unprecedented calamities in the history of the financial markets. All these descriptions were not without justifiable reasons. Consider the following events and statistics:

- As of 9 October 2008, the Dow Jones Industrials was down 36.29 percent; the S&P 500 was down 39.10 percent, and the NASDAQ was down 37.81 percent since the beginning of the year. By comparison, the MSCI EAFE Index (representing developed countries outside of the United States) was down 41.37 percent while MSCI EMF Index (emerging markets) was down 50.31 percent.[1]
- The week of October 6 was described as the worst week for U.S. stocks since the Great Depression ended. The Dow Jones was down 18.15 percent and the S&P 500 was down 18.19 percent in the span of five business days. By the end of that week, the S&P 500 was down 42.5 percent from all its all-time closing high, making it the third worst bear market of the last half century.[2]
- The Chicago Board Options Exchange or VIX Index, commonly known as the fear index, rose above 70 for the first time in its history. It had never breached 50 before the week of October 6, 2008. And, Friday, October 10, 2008, the Dow Jones Industrials saw the largest one-day swing in history and traded through a range of 1,040 points.[3]
- Up until 2008, the worst performing decade ever for the S&P 500 was the 1930s and it was down a mere 0.3 percent in total return for the entire 10-year period. The current decade beginning in 2000 and through October 10, 2008, the S&P was down 29 percent in aggregate for the almost 9-year period.[4]
- The U.S. Treasury and the Federal Reserve Bank spearheaded an unprecedented global response to what could prove to be the worst financial crisis in history. Well-known, established financial names such as

Fannie Mae, Freddie Mac, Lehman Brothers, Merrill Lynch, AIG, Washington Mutual, and others were seemingly placed as footnotes to history as the Federal Reserve virtually doubled its balance sheet within weeks to rescue the financial markets.

- The national debt grew to unprecedented levels in 2008. To illustrate this point, aggregate debt to Gross Domestic Product (GDP) rose from 150 percent in the early 1980s to 350 percent by the end of 2007.[5]
- 12 million households, out of a total of 76 million households nationwide that own their home, have mortgages in excess of what their house is currently worth. Florida and Nevada have been the hardest hit. Home prices in Miami and Las Vegas fell respectively by 28.2 and 29.9 percent on an annual basis as of July 2008.[6]
- It is estimated that as of beginning of October 2008, Americans lost an estimated $2,000 billion in their defined benefit 401(k) pensions over the previous 15 months.[7]
- For those who depend on stock dividends to supplement their income, 2008 saw a 557 percent year-over-year increase in companies cutting their dividend in the third quarter. Analysts estimate the total cuts cost investors $22.5 billion.[8]

No wonder that a whopping 53 percent of respondents over age 60 stated that the economic conditions of 2008 were the worst they had experienced. The survey was even taken before the chaotic events of late September/early October of 2008.[9]

Even though the reasons behind the collapse of the financial markets will undoubtedly be the subject of books and journal articles in years to come, JP Morgan Asset Management aptly described the genesis of the crisis as having precipitated by the lack of credit. "Credit is like the oxygen for the economy," because whether an individual needs to buy a car or home, a small business needs to expand to a second location, or a large corporation needs to build a factory, most of these acquisitions are financed through borrowing, not cash.[10] The lack of trust and confidence in lending markets chocked off the ability of consumers and businesses to finance such projects, thus posing a serious hazard to the economy and precipitating in the near-collapse of the financial markets.

The good news is that unlike the era of the Great Depression, the government, represented by the Federal Reserve and the U.S. Treasury, and the U.S. Congress which controls spending in the United States, moved with full force, albeit, with incremental and sometimes hesitating steps. The $700 billion Troubled Asset Relief Program (TARP) was approved by Congress in an attempt to establish liquidity, bail out banks, and buy illiquid mortgage-related securities which, along with the collapse of the housing market and the subprime crisis, led to the financial crisis of 2008. The Federal Reserve was extraordinarily innovative in expanding its balance sheet, lending to both depository and non-depository institutions through its discount window, purchasing commercial paper and accepting a variety of collateral over a variety of time periods for these loans. President George W. Bush stated that his administration was taking "unprecedented and aggressive" steps to address the financial crisis.[11] He said that the U.S. government would purchase equity in financial institutions, guarantee new bank debt, and expand insurance for non-interest-bearing accounts along with increasing substantially the federal insurance on bank deposits. These and other actions by the government, the President declared, "are not intended to take over the free market, but to preserve it."[12]

Given these extraordinary steps, the market is bound to form a base from the October lows. As Pete Seeley, a respected economist with MSIM, noted, "There is a genuine note of hope and optimism . . . Equities are entitled to rally over the next several months. But investors should not get complacent."[13] John Authers of the *Financial Times* described the "U.S. Treasury's move to buy stakes in the biggest U.S. banks as ending the risk of a general banking collapse."[14] As a result, the cost of insuring against default by the largest U.S. banks was roughly cut in half in a matter of days.

What all this means to the investor is a wake-up call, a reality check and a need to focus on the long term. History has shown that fluctuations are part of the market cycle and that long-term investment plans should not be derailed by market fluctuations, even violent ones as we have seen in 2008. Between 1937 and through 2007, the S&P 500 Index, an indicator of the broader U.S. market, delivered an average return of 10.7 percent. The Index experienced 53 positive years (13 of those delivered annual returns ranging from 30.34 percent to 52.27 percent) compared with 28 negative years (only three of those exceeded 22.10 percent in negative returns).[15] Yes, you might discover in down times that your risk tolerance is in reality much lower than you had assumed. Reviewing your allocations by possibly lowering your equity exposure and not succumbing is the way to go. Market timing is dangerous and could derail your long-term growth plans. Selling at the bottom of the markets and parking your investments in cash is a huge mistake. It will rob you of the opportunity to recover when the markets recover.

Although investing is only one component of wealth management, it is nevertheless a critical component. The chapter on investing will provide you with time-proven strategies on how to invest keeping in mind that no one allocation or formula works for everyone. Consult your wealth advisor, conduct a review, and learn from history where after each downturn or recession, no matter how severe, the markets have always recovered.

Wealth management is not only about investing. It is multifaceted and a critical component of your overall wealth being. Use the book as an informational guide to help you build a secure and stable future for yourself and your loved ones.

Acknowledgments

I could not have written this book without the support of innumerable number of people and institutions.

I begin with acknowledging the role of those academic institutions that have invested in my education. The work ethic that I developed at LaSalle High School in Jerusalem's Old City laid the foundation for my future and advanced learning. I was the recipient of a presidential scholarship at Brigham Young University, where I earned my bachelor's degree and was fortunate to have received a full scholarship at Harvard University, where I earned both my master's and PhD degrees.

My investment and financial training took me through prestigious institutions such as the Wharton School of Business, the Business School at the University of Chicago, the American College, and Canon Financial.

The people who deserve my gratitude are those who have helped me learn the business and the concepts, edit segments of this book, and make its writing and publication possible. Among those people of note are: Steve Moore, who was the first to help me understand the need for wealth management and taught me the value and multifaceted uses of insurance; estate-planning attorney John C. Vryhof, who meticulously edited the chapter on asset protection strategies; Ann Couch, a respected CPA, who patiently answered my frequent queries regarding tax and accounting issues; John Sabino, who reviewed the chapters on estate planning and retirement; Dr. Mark Zener, a prominent trust consultant, whose many presentations that I attended helped me understand the complex concepts of wealth management; Mag Black, Bob Magel, Robert Gaines, Kenneth LaFleur, John Kazanjian, Jeff Welday, Henry Kaplan, Anthony Davidow, John Jaber, James Cadet, Esther Grantham, and Sharon Lilikes, who either encouraged me as I was writing this book or who ultimately facilitated its approval for publication by the prestigious Wall Street firm for whom I work; Peter J. Tanous, a prolific author himself, who read the first chapter I wrote and urged me to finish the manuscript and get it published; Theron Raines, someone whom I have never met in person who became my agent and worked hard to secure a prestigious publisher for the manuscript; my associate Adam Sowa and my assistant Rebecca Pekala, who understood my bizarre schedule and erratic working hours that allowed me to dedicate time for my academic and intellectual pursuits; and my special and dedicated assistant Barbara Warnecke who was always ready to help with those tasks that no one wanted to work on.

I cannot but be grateful for my children—Leila, As'ad, Jubran, and Remzi, who took pride in my work and understood when I had to miss out on spending time with them while I was working on this book, literally seven days a week. My mother, Filomene, watched over me from across my huge writing pad laden with piles of books and research papers, and kept asking me if I needed something to eat or more hot coffee. Also, I am fortunate to have an understanding wife, Sibel Uysal, who as a PhD student and a professor-to-be, supported my scholarly pursuit even though it took me away from spending time with her.

Finally, I am thankful for all those individuals, families, and institutions that have placed their trust in me and afforded me the privilege of helping them with all their wealth management needs. Among those who have been strong advocates, special thanks are owed to Carl Hasty, Dr. Walid Alami, Dr. Seuss Kassisieh, Dr. Jacob Musallam, Dr. Maria Colombo-Goldstein, Ahmad Ouri, Dr. Gabe Reuben, Dr. Michael Esber, Felicia Windsor, Bill Chastain, Waleed Hawileh, Bill Jordan, Dr. Dan Beruti, Mack Rayyan, Maher Arekat, Dr. John Swain, Sam Khazen, and Dr. Fadia Habib.

CHAPTER 1

Wealth Management

The Cornerstone of Your Future Security

People often refer interchangeably to investing and wealth management as though they are one and the same. Investing and wealth management are not the same. Investing is only one component, albeit a very important one, of wealth management. According to a study by CEG Worldwide and sponsored by Dow Jones & Co., wealth management is defined as a "consultative process that engenders close client relationships and provides customized solutions tailored to individual needs."[1] Based on the report's criteria, only 6.6 percent of surveyed advisors fit into the wealth management mold, while the rest are investment generalists. Wealth advisors have fewer clients—an average of 101—compared to 269 for the generalists, but their average assets under management are almost twice the assets managed by the generalists. Wealth managers tend to specialize in a particular type of a client; implement a formal review process with prospective clients; provide formal action plans; generate greater number of client referrals; and outsource a much larger percentage of their money management business.[2]

In this chapter, we will identify the 15 most common components of wealth management; discuss the composition of your wealth management team; and concentrate on helping you set your goals and objectives, since all plans have to begin by identifying the needs and charting a course of action to reach your desired objectives.

The Components of a Wealth Management Plan

Wealth management is a comprehensive and disciplined approach geared to meeting your financial and other related wealth-planning needs. The goal of wealth management is to maximize your financial well being through proper planning and by adhering to sound investment principles. It is intended to benefit you, your family, the people you care for, and the causes you believe in. Wealth management is an ongoing and lifelong process, given the changing tax laws, applicable rules and regulations, and your changing goals, priorities, and needs.

Wealth management entails the following 15 steps:[3]
1. Recognize the need for wealth management planning.
2. Identify the components of a successful wealth management plan.
3. Select your wealth management team and define each member's role.
4. Adhere to well-established, scientific, and appropriate investment principles.
5. Establish the legal foundation to execute one's wishes to provide the maximum possible benefits to the heirs through the creation and implementation of an estate plan.
6. Update your beneficiaries and accurately title your assets (bank accounts, home(s), life insurance, and IRA beneficiaries).
7. Properly manage your liabilities/debt.
8. Learn and adopt good financial management habits such as having a budget, living within one's means, and learning to save.
9. Plan for your retirement, health, and long-term care needs.
10. Contribute to the well-being of others by gifting during your lifetime or at death in a tax-advantageous manner.
11. Minimize and manage your tax liabilities.
12. Develop a business succession plan and/or deal with company stock option issues and highly concentrated investment positions whether in specific stocks or certain sectors of the market, such as real estate.
13. Develop and implement an asset protection strategy.
14. Utilize insurance to mitigate against catastrophic losses and to leverage premiums paid for a host of insurance uses and benefits.
15. Select a wealth advisor to oversee your wealth management process and plan implementation.

All of these issues have to be dealt with over the span of your lifetime. They need not be—nor can they realistically be—addressed all at the same time. Wealth management is an evolving and continuous process based on your age, health, wealth, personal and business conditions, goals, and family dynamics.

The Wealth Management Team

No one individual or expert, no matter how knowledgeable they might be, is capable of designing, structuring, and implementing a wealth management plan. In fact, you need a team that includes five specialists:

1. An estate planning lawyer
2. A tax advisor, accountant, or CPA
3. A trust officer or a trust consultant
4. An insurance specialist
5. An investment advisor or, preferably, a wealth advisor

You need a lawyer in order to draft the legal framework of an estate plan—a will, a trust or trusts, and durable powers of attorney—critical components of a wealth management plan. Laws and regulations affecting estate plans differ from state to state. Normally, the state where you reside most of the time is the state whose laws would apply to your estate. Moreover, regulations are constantly changing, either due to the introduction of new laws or because of IRS rulings and interpretations of existing laws. A lawyer, preferably an estate planning specialist, needs to be abreast of the changing legal landscape to ensure the continued legality of an estate plan particularly if it is ever challenged in the courts.

Similarly, tax laws and regulations are constantly changing. A qualified accountant is needed to recommend and implement the tax-related provisions of an estate plan. The key function of an accountant or a tax expert is to help minimize any of your tax liabilities either during your lifetime or at death. Tax avoidance, however, is illegal under U.S. laws.

A trust officer or a trust consultant is an individual that can, along with an estate planning lawyer and a tax advisor, help identify your needs and recommend the type of trust or trusts that would best help you execute your wishes. There are revocable and irrevocable living trusts, there are spendthrift and generation-skipping trusts, and others. Each trust performs a specific function within your overall wealth management plan.

As we will discuss in a subsequent chapter, insurance is an important tool in wealth planning and management. Like other members of the wealth management team, an insurance expert will bring to the table his own unique view of mitigating risks through insurance and, when it comes to estate planning, utilize life insurance in the process of the efficient and proper transfer of your assets. The insurance agent can navigate through the various insurance proposals, negotiate with insurance companies, evaluate insurance offers, and recommend the choice most appropriate to your needs and best meets your goals.

The investment advisor is the professional that will be given the responsibility of recommending and implementing your various investment strategies. Over the past few years, investment advisors have taken on expanded roles. They are no longer merely stockbrokers. Many are now trained as financial planners and/or wealth advisors. The difference between an investment advisor and a wealth advisor is usually defined by the scope of advice and expertise offered to the client. An investment advisor's main responsibility is usually investing, while a wealth advisor can act, through proper training, as the quarterback for a client's wealth management effort. The wealth advisor is the one that would coordinate the wealth management team and its activities. Even though the primary role is that of an investment professional, a wealth advisor can take on the added responsibility of coordinating and leading the efforts of the entire wealth management team.

Most people tend to think that it is their net worth that determines whether there is a need to have an estate plan. If everything you own is to pass on to your spouse, then, you might argue, there is no need to have an estate plan. However, what happens if your spouse dies before you do, or if both of you die together in an accident? What will happen to your children and all the assets that you leave behind? What if you are in an accident, on a respirator, and someone needs to make medical decisions for you? Unless you indicate your wishes in a durable power of attorney, most likely a stranger, the state, will be the one making those decisions for you. The tax consequences of not having an estate plan in place could be devastating, even if the issue of who is to inherit your assets is clearly defined. In putting together a wealth management strategy, there can be no shortcuts. You need a team with defined, yet complementary, responsibilities.

The Five Phases of Wealth Management

There is no uniform rule to dissect the wealth management phases. For the purpose of our discussion here, I have divided them into five phases:

1. Recognition/Awareness/Discovery Phase
2. Wealth Accumulation Phase
3. Wealth Planning Phase
4. Wealth Preservation Phase
5. Wealth Transfer Phase

Phase I: Recognition/Awareness/Discovery Phase

You have just graduated from school or college. You are likely burdened with some debt. You are driving an old, beat-up car. You are debating whether you want to rent an apartment to gain some independence from your parents' loving clutches. You have acquired your first, possibly full-time, job with some type of a career path. You are living paycheck to paycheck, and you are happy that you no longer have to ask your parents for gas money.

At this stage of life, if you are like most young adults, you might think, "Who wants to think about saving and putting away money for retirement in what seems like a million years away?" You want to take that vacation with your buddies, and this time, you might want to stay at a nice hotel instead of crashing in a hostel or camping on a beach.

But, you are maturing, and you begin to realize that you need to work and take life more seriously. You need to set up some goals, such as saving money for a new car, a down payment on a house or a condo, and a little extra cash for emergencies. You are working hard to build a career and you are encouraged, if not obligated, to set some money aside in your 401(k) plan. You talk to your older peers, who tell you that they regret having started financial planning too late in their lives. You begin thinking and, one day you decide yes, it is time to wet your toes in the mature world of setting simple financial goals, and begin saving and investing. You might meet a young financial advisor at a bar or through a friend. You like him/her. You strike up a conversation about goals and investing and you pay the advisor a visit, and thus phase I of your wealth management process begins. You are looking for ideas to get started, and your financial investments are mostly transactional in nature.

Phase II: Wealth Accumulation Phase

Your career progresses, your goals change, you meet someone you want to share your life with, and you realize that it is time to hunker down and be more serious. You are making more money. This phase of your life usually extends from your mid- to late-twenties until your peak years of income—usually in your fifties.

During this phase, you create an investment policy statement, or a plan of action that defines your goals, time horizon, risk tolerance, and other factors such as the desired type of asset allocation and your overall investing strategy. You become more aware of the effects of inflation and taxation on your investments. Especially if you are in a profession such as law or medicine and are subjected to frequent lawsuits by disgruntled clients or patients, you begin paying particular attention to asset protection strategies.

During this phase of wealth accumulation, you are looking for a consultative relationship with your wealth management team, which, as you will discover, will need to include the wealth advisor, the tax lawyer or CPA, the lending/mortgage officer, the trust officer, and the insurance agent.

Phase III: Wealth Planning Phase

The wealth planning phase ushers itself upon you when you establish a family and have children, when you have a thriving business that you have built up, or when you discover that you have accumulated sufficient wealth worth protecting or preserving. You worry about who will take care of your family in the event of your disability or untimely death, who will run or inherit the business, and whether you have sufficient life and liability insurance policies to protect against frivolous lawsuits and financial predators.

Will your wishes be honored after you pass on, and will the government once again tax away your hard-earned accumulated wealth? In this wealth planning phase, you set up an estate plan, come up with a business succession plan, and manage the future wealth being of your family. You do so through significant strategic and, possibly sophisticated, planning. You make choices while you are in good health and are still accumulating wealth so that your wishes are honored and your privacy is preserved.

The earlier the planning phase of wealth management begins, the better you will be served and the more peace of mind you will have. The wealth planning phase can extend from the exploration, to the wealth accumulation, to the wealth preservation, and to the wealth transfer phase of your life. Once you have a wealth plan in place, you will discover that life's changes force you to make adjustments to meet unexpected developments in your life. You might have to change your goals and adapt to your new needs. Some of the pleasant changes in your life could include the birth of grandchildren or the unexpected success of a business, while some unpleasant changes could include a divorce, a death, or an illness of a loved one.

Phase IV: Wealth Preservation Phase

Although human nature is rarely ever satisfied and always wants more, there comes a point in life when you feel that you have accumulated sufficient wealth and your main concern, in addition to growing it moderately or at least beating inflation, is to preserve it. You are cautious with your investments and with your spending habits. You do not want to "gamble away" or risk what you have accumulated. What you have accumulated is what you feel is what you need to live on the rest of your life while maintaining a decent standard of living commensurate with what you have been used to. If you are fortunate, and, after calculating your basic lifetime needs, you feel that you can afford to help your children, loved ones, and your favorite charity, then you begin thinking about the most tax-efficient way to transfer part of your wealth in a way that also satisfies your wishes toward those whom you care about.

Phase V: Wealth Transfer Phase

You are about to retire or are retired. Once you have ensured that you and your spouse's retirement needs—such as health care, long-term care, and living expenses—are secured, you begin thinking about what to do with the rest of your wealth. Should you donate to charity? How much, and in what manner? Should you sell your business to the highest bidders or allow your children or key employees to buy it? How should you distribute your wealth among your loved ones? How much of your wealth should be distributed through gifting during your lifetime and how much should be left in your estate? Do you have a special-needs child or even parents who are still alive? Have you considered your family dynamics and what will happen to the fabric of your family upon your death?

In this and in the planning phase of wealth management, you need to think about the unpleasantness of death. You need to work closely with a network of trusted professionals—wealth advisors, estate planners, tax lawyers or CPAs, insurance agents, and trust officers. You have to educate yourself and be aware of the various options, some of which might be sophisticated, that are available to you and that deal with wealth transfer issues, particularly if you have a sizable estate, younger children, and multiple families due to a previous divorce.

Each phase of wealth management covers a certain period of your life and coincides with personal and business developments. Each phase has its own set of issues and challenges and must be dealt with in a manner that continually helps you attain your desired goals and objectives based on a well-planned, well-thought-out course of action.

This book and its various chapters are intended to help guide you, inform you, and better educate you to allow you to make wise decisions that benefit you, your family, and loved ones in a manner that expresses your wishes and desires privately and away from the public eyes.

The Four-Step Wealth Management Process

Wealth management is a lifelong process. Once you have taken the important step of choosing your trusted wealth management team—the wealth/investment advisor, the tax counselor, the insurance agent, the estate planning attorney, and the trust/charitable giving officer—your wealth management process can then be broken down into four distinct steps:

1. Share information and open up to your trusted wealth management team and let them get to know you so that they can help you identify your needs, goals, time horizon, and risk tolerance.
2. Develop an action plan.
3. Evaluate, select, and implement the elements of your plan.
4. Monitor and adjust your plan as needed.

At the risk of sounding redundant, wealth management is an ongoing process, not set in stone. Both you and your team of advisors should have the wisdom to be flexible to meet your changing needs and to take advantage of opportunities as they arise.

Step 1: Share Information with Your Team so They Can Help You Identify Your Needs and Goals

It is difficult to assess most people's needs because quite often, they do not know or are unaware of what they need or want. The "know your client" rule, or *rule 405,* as it is known among investment professionals and in the financial industry, is one of the most basic and highly emphasized rules. The premise behind it is quite simple. Unless a wealth advisor knows his/her client's goals, needs, fears, aspirations, values, risk tolerance, and time horizon, a wealth advisor is not in a good position to recommend an investment, let alone a wealth management plan, to that client. A wealth advisor must know his/her client well and gather as much information as possible before making any recommendations.

In the wealth management arena, a wealth advisor is not limited to recommending investments or investment vehicles, but that role is more expansive and extends considerably beyond investing. This is one of the main differences between a financial and a wealth advisor.

If you are a prospect and are about to begin a relationship with an advisor, you should be open and answer all the pertinent questions that you are asked. You should provide information pertaining to your name, address, contact numbers, line of work, approximate net worth, date of birth, and Social Security numbers (for you and your beneficiaries). You should answer those questions, as they are required by law to open up a brokerage account for you. If you refuse to answer those questions, your wealth advisor should respectfully turn you down as a client.

How can you expect to be treated by a physician or be defended by a lawyer without revealing pertinent and, sometimes, very intimate and sensitive information about yourself? The same applies to the financial/wealth advising industry. Your refusal to share pertinent information and open up to your trusted advisors could hinder their ability to help you. The more they know about you, the better position they will be in to help you. Each member of your team of advisors is your partner and ally. They are all there to help you achieve your goals. Unless you have a relationship of trust with them, your relationship is doomed from the very beginning.

The information you provide to them should be treated with utmost confidentiality. This information should help your wealth management team to identify your needs and uncover weaknesses and needs that must be addressed. For example, the information that you share could reveal that your existing retirement plan is insufficient to meet your retirement needs, given your current age, accumulated savings, health condition, and your other liabilities. The questions about insurance could demonstrate whether you have sufficient life insurance to take care of your loved ones upon your death or whether there is insufficient liquidity to pay estate taxes. Your family should not have to sell the family business to meet the estate tax obligations.

The getting-to-know-you phase, or the discovery phase, could reveal that you have insufficient emergency funds in the event you become disabled, lose your job, or are faced with having to replace the roof on your home or buy a new car. Based on the information that you as the client provide, it becomes easy to remedy some of these deficiencies. You might end up having to spend less and save more, buy additional life insurance, or refinance the mortgage because rates have dropped and you are still paying above–market rates. You might realize that you need to begin contributing to a 529 education plan to help save for your children's college education.

A major dilemma that faces many financial/wealth advisors arises when you, the client, are unwilling to share some other basic information. For example, we know that, on average, most clients have three brokerage relationships and, in most cases, do not share that information with their financial or wealth advisor. This is like having three primary care physicians. A patient goes to each physician for a different ailment, or even for the same one. Each physician prescribes medication, completely unaware of what the other physician is prescribing to the patient. This situation could end up being hazardous to the patient's health if the medications interact in a detrimental way.

You, as a client, need to be forthright about revealing what you own and with whom. As a client, you cannot omit basic and relevant information. And, at times, you will find that you have no choice but to reveal all this information. For example, when you apply for a mortgage and/or life insurance, you have no choice but to reveal information that you would rarely share with your wealth advisor. When applying for a mortgage, pulling up your credit history is required. Your credit report will reveal all the reported liabilities that you have, the debts that you owe and to whom, and whether you have had problems paying off these or other debts. And, if you deal with a mortgage broker, in most cases you will have to reveal all your assets and where they might be, because producing this information is usually a requirement, if not a condition, to approving your request for a loan.

If the wealth advisor is a licensed life insurance agent, as most are these days, then an insurance application will reveal your health history, with all the details of past ailments and surgeries.

There are other nonstructured ways of getting to know one's client. They might not follow a textbook path, but ultimately, the information acquired should help in getting to know you, the client, and thus help you identify your needs. One of these ways is to spend as much time as possible together, outside the office setting, and ask each other open-ended questions. Over time, you will end up sharing with each other your fears, concerns, goals, and dreams. You will also get to know your advisor's work ethics, social skills, desire to learn, ambitions, and personal and professional goals.

In short, if you as the client expect to be well advised by your wealth advisor, you need to open up and share your goals, needs, aspirations, fears, concerns, and expectations with your wealth advisor. In return, the wealth advisor needs to be sensitive to your openness and never ever misuse or reveal the information or those deep-seated emotions and intimate goals. Not only would that be unethical, but also it would be illegal.

Therefore, it is necessary before implementing an action plan to have a complete snapshot of the following:

- Your current assets, including real estate, and other nonsecurity holdings
- Your employment situation
- Your current saving strategies
- Your other advisors
- Your current tax information
- Your current estate planning efforts
- The people you care about
- Your charitable inclinations
- Any tangible objectives that require money and financial planning to achieve[4]

You and your wealth management team then need to analyze the following:

- Your current portfolio of assets
- How each component fits with your objectives
- The tax efficiency of each component
- The risk/reward aspect of each component
- The suitability of each component[5]

Step 2: Develop an Action Plan

Upon the completion of the discovery phase, you and your wealth advisor will need to identify and prioritize your goals and objectives. These could include the following:

- Retiring in comfort at a standard of living similar to the latter years of working career

- Ensuring that your surviving spouse is provided for the rest of his/her life
- Providing for your children's education and possibly paying for the weddings and a down payment on a first home
- Planning for the sale of your business sale or putting in place a succession plan

The work then begins in strategizing and designing an action plan that is tailored to meet stated goals, objectives, needs, values, and desires.

Designing an action plan is not easy. It has numerous components, which include creating an investment policy statement that relies on your stated guidelines and that is centered on a number of important factors:

1. Your goals, objectives, and values.
2. Your tax situation—How sensitive are you to taxes, and how will you incorporate your long-term tax considerations into your plan?
3. Your estate planning issues, including your legacy objectives, your privacy, your income needs in retirement, and whether your heirs might be subject to estate taxes given the size of your estate and the level of estate planning that you have already conducted.
4. Your investment risk awareness—Are you aware of the various investment risks that you might face? These could include market risk, concentration risk, interest rate risk, credit risk, volatility risk, inflation risk, just to name a few.
5. Your life planning risks—Have you made provisions for your life risk (death), disability risk, health risk, and long-term care risk?
6. Litigation risk—Have you implemented an asset protection strategy to help you in the event you get sued? Do you have sufficient property, liability, and umbrella insurance coverage? Has your estate plan been devised to help protect your assets, or does it need to be revised?

Step 3: Evaluate, Select, and Implement Your Action Plan

Once your investment policy statement is in place and once you have reviewed your other wealth management issues, you then need to begin evaluating your options and implement the recommendations.

With regard to the investment aspect of your plan, you and your wealth advisor can review a number of investment options that would meet your financial needs, objectives, risk tolerance, and time horizon. You could decide to divide up your investment portfolio into various buckets: the liquid (cash) bucket to ensure that your liquidity needs are met, the conservative bucket with an eye on preserving the assets allocated to that bucket, the moderate bucket to help at least beat inflation, and the moderately aggressive bucket to help grow that portion of the portfolio to allow for future growth of your overall portfolio. Each bucket would most likely end up with a different asset allocation strategy. Wealth managers tend to use outside money managers, not individual stock selection. They tend to look at the overall return of the entire portfolio as opposed to individual buckets within the portfolio. They tend to take a consultative macro approach to investing rather than a tactical, short-term approach.

Your wealth advisor should provide you with options pertaining to each investment bucket, and you should both agree on a strategy (asset allocation) for each bucket that clearly meets your needs, goals, risk tolerance, and time horizon. Usually, there is little activity in these types of portfolios. Each bucket should have its own return expectation over time, largely depending on the investment strategy implemented.

The aspect of your plan that does not deal with investment issues would deal with estate planning issues—Is your estate up to date? Should you have another estate planning lawyer review it for you? Do you have a gifting strategy to help those whom you care about and to allow you to minimize estate taxes over time? Have you reviewed your life insurance policies, and should you consider exchanging those for new ones given that the cost of life insurance has decreased over time? Do you need the life insurance proceeds for your surviving spouse, or should you establish an irrevocable life insurance trust for your children and grandchildren? These and other issues need to be reviewed, options should be explored, and decisions made to improve your overall wealth management plan.

Step 4: Monitor and Adjust Your Plan as Needed

No wealth management plan, no matter how well designed and implemented, should remain without, at the very least, annual reviews. Change is a constant in life. This change could relate to your health, to your family dynamics, to the birth of a grandchild or two, to a serious downturn in the market, to changing laws and regulations that affect income and other taxes, including estate taxes. You could have decided to move to another state where the laws are different and adjustments would be required to some aspects of your wealth management plan. Your spouse could have died prematurely.

You and your wealth advisor should be in constant touch, as often as needed, but certainly at least once or twice a year to review where things are and if there had been any changes in your life. Communication is a key ingredient to a great relationship between you and your wealth advisor and, in turn, with your wealth management team. Stay in touch and talk with one another. Yours is not a transactional relationship. It is a lifelong relationship based on trust, communication, and a commitment to advancing your goals and meeting your needs.

Concluding Remarks

Wealth management and financial investing are no longer interchangeable. We live in an increasingly complex world that requires the expertise of a group of individuals who can help you maneuver through the maze of wealth management issues. Wealth management needs include: designing and implementing a successful investment strategy; creating an estate plan; learning to save and manage debt; planning for a comfortable retirement; utilizing insurance to mitigate potential threats; planning your gifting strategy to maximize its value; implementing asset protection strategies; taking advantage of tax planning and tax-saving strategies; and recognizing that you need a wealth management team and knowing how to select that team.

These are all necessary ingredients to having a successful wealth management plan. The needs, goals, and strategies for each wealth management phase are different, and you need someone alongside you to help you decipher the changes and adapt accordingly. If you have at least begun the process of wealth management, you are one of the lucky few. It is somewhat sad to note that only 1 in 50 high-net-worth families are receiving the comprehensive financial and wealth management planning that they need.[6] You do not have to be a millionaire to require a wealth management plan; the need for wealth management (not just investing) in these days is a universal need for people from all walks of life. Wealth management is a cornerstone to your future well-being and financial security.

CHAPTER 2

The 15 Ingredients of a Successful Investment Strategy

The prolific and highly respected Jerome Siegel, a distinguished professor at the top-ranking Wharton School of Business, calculated the total real return (after inflation) of several indexes over a 205-year period.[1] The results are as follows for U.S.$1.00 invested on December 31, 1801, through December 31, 2006:[2]

Investment Vehicle	Cumulative Real Return
Stocks[3]	$754,511.00
Bonds[4]	$1,083.00
Treasury bills[5]	$300.00
Gold[6]	$1.95
Dollar[7]	$0.06

Even though these investment results are eye-opening, quite compelling, and establish a clear long-term trend, investing is a complex and an ongoing process that entails wise decisions, appropriate time horizons, changing needs, objectives and risk tolerance, not succumbing to fear and greed, discipline, employing multiple strategies and investment vehicles, diversifying, asset allocating, rebalancing, dollar cost averaging, understanding the risks, recognizing the value of time and the effect of taxes and inflation, and accepting the potential of loss and heart-wrenching volatility. Having acknowledged the complexity of investing, the volatility and potential for loss, investing can, nevertheless, be quite rewarding.

If we let history be our guide and unequivocally recognize that past performance is no guarantee of future results, we will discover that in the twentieth century, 73 years produced positive returns among large stocks by capitalization, with an average annual return of 22.2 percent. By comparison, 27 years had negative returns, among the same large stocks, with an average negative return of 12.2 percent.[8]

In short, the odds of making money in a hundred-year span in large-capitalization stocks were 73 to 27. The positive years resulted in considerably higher average returns (+22.2 percent) than the negative years (−12.2 percent). The data are quite telling and reveal a clear pattern of favorable odds (over time) for positive returns. Recognizing the favorable odds, over time, of positive returns in the stock market represents one element in devising a comprehensive investment process.[9] Looking back at the history of the markets in the 20th century, there was one decade—the 1930s—when the returns on large-cap stocks had a negative return. From January 2000 through June 30, 2008, the S&P 500 Index was down on average 1.6 percent per year and even worse after the market meltdown of September of 2008. These two decades are, however, more the aberration than the norm with regard to the performance of large-cap stocks.[10]

The following are the 15 ingredients of a successful investment strategy that can help you map out a path of success but only if applied in tandem and with proper, timely, and disciplined implementation.

To succeed as an investor, you need to do the following:
1. Define your goals and timeline.
2. Develop a strategy and establish a process.
3. Diversify.
4. Asset allocate.
5. Invest worldwide.
6. Dollar-cost and value average.
7. Rebalance.
8. Control your behavior—be disciplined.
9. Put time on your side—be patient.
10. Understand how to manage and measure risk.
11. Recognize the effect of taxes and inflation.
12. Utilize multiple investment products/vehicles.
13. Monitor your plan and make necessary changes.
14. Seek professional advice.
15. Avoid the most common investor mistakes.

The objective of this chapter is to highlight the components of a successful investment strategy. It is not intended to provide financial or investment advice, as this type of advice is dependent on a multitude of factors that are specific to individuals, institutions, or foundations and include goals, objectives, time horizon, risk tolerance, and many other varying and changing elements. You should always recognize that past performance cannot be used as an indication of future results and that a security or an investment, by its very definition, carries the risk of loss. And, even though the Internet has allowed people—most of whom lack the knowledge and the proper training—to buy and sell securities on their own, there is a tremendous value to a structured process of investment guided by a seasoned, licensed, and experienced financial or wealth advisor.

Investing is not about hunches and feelings. With the advent of technology and advanced computing capabilities, investing has become more scientific in nature with rules that, if properly implemented, could lead, with a good measure of probability, *yet with no guarantees,* to favorable results. Altogether, these basic and time-tested rules of investing provide a realistic road map to successful investing.

Define Your Goals and Timeline

To embark on a successful investment plan, you need to begin by identifying the primary purpose for investing, your investment timeline or horizon, and your cash needs during that period. Most people invest to accumulate wealth, ensure a comfortable retirement, finance children's education, make a major purchase, or generate current income. The way you and your advisor would invest depends to a large extent on when you would expect to begin withdrawing funds for your primary investment objective. If you need the funds in 10 to 20 years or longer, you are a long-term investor and you can afford to be more aggressive because you have sufficient time to ride out negative returns and cycles in the market. If, however, you will need to withdraw funds within 5 to 10 years, you have an intermediate time horizon and your investment strategy should be moderate and less aggressive. If you need to tap into your investments immediately or within a period of less than 5 years, you should be a conservative investor.

In addition, once you begin withdrawing funds for your primary investment objective, how long you anticipate the withdrawals to continue is critical to determining your overall time horizon. The longer you will need to withdraw funds, the more aggressive you will have to be. Other factors that can help gauge your investment time horizon include your age, the number of individuals that are dependent on you, when you plan to retire, how stable is your employment, and what assets and how much do you currently have.

Develop a Realistic Strategy and Establish a Process

Investing is a marathon, not a sprint. Your strategy should be realistic, and you should manage your expectations. A realistic strategy should help you chart the course to reach your goal within your expected time frame. Once you have identified your goal, you need to determine the following:

- How much do you currently own that you can apply toward your goal?
- How much do you need to save on a monthly basis?
- What is your assumed rate of return?
- Is your stated risk tolerance realistic?
- What products or investment vehicles are more likely to help you attain your goal?
- What process will you implement to monitor your performance and gauge whether you are on the right track?

For example, if you are a professional, 40 years old, with an annual income of $200,000, currently have $250,000 in retirement and other savings, and plan to retire at age 67, it is not difficult to calculate how much you would need to put away each month in your retirement and other savings plans in order to have sufficient money at age 67 to maintain your current standard of living throughout your retirement years based on your life expectancy. If you assume that your combined investment portfolios will return an average of 8 percent annually, and account for annual inflation, you and your financial/wealth advisor would then be able to calculate your required monthly contributions to meet this specific goal. You need to determine the asset allocation that will help you reach your goal and the type of investments (stocks, bonds, cash, and alternative investments) that you should utilize. Understandably, your needs and circumstances could change over time. You need to be both flexible and realistic in order to adapt to keep pace with changing needs and new opportunities. Meet with your wealth advisor and together design a road map that will help you attain your multiple goals.

Diversify

In investing, you should embrace and manage risk, not avoid it. Risk taking, or investing, is the only way you can make money over time after accounting for inflation. Risk management through diversification was the core thesis articulated in a groundbreaking paper that was published in June 1952. Written by Harry Markowitz and titled "Portfolio Selection," the paper earned Markowitz a Nobel Prize in Economics in 1990. In the paper, Markowitz suggested that constructing a portfolio of two or more risky investments that have a low historical correlation, one could lessen the portfolio's overall risk. When adequately diversified, a portfolio's asset allocation can help minimize risk and enhance reward.[11]

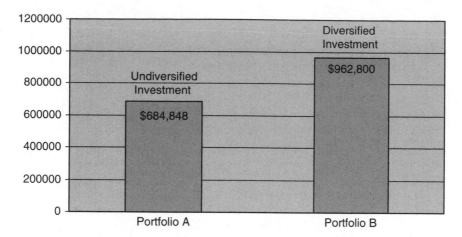

FIGURE 2.1 The Power of Diversification

You often hear the advice, "Do not put all your eggs in one basket." This represents the simple concept of diversification. Let us say that you own only one stock and it performs poorly. The impact of this poor performance will be devastating on your portfolio because your portfolio lacks diversification. But if you own 60 stocks and 1, 2, or even 10 performed poorly, then their effect on your overall portfolio will be less severe because your other 50 stocks performed better. That is the simple logic behind diversification.

To illustrate the benefits of diversification, take two portfolios of $100,000 each and invest them utilizing two different investment approaches (see Figure 2.1). In portfolio (A), you invest $100,000 in an 8 percent fixed rate investment. Over a 25-year period, and disregarding the effect of taxes on your returns, your $100,000 will grow to $684,848.[12]

Portfolio (B), also with an initial investment of $100,000, is invested equally among five different vehicles ($20,000 each). The returns on each of the five different investment vehicles, over a 25-year period and ignoring the impact of taxes on the returns, are as follows:

- *You completely lose your first $20,000 investment.* After 25 years, it is now worth zero.
- *You break even with your second $20,000 investment.* Your return is 0 percent. The ending value of this investment vehicle is $20,000.
- *You earn 5 percent per year on your third $20,000 investment.* The ending value of this investment vehicle is $67,727.

- *You earn 10 percent per year on your fourth $20,000 investment.* The ending value of this investment vehicle is $216,694.
- *You earn 15 percent per year on your fifth $20,000 investment.* The ending value of this investment vehicle is $658,379.

Even with the disparity in investment returns among the five different investment strategies within Portfolio B, the diversified strategy grew to $962,800 or 40 percent more than the undiversified, fixed income portfolio, which returned $684,848. Mind you, the 8 percent fixed income rate that we assumed in this illustration is significantly higher than actual fixed income historical returns.

Diversification within a portfolio does not mean investing in more than one stock. Within your overall portfolio, you can diversify at different levels and in a number of specific ways.[13] You can diversify at least seven different ways:

1. Among the three primary asset classes—stocks, bonds, and cash
2. Among the different stock capitalizations—large cap, mid cap, and small cap
3. Among the different stock investment styles—value and growth
4. Among the different types of fixed income securities—corporate bond, high yield, senior loan, municipal bond, government bond, and U.S. Treasury bills
5. Among domestic and international stocks and bonds
6. Among international stocks and bonds—developed vs. emerging markets
7. Among other types of investments or alternatives—real estate, managed futures, venture capital, private equity and hedge funds

Diversifying by combining asset classes so that some are not correlated with others should, in theory, help smooth returns and minimize volatility. Please note that diversification does not assure a profit, nor does it protect against a loss.

Correlation—A discussion of diversification (and asset allocation) cannot be complete without understanding correlation. If you invest in two portfolios that have similar risk (volatility) and return characteristics, then both of your portfolios will go up and down in a similar manner. In other words, they are positively correlated. In this case, even though you have two portfolios, you have not achieved diversification. However, if you select two portfolios that move inversely of each other, meaning that when one portfolio goes up, the other comes down, then you are achieving diversification. Unfortunately, in our investment world, perfectly negatively correlated investments (a desired outcome) are rare. In the real world, the most we can hope for are investments with negative or the least positive correlation. At times, these investments might go up and down at the same time (the diversification effect is weak), but at other times, they might move in opposite directions but not uniformly, indicating periods of lower correlation and a strong diversification effect on the portfolio.[14] A diversified portfolio is composed of investments that exhibit negative or the least positive correlation. Correlation—or, more precisely, low or negative correlation—is achieved through diversification and is intended to smooth the volatility of your portfolio in search for attractive long-term performance.[15]

The correlation between asset classes is not a constant and has shifted over time. International markets, for example, have become increasingly more correlated to the U.S. markets due to globalization. Between 1980 and 1989, the correlation of the S&P 500 Index to the EAFE Index was 0.58. This relationship became more correlated between 1990 and 1999 and was 0.75. Then, between 2000 and 2006, the correlation of these major indexes representing the U.S. domestic and international markets saw an increase to 0.84. This essentially means that investors now have to look to other asset classes in order to enhance their diversification and decrease the correlation between the various asset classes in which they are invested.[16]

Highly correlated markets may spell doom for portfolio diversification. A recent study led by Richard Bernstein, chief investment strategist at Merrill Lynch, found that with the globalization of the world markets, many asset classes are losing their correlation advantage. As of January 31, 2008, developed market stocks, represented by the MSCI EAFE Index, and small-cap U.S. stocks, represented by the Russell 2000 Index, are now highly correlated with the U.S. large-cap stocks, represented by the S&P 500 index. The five-year rolling correlation figures amount to 93 percent and 91 percent respectively.[17] In other words, all these asset classes will likely rise or fall in tandem.

Other classes that have historically provided advantageous negative correlation are also losing their edge. Over the past two years, U.S. Treasuries went from having a strong negative correlation (−58 percent) compared to the S&P 500 Index, to virtually no correlation (−1 percent). Additionally, commodities and gold went from having moderate positive correlations two years ago (33 percent and 26 percent), to slightly negative correlations (−26 percent and −3 percent) with today's S&P 500 Index.[18]

Asset Allocate

The strategy of investing in different types of asset classes is called *asset allocation*. Since there is a certain element of risk involved with any type of investment, the challenge is to create an asset mix to balance the amount of risk you are willing to accept in exchange for potential higher rewards. Even though asset allocation can help minimize risk and enhance returns through diversification, it does not guarantee a profit or protect against loss.

Historically, there is a rotation among the best- and worst-performing asset classes on a year-to-year basis. Rather than try to predict which asset class will become the best performer, *modern portfolio theory* (MPT), developed by Nobel Prize winning economist Harry Markowitz, suggests that investors should maintain broad exposure across multiple asset classes. MPT quantifies the relationship between risk and return. MPT demonstrates that by combining different asset classes (diversifying), investors can minimize the risks of investing while maximizing returns. It was Markowitz's position that a portfolio's risk could be reduced and the expected return could be improved if investments having dissimilar price movements (low correlation) were combined.[19]

Building upon the work of Markowitz and others, Gary Brinson, Randolph Hood, and Gilbert Beebower studied the impact of asset allocation on the performance of a portfolio. In a 1986 article published in the *Financial Analysts Journal*, the authors concluded that asset allocation contributed the most to a portfolio's performance (see Figure 2.2).

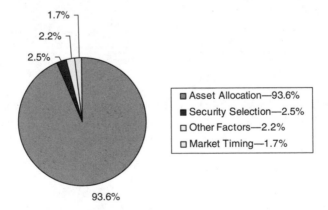

FIGURE 2.2 **Factors Affecting Portfolio Performance**

Source: Brinson, Gary P., Hood, L. Randolph, and Beebower, Gilbert L., "Determinants of Portfolio Performance," *Financial Analysts Journal*, Vol. 42, No. 4 (July/August 1986), pp. 39–48.

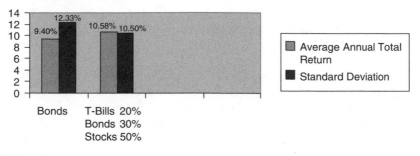

FIGURE 2.3 Asset Allocation Reduces Risk and Enhances Return

Asset allocation works. In the hypothetical illustration in Figure 2.3, a one-bond long-term government portfolio with a maturity near 20 years has an average total return of 9.4 percent and a standard deviation (risk level) of 12.33 percent. When this hypothetical portfolio is diversified among a number of asset classes including T-bills (20 percent), bonds (30 percent), and stocks (50 percent), the average annual total return increases to 10.58 percent and its standard deviation (a measure of risk) decreases to 10.50 percent.[20]

Asset allocation can range from very basic such as allocating among stocks, bonds, and cash to highly sophisticated. A highly sophisticated allocation might include exposure to different asset classes (stock, bonds, and cash), different stock capitalizations (large, mid, and small cap), different investment styles (value and growth), different types of bonds, international stocks and bonds, and alternative investments.

An Asset Allocation Shift Is Underway to Alternatives

An alternative investment "generally refers to any investment in which successful performance does not depend on continued upward movement in the stock market."[21] As an asset class, alternative investment has its own set of asset classes, which include hedge funds, funds of funds, managed futures, private equity, real estate, real assets and exchange funds.[22]

Alternative investments may benefit investors because they have the potential to provide alternative risk-adjusted returns; diversify and reduce overall portfolio volatility; and employ sophisticated money management. Historically, some strategies have exhibited low correlation to traditional investments.[23]

A recent study by the strategic consulting firm Eager, Davis and Holmes has revealed that a significant asset allocation shift is underway, particularly among institutional investors. The study found the following:

- Institutional investors moved three times more money into alternative investments in 2006 than the average for the previous five years.
- Alternative investments accounted for about 40 percent of hires in 2006, compared to an 18 percent average over the previous five years.
- Investors put 33 percent of the money to work in alternatives, triple the average between 2001 and 2005.[24]

Glenn Davis of Eager, Davis and Holmes noted, "If we step back and look at the big picture, we are mid-stream in the biggest fundamental asset allocation realignment in the last 20 years... The movement to alts [alternatives] is as big as the movement to international that gained traction in the 80s or the movement to equities with the passage of ERISA."[25] Institutions are showing more interest in private equity than hedge funds. Private equity formed about three-fourths of the alternative placements in 2006, gaining share from hedge funds and other alternatives relative to past years.[26]

A look at two of the most successful endowments in the United States—those of Yale and Harvard Universities—reveals that Yale's allocation to alternatives in its endowment is a staggering 70 percent, while Harvard's stands at 62 percent.[27] The reason for this high allocation to alternatives is because institutional investors are expecting a lower return environment for stocks and bonds, going forward.[28]

Investing like an institution, even though you are an individual investor, is not a task for the amateur. With the help of a financial/wealth advisor and after taking into account your goals, assets, time horizon, risk tolerance, cash flow needs, and tax concerns, a personalized asset allocation is then created, regularly monitored, and readjusted as the need arises. Deciding on your asset allocation, in the view of most experts, is the most important task that you and your advisor have to decide upon. That is because the proportion in which you hold stocks versus bonds versus cash versus alternatives generally has a greater effect on your portfolio's returns and its volatility than the individual investments you choose.

Asset Allocation and Diversification Lower Volatility

An important byproduct of diversification and asset allocation is the lowering of the volatility of a portfolio. From 1950 to September 2007, the average annual return of the S&P 500 Index was 9.12 percent with a standard deviation (risk/volatility level) of 14.11 percent. In the same time period, an investment with the same monthly average return that had a lower volatility (or a standard deviation of 7.05 percent) created over 54 percent more wealth. In other words, the growth of $1.0 million from 1950 to September 2007 with a high volatility level resulted in a portfolio value of $141,869,321. By comparison, the same $1.0 million would have grown to $218,557,960, when the volatility over that same period of time was cut in half. High volatility is detrimental to the growth of a portfolio over time. Diversification and proper asset allocation lower a portfolio's volatility and allow it to potentially grow faster over the same period of time.[29]

Invest Worldwide

In today's evolving global economy where opportunities for investments are abundant throughout the world, it is hard to believe that 87 percent of American investors do not have any money invested in international stocks.[30] This is perplexing, given that 56 percent of the world's stock market opportunities come from countries outside of the United States, compared to just 34 percent in 1970.[31] Even domestic companies represented by the S&P 500 Index generate 46 percent of their revenues outside the United States, while technology stocks in the index produce 56 percent of their revenues overseas.[32]

Traditionally, those U.S. investors who purchased international equities viewed it as a basic building block of a well-diversified portfolio. Today, the structural changes brought on by a rapidly globalizing world present a more compelling reason for investors to increase their allocations to non-U.S. investments. The United States represents a shrinking share of the world's investment opportunity set. Other countries, economies, and markets are becoming increasingly important drivers of global growth. As a result, international investing has become not only an opportunity but also a necessity for a well-diversified portfolio.

A 2007 study revealed that 43 percent of financial advisors now recommend an international allocation of 11 to 20 percent for a 65-year-old risk-neutral retiree investor with $500,000 investable assets, as part of a diversified portfolio. 17 percent of advisors would recommend an even higher allocation of up to 30 percent to suitable clients, because international funds may help reduce risk and protect portfolios against inflation during a possible 30-year retiree horizon.[33]

The nature of international investing has changed dramatically over the past decade. The world's economies are more closely linked than they have ever been before. Well-managed companies exist throughout the globe, and not just in the United States. And, if you as an investor are to benefit, your portfolio should include a significant allocation to international companies diversified across many regions, industries, and sectors.

The many benefits of international investing include the following:

- Diversification
- Hedging against a falling dollar
- Potential for higher returns
- Potential for less portfolio volatility
- Access to dominant players

Diversification

If you were to go to a grocery store, you would not want to limit yourself to shopping in less than half of the store irrespective of what you would be missing out on. International investments offer exposure to the different economic cycles, and growth potential of international markets, providing attractive diversification to your investment portfolio. Non-U.S. stocks constitute about 70 percent of the world equity market's capitalization. Non-U.S. economies also account for approximately 70 percent of global output as measured in local currency terms.[34] As a U.S. investor, you have to seek to benefit from this global growth. Besides, had you been investing only domestically in the most representative domestic index, the S&P 500, your annualized return since the year 2000 through the end of 2007, would have been a mere 1.6 percent—certainly far from the long-term average domestic stock market return and considerably less than the returns generated by the most representative international markets.[35]

Currency Hedging

Investing in foreign markets allows U.S. investors to hedge against any future declines in the value of the U.S. dollar. From the end of 2001 through 17 March 2008, the U.S. dollar fell 43 percent versus the euro and dropped 26 percent versus the Japanese yen. The last time the U.S. Federal Reserve intervened and purchased dollars to boost its sagging value was in 1995.[36] U.S. investors who own shares in foreign stocks or funds increase their gains when the dollar weakens because that makes non-U.S. assets more valuable when translated into dollars. The EAFE (Europe, Australia, and the Far East) Index, a major global benchmark from Morgan Stanley Capital International, gained 15 percent in local currency terms between September 2006 and September 2007. But Americans who invested in the same stocks as are those in the EAFE saw their holdings rise 25 percent (not 15 percent) because of the weakening dollar during that same period.[37] This is also a reason why U.S. investors find investing in U.S.-based large multinational corporations attractive because many of these generate significant revenue from their investments overseas. And, many experts believe the large U.S.

current account deficit poses a long-term threat to the value of the U.S. dollar.[38]

Potential for Higher Returns

Investments in foreign markets entail special risks such as currency, political, economic, and market risks. The risks of investing in emerging-market countries are even greater. However, international investments can offer the potential for higher returns than are generally available in U.S. markets. This is because many of the world's fastest growth stocks markets are outside the United States. According to Morningstar data ending May 31, 2005, international equity funds in the United States far outperformed the S&P 500 Index for the preceding three years. Almost 98.4 percent of international funds outperformed the S&P 500 Index over the prior five years.[39] However, this should not be a reason to abandon diversification and proper asset allocation, because if we examine the 20-year annualized growth rate of the S&P 500 to the EAFE, we will find out that the S&P 500 grew at 11.8 percent a year compared to 7.9 percent over the same period from December 31, 1987, to December 31, 2007.[40]

Potential for Less Portfolio Volatility

Foreign markets seldom move in line with each other, or with the U.S. markets. Adding international stocks to a portfolio of domestic stocks can temper the ups and downs of market swings. Over a 35-year period (January 1, 1972, to December 21, 2006), a portfolio mix of 60 percent S&P and 40 percent EAFE had an annualized return of 11.81 percent with a standard deviation of 16.95 percent. Over the same period, a portfolio made up of 100 percent S&P 500 had an annualized return of 11.35 percent with a 17.22 percent standard deviation. Conversely, a portfolio made up of 100 percent EAFE had an annualized return of 11.75 percent with a 21.7 percent standard deviation. Constructing a portfolio with a 60/40 mix (60 percent S&P 500 and 40 percent EAFE) resulted in a portfolio that had a higher return at 11.81 percent with a lower standard deviation at 16.95 percent.[41] The message is clear—adding an international component to your portfolio would have provided you a higher return with a lower standard deviation (a measure of risk).

Access to Dominant Players

Investors often look for the dominant players in a particular industry or market sector. More than half of the world's largest 500 largest companies are headquartered outside the United States.[42] According to data from

T. Rowe Price Group Inc., the majority of the top 10 companies in sectors such as electronics, finance, mining, and telecommunications are foreign firms.[43] Many foreign companies are global leaders in key growth industries of the twenty-first century.[44] Twenty-three of the 30 largest oil companies (including BP and Shell) are based outside the United States. Seven out of the 10 largest telecommunications firms are foreign.[45] Even though Americans spend heavily on products and services of foreign companies, many of which are common household names such as Sony, Canon, Bayer, and Honda, Americans either resist or overlook investing in those same foreign companies.

Diversification across industries is the best way to reduce overall risk in an international portfolio. Investing in an industry has provided more diversification benefits than the country chosen.[46] Also, correlations of U.S. and EAFE equity returns are relatively high, indicating fewer diversification benefits. Many non-EAFE market stocks have lower correlations with U.S. stocks, thus providing valuable risk reduction advantages.

Investors can no longer afford to overlook a significant allocation to the international markets. They should focus on industries rather than countries, and should expand beyond EAFE stocks to gain added diversification benefits. There have been significant improvements in corporate governance and market transparency, adding further to the attractiveness of international markets.[47] In remarks to the spring 2007 conference of the Investment Management Consultants Association (IMCA), Jeremy Siegel, a prominent professor at The Wharton School of Business, concluded that "growth in the developing world will offset slowing in aging economies and support future equity prices." He also added that equities "should be 40 percent international," and warned not to "jump into emerging markets without examining valuation."[48]

Dollar-Cost and Value Average

No investor can perfectly time when the markets bottom or peak. Trying to time the market is like attempting to foretell the future—good luck! Alternatively, two strategies that have often been used are dollar cost averaging and dollar value averaging.

1. **Dollar-cost averaging** is "a technique designed to reduce market risk through the systematic purchase of securities [stocks, stock funds or bond funds] at predetermined intervals and set amounts."[49] Instead of investing assets in a lump sum, which assumes that you have the funds to do so, you invest a fixed dollar amount ($250, for example) on a

regular basis (usually biweekly, monthly, quarterly, semiannually, or annually). You invest this amount in a predetermined stock or fund whether the market is up or down. If you buy when the fund's price has declined, you end up buying slightly more shares with your fixed income investment amount. If the market is up, you end up buying slightly less shares. This strategy results in lowering the average cost of the fund, assuming the fund fluctuates up and down, which, as you know, is the norm for a fund or a stock. The strategy reduces the risk of investing a large amount in a single investment at the wrong time.

Most of us who contribute to retirement plans unwittingly participate in this strategy because money is deducted on regular intervals (usually semimonthly or biweekly) from our paychecks to contribute to one or more funds and, often, to purchase our company stock. For example, if you invest $1,000 in a stock fund at $34 a share, you get 29.4 shares. If the price fluctuates the next pay period and falls to $27 a share, the same $1,000 will now buy you 37 shares. Your average cost price over these periods becomes $30.5 a share and you would have bought 66.4 shares. Had you invested your $2,000 altogether, you have bought 58.8 shares instead.

2. **Value averaging** is a variant of dollar-cost averaging. With value averaging, you set a dollar target for your investments, let us say you want your account to rise by $1,000 a month. If your initial $1,000 purchase went down in value the next month to $950, you then contribute your regular $1,000 and then add another $50 to make up for the previous month's shortfall. Essentially, value averaging makes you invest more when the market is down ($1,050) and less (the minimum $1,000) when the market is up. This means that value averaging entails monitoring your investment regularly and in a disciplined fashion. With dollar-cost averaging, you set the amount to be invested, you decide on the frequency, you select the stock or fund you want to invest in, and you forget about it until your next scheduled review, which could be once a year.

An article in the American Association of Individual Investors (AAII) revealed, via computer simulation, that value averaging would outperform dollar-cost averaging 95 percent of the time.[50] According to John Markese, the president of AAII, despite the criticisms voiced against these two strategies, he states that, "You'll never get rich, but you'll be invested in a disciplined manner."[51] Even those who do not advocate dollar-cost averaging admit that they are not against the principle of investing small amounts of money on a regular basis. Writing for CNNMoney.com, Walter Updegrave concludes, "This sort of systematic investing makes perfect sense, if for no other reason than it assures we save rather than spend the money."[52]

In short, if you cannot afford to invest a large sum in a fund or a stock that you like, dollar-cost averaging and value averaging provide you with a structure to invest regularly in a disciplined manner, with the objective of helping you reduce market risk. Ideally, if you use either strategy and increase your systematic contribution by 5 or 10 percent a year, your account will be worth more over an extended period of time.

Rebalance

Rebalancing is bringing your portfolio back to your original asset allocation mix. Rebalancing on a regular basis is necessary because over time, some of your investments may become out of alignment with your original investment goals. Some of your investments will grow faster than others and will, as a result, make up a larger percentage of your overall portfolio, thus altering your original asset allocation.

Why Should You Rebalance?

The primary objective of rebalancing is to manage risk by maintaining effective diversification. By ensuring that your portfolio is not overly dependent on one or more asset classes, you control risk by "curtailing overweighting and underweighting—thus reaping the full rewards of effective diversification in your investment strategy."[53] Rebalancing forces you to sell high and buy low—a fantastic investment principal that the vast majority of us can rarely ever properly time. With rebalancing you realize your gains or sell a portion of your winning asset classes and you buy your undervalued asset classes and, as a result, help reduce the overall volatility of your portfolio. Rebalancing also allows you to review the investments within each asset allocation category and to assess whether any changes need to be made.

How Can You Rebalance?

There are three basic ways to rebalance your portfolio:

1. You can sell off investments from overweighted asset categories and use the funds to beef up or purchase underweighted investment assets.
2. You can add new funds to shore up those investments that have underperformed.

3. If you are making continuous contributions to your portfolio, you can change your allocations so that more of your funds go to the underweighted asset class.[54]

When you rebalance, be mindful of possible transaction fees or potential tax consequences. For tax-deferred accounts, shifting assets from one category to the other should not have any tax consequences. For taxable accounts, it is best to add new contributions to the underweighted asset classes and thus avoid incurring taxes. If you do not have the funds to do so, you would have to sell from the outperforming asset classes to fund the underperforming ones. If taxes will occur upon a sale, try to wait until you avoid having to pay short-term gain taxes so you may pay incur long-term capital gains.

When Should You Rebalance?

There are many views and theories to support rebalancing at different intervals. Here is a summary of the most common intervals for rebalancing:

- *Calendar rebalancing.* You pick a time period—quarterly, semiannually, annually or over a 3-, 5-, or 10-year periods—and rebalance at the end of each period, no matter what the market is doing. In a UBS study published in 2003 covering a period of 20 years ending in September 2002, a hypothetical portfolio composed of 60 percent fixed income (Lehman Treasury Index) and 40 percent Large Cap Equity (S&P 500) was created to study the effect of rebalancing monthly, semiannually, and annually (see Table 2.1).

  The rates of return achieved under the hypothetical scenarios outlined in Table 2.1, including when the portfolio is not rebalanced, are virtually identical with the annual rebalancing achieving the highest return. However, a rebalanced portfolio demonstrated significantly lower volatility as measured by standard deviation.

TABLE 2.1   The Effect of Automatic Portfolio Rebalancing

Rebalancing Frequency	Annual Return Percent	Annual Standard Deviation Percent
No rebalancing	11.32 percent	9.7 percent
Rebalancing monthly	11.38 percent	7.39 percent
Rebalancing semiannually	11.57 percent	7.35 percent
Rebalancing annually	11.60 percent	7.42 percent

Source: The Importance of Automatic Portfolio Rebalancing, UBS Global Asset Management, 2003.

Table 2.2   Effect of Rebalancing When Asset Mix Shifts

Rebalancing Frequency	Annual Return Percent	Annual Standard Deviation Percent
No rebalancing	11.32 percent	9.7 percent
Rebalancing at 5 percent	11.54 percent	7.47 percent
Rebalancing at 7.5 percent	11.48 percent	7.67 percent
Rebalancing at 10 percent	11.58 percent	7.74 percent

Source: The Importance of Automatic Portfolio Rebalancing, UBS Global Asset Management, 2003.

- *Targeting rebalancing.* In this methodology, rebalancing occurs when an asset mix shifts by a certain percentage point—for example, 5, 7.5, or 10 percent from its target mix (see Table 2.2).

    Utilizing this approach, the average annual returns are virtually identical; however, the risk level decreased considerably when rebalancing occurred whenever the asset mixed deviated between 5 and 10 percent.

- *Tactical rebalancing.* A study conducted by Crestmont Research in 2003 has concluded that it is more advantageous to rebalance a portfolio more frequently in secular bear markets and less frequently in bull markets in order to enhance returns. During the secular bull market of 1982 to 1999, if you rebalanced biannually as opposed to annually or less frequently, the portfolio would have had an added advantage of 0.3 percent, compared to rebalancing annually. By comparison, in a secular bear market (1966 to 1981), if you rebalanced a portfolio more frequently or annually, the portfolio would have had an added advantage of 1.3 percent.[55]

    The most important lesson is that rebalancing adds the potential for downside protection by significantly lowering the risk level or standard deviation of a portfolio without necessarily sacrificing return. If we use the same hypothetical portfolio referenced above (60 percent fixed income and 40 percent large cap equity for the 20-year period ending September 2002), with no rebalancing, an investor would have suffered a maximum loss of 15.82 percent for any rolling 12-month period. By comparison, with periodic rebalancing, an investor would have been able to reduce the maximum loss by at least two-thirds, to −5.13 percent or less—relative to the investor who never rebalanced. In short, rebalancing can reduce maximum loss in down markets.[56] Benefit from rebalancing and employ automatic portfolio rebalancing as a powerful risk management tool.

Control Your Behavior—Be Disciplined

The most important component of a successful investment plan is the investor himself or herself. Investors make money in up and down markets. Therefore, it is not only the product or the investment vehicle that necessarily determines success or failure; it is the investor's behavior and decisions that determine the outcome of an investment.

In an investment policy statement or the written plan, it is the investor that spells out her goals, her time horizon, her risk tolerance, her expectations of return, the amount to invest, when to invest, and how to invest, hopefully guided by a seasoned and trustworthy advisor. The vast majority of investment decisions are made by the investor. Few investors, except those who invest in mutual funds or through money managers, relegate the authority of decision making to their advisor through a discretionary agreement giving the advisor the right to select what to buy and sell and when.

Even investors with a solid investment policy plan that defines their long-term objectives and quantifies their risk tolerance are often unreasonably bullish when the markets are on the rise and frantic and fearful in times of volatility or declining markets. To achieve your desired results, you should stay the course, especially when the markets become volatile. Too often investors attempt to predict the market and a recent study has found that investment return is heavily dependent upon investment behavior (see Figure 2.4).

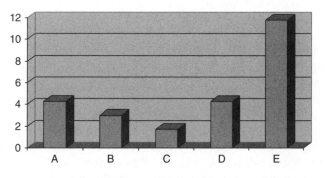

FIGURE 2.4 **Investors' Average Annualized Return (Percent) 1987–2006**

A = Average equity fund investor (4.3 percent)
B = Inflation (3.0 percent)
C = Average fixed income fund investor (1.7 percent)
D = Treasury bills (4.3 percent)
E = S&P 500 Index (11.8 percent)
Source: Dalbar and Mellon Analytical Solutions (July 2007).

Even though the S&P 500 Index returned 11.8 percent over this 20-year period, the average equity investor managed to return a measly 4.3 percent over the same period. Equity investors only slightly outpaced inflation. The average equity investor remains invested for 4.3 years compared to 3.7 years for the average fixed income investor, clearly a short period of time and inconsistent with a well-planned, long-term strategy:[57]

> *Occasional outbreaks of those two super-contagious diseases—fear and greed—will forever occur in the investment community . . . We never try to anticipate the arrival or departure of either disease. Our goal is more modest: We simply attempt to be fearful when others are greedy and greedy when others are fearful.*

> —Warren Buffet, Berkshire Hathaway, Annual Report, 1991

Fear and greed are the likely culprits and could explain why the investor's average annualized returns are substantially less than those of the S&P 500 or a well-planned pension fund.[58] Wealth advisors and professionally managed accounts can help reduce making emotional buy and sell decisions.

Citigroup Smith Barney's affluent investor survey of 585 investors with $100,000 or more in financial assets revealed what investors thought were their biggest mistakes:

- 13 percent—Investing too much in one company/sector
- 10 percent—Not pulling out of poorly performing investments
- 8 percent—Getting rid of investments too quickly
- 8 percent—Not contributing enough to retirement funds
- 6 percent—Being too conservative[59]

A study by MFS Investment Management revealed that 57 percent of working Americans are concerned that they may become too conservative with their investment allocation during their retirement years.[60]

To these mistakes, I would add misplaced self-reliance and chasing returns. Investors need to educate themselves on what it entails to have a successful investment process. However, overconfidence in one's ability to do what it would take years of study, preparation, and experience for a professional advisor or money manager to achieve is a huge mistake. You simply cannot be your own physician or lawyer as much as you should not attempt to be your own wealth/financial advisor. I would challenge average investors to deny that, in the past, they have often determined their investment selection, especially when it came to their 401(k) or other retirement plans, primarily on the basis of past performance. Rearview mirror investing is dangerous, especially if you lack the tools to determine which stock or fund to select in a particular sector, your asset allocation structure, the quality of the investment team if you are looking at mutual funds or individual money managers, whether the fund you are looking at has deviated from its stated goal, and whether it is being compared to the wrong index.

In short, individual investors suffer from seven deadly sins: emotion, disorganization, myopia, impatience, greed, arrogance, and cowardice.[61] I would add to that list: misplaced self-reliance and rearview mirror investing, or chasing returns.

Put Time on Your Side—Be Patient

Time is a critical component of an investing strategy. It is the investor's greatest ally. History has taught us about the value of time:

1. *The earlier or the longer you invest, the more you will be rewarded. The earlier you invest, the more you will accumulate.* Assume that an "early investor" contributed $2,000 annually for 10 years, beginning at age 25 and stopped contributing at age 35. The total amount contributed over this 10-year period will be $20,000. At age 65, assuming an annual return of 8 percent and excluding the effect of any applicable taxes, this investor will end up with a total of $314,871. The "late investor" begins at age 35 and keeps contributing $2,000 a year for 30 years for a total investment of $60,000. By age 65, assuming an annual return of 8 percent and excluding the effect of any applicable taxes, this "late investor" will end up with a much lower amount of $244,692. The early investor used the power of compounding and ended up with substantially more money than the late investor even though the former contributed to his nest egg one-third of what the late investor contributed.[62]

2. *The market is up more years than it is down.* Between 1950 and 2006, the S&P 500 Index was up 77 percent of the time (44 out of 57 years). It was down 23 percent of the time (13 out of 57 years).[63]

3. *In positive years, the market is up a larger percentage than it is down in negative years.* Using the same time period (1950 to 2006), when the market, represented by the S&P 500 Index, the average annual return was 20.4 percent. When it was down, it was lower an average of 10.66 percent. Over the 57-year period, the average annual return of the S&P 500 Index was 13.32 percent.[64]

4. *The odds of negative returns decrease with time.* The probability of negative returns for the S&P 500 Index decreases with time.[65]

1 day	46 percent (probability of negative return)
1 week	42 percent
1 month	35 percent
1 quarter	.27 percent
1 year	18 percent
5 years	17 percent
10 years	0 percent

5. *Time in the market, not timing the market, is what matters.* No one
    can predict the performance of the financial markets from year to year,
    month to month, or even day to day. There is no "perfect" time to
    invest in the market. The key to long-term investment success is not
    when to invest but that you *do* invest. To illustrate this point, compare
    the hypothetical returns of a $5,000 annual investment in the stock
    market, represented by the S&P 500 Index, for the 30 years through
    December 31, 2006, using three different strategies (see Figure 2.5):

    ■ Investing on the worst day of each year, the day the market peaked,
      yielded $1,325,961 (12.3 percent a year).
    ■ Investing on the first day of each year yielded $1,547,279 (12.7 percent
      a year).
    ■ Investing on the best day of each year, the daily market low of the
      year, yielded $1,648,567 (13.2 percent a year).

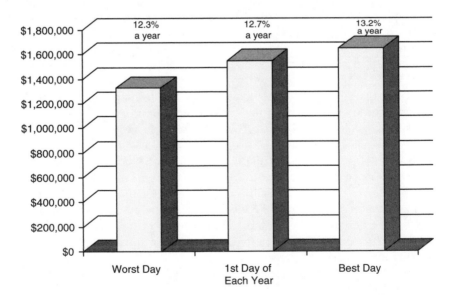

FIGURE 2.5 How $5,000 a year has grown over 30 years[66]

From these data, you might conclude that since no one can predict the worst or best day to invest in a year, had you picked the first day of the year, you would have eliminated the guessing game and your performance would have been in between the best and worst day to invest.

Another way to illustrate the benefits of being fully invested and not attempting to time the market is again by looking back at history. As history has shown, missing out on the best days of market performance—whenever they occur—can significantly affect your investment return. As Table 2.3 reveals, missing the 20 best days in the stock market instead of being fully invested from December 31, 1991, through December 31, 2001, reduced the average annual total return from 10.65 percent to 2.63 percent. The lesson to be learned is that it is better to stay fully invested in the market than attempt to time it.

If we take another 10-year period of the market (December 31, 1997, through December 31, 2007) and started with a hypothetical $10,000 investment in the S&P 500 Index, if you remained fully invested your return would have been $15,131 (+4.3 percent average annual return). Compare that with missing the best 40 days of the market, your portfolio would have lost 64.1 percent with an ending value of $3,590 (see Table 2.3).

Consider, also, the 2,524 business days during this decade:

- None of the market's 10 best days were consecutive.
- Five of the 10 best days were in one year.
- Six of the years did not have any of the 10 best days.[67]
- 8 of the 10 best percentage-gain days for the S&P 500 in the last 50 years took place during bear markets. A bear market is defined as a market drop of at least 20 percent. The 10 days on either side of the peak or trough in the index were counted as part of the bear market period.[68]

TABLE 2.3   Trying to Time the Market Can Be Costly (December 31, 1991–December 31, 2001)[69]

Period of Investment	Average Annual Total Return	Growth of $10,000
Fully invested	10.65 percent	$27,526
Missed the 10 best days	5.99 percent	$17,887
Missed the 20 best days	2.63 percent	$12,968
Missed the 30 best days	−0.08 percent	$9,920
Missed the 40 best days	−2.48 percent	$7,782

TABLE 2.4   Return on $1,000 Invested in the S&P 500 Following Tragic Events

Historic Event	5 Years Later	10 Years Later	Through 12/31/2006
Pearl Harbor attack (12/1941)	$2,046	$44,485	$1,790,695
JF Kennedy assassination (1963)	$1,790	$1,973	$82,504
Dow falls −22.6 percent on 10/19/87	$2,188	$5,635	$9,788
Tech bubble burst on 3/24/00	$829		$1,038
9/11/2001 attack on United States	$1,298		$1,425
U.S. invades Iraq (3/20/2003)			$1,735

Source: "Bull and Bear Markets Come and Go. Successful Investors Stay the Course," *American Funds*, 2007, p. 4.

There is only one strategy to ensure capturing the best days. Do not market time. Stay invested for the entire period.

6. *The market recovers following historical tragedies.* Historically, U.S. stock prices drop following a national tragedy, but over time, returns become positive. If investors sell during downward price pressures, they may realize short-term losses and risk missing out on a potential recovery. Investors who base their decisions on emotions, whether it is greed or fear, tend to lose out. Whether it is the bombing of Pearl Harbor, the assassination of President John F. Kennedy, the Dow falling 22.6 percent in one day, the technology bubble, the September 11, 2001, terrorist attacks in the United States or the U.S. invasion of Iraq, the market recovered with the passage of time (see Table 2.4).

7. *There are a few notable "timing" trends.* Some analysts have studied market and performance data in an attempt to identify "timing-related" trends. For example, the three months of October/November/December have generated 63 percent of the entire total return achieved by the S&P 500 Index in the 17 years from 1990 to 2006.[70] Through 2006, September has returned an average of minus 0.7 percent for the S&P 500 when calculating the S&P 500 average monthly return since 1970. The average monthly return for the S&P 500 Index during that same period has been positive for all other months.[71] In the past 12 U.S. presidential terms, large-cap stocks have gained 23.8 percent on average during the third year of the four-year cycle. In year one, two, and four they averaged 8.3 percent.[72] Election year equity market performance has tended to be strongest with a Republican president in the White House, while the first three years of an administration have seen higher returns under Democrats.[73] Defense stocks have outperformed the S&P 500 in the last eight election years by an impressive average of 19.4 percent.[74]

Some analysts believe that you should pay attention to the current state of the market when you buy stocks. They believe that you should buy stocks when the major indexes are showing signs of accumulation (during heavy volume price increases) and sell stocks when they are showing signs of distribution (heavy volume price declines). According to the proponents of this approach, three-fourths of all stocks follow the market's trend, and you should not go against the trend. This kind of market timing assumes that you have to watch the market's trend each day or essentially time the market using heavy volume price increases and price declines.[75] This approach ignores the effect on taxes, a long-term investment strategy, the cost of buying and selling, and a heavy dose of good luck.

Even though these are clearly identifiable trends, they are only trends that should be noted but in no way should replace a comprehensive and well-studied approach to investing.

Understand How to Manage and Measure Risk

Investing is a personal matter and varies from one person to the next. No single investment or strategy is right for everyone. A major element of investing is understanding risk and your own risk tolerance. With investing, there exists the potential for losing all or a portion of your initial investment. A successful investment strategy gauges how comfortable you are with risk. Often, investors misjudge their risk tolerance. If the markets are rallying and are experiencing a period of lower volatility, investors tend to believe that they have a higher risk tolerance. The more accurate gauge of risk tolerance manifests itself when the markets have sustained a fairly long period of negative returns accompanied by a high level of volatility. Undisciplined investors with misjudged risk tolerance tend to sell in fear, at or close to the bottom of the market, because they are invested more aggressively than their true risk tolerance can bear.

> *"If your stocks worry you, sell to the sleeping point.*
> *Be bullish in a bull market, but don't be either a bull or a bear all the time.*
> *The market always does what it should do, but not always when."*
>
> —Joseph D. Goodman, *Forbes* magazine columnist[76]

Stocks and bonds have different measures of risk.

Stock Risk Measures

Stocks are subject to two types of risk—market risk and nonmarket risk.

Market risk is the risk that movements in the overall stock market will affect a particular stock's price. If markets are on the rise, stocks tend to increase in price, sometimes irrespective of the fundamentals. Conversely, the stock price of fundamentally sound companies tends to suffer in a declining market.

Nonmarket risk, or specific risk, is the risk that events specific to a company or its relevant industry sector will negatively affect the stock's price. For example, the aviation industry is directly affected by the price of oil. Whenever the price of oil rises, the aviation industry is negatively affected, and vice versa. Nonmarket risk can be reduced through diversification, or owning several different stocks in different sectors of the market that demonstrate little correlation to each other.

You can measure a stock's historical response to market movements and select those with a level of volatility that you and your advisor are comfortable with. Standard deviation and beta are two tools commonly used to measure stock risk.

Standard deviation is statistical measure of volatility. Standard deviation = volatility = unpredictability = risk.[77] Standard deviation measures a stock's volatility or total portfolio risk, regardless of the cause. It indicates the extent to which an investment's return deviates from the expected normal return. In other words, it tells you how much a stock's short-term returns have moved around its long-term average. A volatile investment would have a high standard deviation because its range of performance has been very wide. What you need to take away is that the smaller the standard deviation, the lower is the volatility associated with the stock, and the higher the standard deviation, the higher is the volatility associated with the stock. If you have a choice, choose a portfolio that gives you an 8 percent return with a standard deviation of 10 instead of a portfolio that gives you an 8 percent return with a standard deviation of 14. Small-cap stocks tend to have a larger standard deviation than large-cap stocks, while growth stocks tend to have a larger standard deviation than value stocks.[78] In performance measurement, it is generally assumed that a larger standard deviation implies that greater risk was taken to achieve the return.

Beta is a statistical measure of a portfolio's sensitivity to market (index) movements or the impact that stock market movements have historically had on a stock's price. The beta of the market is 1.0 by definition. If we take the S&P 500 as the index (which, by definition, has a beta of 1), then a stock with a beta of 1 means that, on average, the stock moves parallel with the S&P 500—the stock should rise 10 percent when the S&P 500 rises 10 percent and should decline 10 percent when the S&P 500 declines 10 percent. If a stock's beta is greater than 1, this indicates that the stock should rise or fall to a greater extent than the S&P 500 Index. Roughly speaking, a security with a beta of 1.5 will move, on average, 1.5 times the market return. In other words, the stock is more volatile than the market. A beta less than 1 means the stock should rise or fall to a lesser extent than the S&P 500. In this case, the stock is less volatile than the market. Beta represents the type of risk (systematic risk) that cannot be diversified away.

$$\text{Total risk} = \text{Market risk} + \text{Nonmarket risk}$$

Total risk is measured by factors like standard deviation.
Market risk is measured by beta (market risk relative to a benchmark) and cannot be diversified away.[79]

Standard deviation and beta are the most often used risk measures. Sharpe ratio and information ratio are, by comparison, risk-adjusted measures.

   Sharpe ratio measures risk-adjusted performance by determining the reward per unit of risk. The higher the Sharpe ratio, the more efficient or the more return you earn per unit of risk. Sharpe ratio assesses both risk and return in one measure. It is more appropriate for investors concerned with absolute performance. If you compare two portfolios that have the same return, you need to find out the level of risk that was taken by the portfolio managers to achieve their returns. Clearly, the portfolio that achieved the same return with lower risk is the preferable portfolio. This would be reflected in a higher Sharpe ratio for the portfolio. If you see a negative Sharpe ratio, that means that the portfolio has underperformed the Treasury bill (T-bill), and that is not a desirable portfolio.[80]
   Information ratio also measures risk-adjusted performance by determining the reward per unit of risk. As an investor, no matter what your aversion to risk, you should seek the highest information ratio possible. Information ratio and Sharpe ratio share the same concept; however, they are calculated using different measures.

Fixed Income/Bond Measures

The most common fixed income or bond measures are duration, yield, and maturity.

> **Duration**—Interest rates and bond prices move in opposite directions. This can significantly affect a bond's market value. Duration calculates how much a bond's price will move for every 1 percent change in interest rates. If a bond's duration is 4.5 years, the price of the bond will fall 4.5 percent for a 1 percent rise in interest rates. And, if a portfolio manager expects interest rates to decline by 0.5 percent and holds a portfolio with duration of five years, the portfolio's market value would be expected to appreciate by 2.5 percent. Bonds with one to four years of duration are considered short-term bonds, while those with four to seven years are considered intermediate bonds, and those with more than seven years of duration are considered long-term bonds.[81]
>
> **Maturity** takes into account the life of the bond while duration also takes into account coupon payments. A bond's duration is typically shorter than its maturity.
>
> **Yield** is the cash flow as a percent of the purchase price. Current yield is calculated by dividing the bond's annual interest rate by the purchase price. Therefore, the components of total return for a bond are its price appreciation plus its yield.

Bond investing is subject to certain risks, including *credit risk, interest rate risk, income risk,* and *foreign risk.* **Credit risk** is the risk that an issuer of a bond will be unable to make interest and principal payments when due. Lower-rated bonds tend to pay higher interest but are generally considered speculative and carry greater credit risk. **Interest risk** is the risk that interest rates will rise, causing bond prices to fall. **Income risk** is the risk that the fund's income will decline if market interest rates fall. If you invest in foreign issuers and non-U.S.-dollar denominated instruments, you are subjecting yourself to foreign risk. **Foreign risk** is the risk that foreign securities will be more volatile than U.S. securities due to factors such as adverse economic, currency, political, social or regulatory developments in the foreign country, including government seizure of assets, excessive taxation, limitations on the transfers of assets, the lack of liquidity, or regulatory controls or differing legal and/or accounting standards.

Stock risk measures and bond duration, yield, and maturity measures can provide important information about your portfolio's volatility. If your portfolio is riskier than you realized, you might want to take steps to reduce that risk. In short, when investing, you cannot only concentrate on the returns, but you have to also take a hard look at the level of risk that you are taking in order to achieve your desired return or reward. Understanding risk and being able to quantify it, if possible, are critical components of determining your investment strategy.

One of the great pieces of investment wisdom was uttered by Baron Rothschild some 200 years ago. He advised, "Buy on the sound of cannons and sell on the sound of trumpets."[82]

Investors across the ages have made fortunes buying when others were in a state of panic. Investors did not have a fairly reliable gauge to foretell when fear was at its most. If they waited for a definitive sign that fear had subsided, they might have missed most of the upside potential. Then, in 1993, the **VIX Index**, otherwise known as the **Volatility Index**, was introduced in a published paper by Professor Robert E. Whaley of Duke University. The Chicago Board of Options Exchanges (CBOE) Volatility Index, more commonly known by its ticker symbol VIX, is also known as the *fear gauge*. The VIX is an implied volatility index that measures the market's expectation of 30-day S&P 500 volatility implicit in the prices of near-term S&P 500 options. Traders have found the VIX to be very useful in trading. It provides excellent opportunities for both hedging and speculation. One advantage of the VIX is its negative correlation with the S&P 500. Since 1990, the VIX has moved opposite the S&P 500 Index 88 percent of the time. This makes it an excellent diversification tool and one of the best tools for market disaster insurance.[83] The VIX has spelled out some of the best buying opportunities of recent years. When the VIX hit an intraday high of 37.57 on January 22, 2008, its highest since October 2002 (38.5), stocks staged a massive turnaround that day and an even bigger one on the next day, with the Dow Jones Industrials swinging over 600 points from its bottom to its close.[84] Between 1995 through the end of 2007, the average VIX level has been 19.8.[85]

Factor the Effect of Taxes and Inflation

Over time, the great enemy of investors has been inflation and, with the evolution of taxation into a permanent feature in our daily lives, taxes have emerged as an equally great threat to the growth of investments and the building of wealth.

Inflation has gone up +115 percent over the last 25 years, or +3.1 percent per year. An item costing $1 on December 31, 1982, would cost $2.15 on December 31, 2007. If you were living on a fixed income over the past 25 years, you would only have 46 percent of your purchasing power today, compared to what you had at the end of 1982.[86]

To help you mitigate the threat of inflation, the asset mix in your investments is critical. If your investments are primarily in fixed income instruments such as money market funds and bonds, you would have historically generated more consistent (albeit lower) returns than stocks. Your principal, had you invested in bonds, would have seen *some* fluctuation, but considerably less than fluctuations or volatility experienced by stocks. And, you would have received a stream of income from those bonds. However, stocks in general have historically been superior contributors to building and protecting wealth from inflation, as compared to government bonds or U.S. Treasury bills.

Had you invested $1 in 1926 in stocks, bonds, and Treasury bills, your investment by 2006 would have grown as follows:

- $3,077.33 (invested in the S&P 500 Index)
- $71.69 (invested in long-term government bond)
- $19.29 (invested in U.S. Treasury bills)
- $11.20 (U.S. inflation index)[87]

The effect of taxes and inflation on the return of an investment can be easily demonstrated with the following example. Even though you might have earned an average of 9.54 percent on your investment every year, your "real" rate of return would have been reduced by taxes and inflation. Depending on your situation and income tax bracket, as much as 35 percent of your 9.54 percent compound annual return could have been paid in federal taxes, leaving you with a real return of 6.20 percent.[88]

Then, if you calculate the effect of inflation on your earnings and assuming that inflation averaged 3 percent over the same period that you earned your 6.20 percent compound annual return after taxes, your inflation-adjusted, after-tax return will in reality be 3.11 percent.[89] Although this example uses the highest federal income tax return, which does not apply to every investor, this illustration clearly demonstrates the impact that both taxes and inflation can have on your return.

In summary and using the previous example:

- A 9.54 percent return is reduced to 6.20 percent adjusted for federal income tax.
- The 6.20 percent return adjusted for inflation is further reduced to 3.11 percent.

To help you fight inflation when investing, you must pay careful attention to the makeup of your portfolio. Historically, stocks, more so than almost all other investments (including most real estate investments), have beaten inflation. In February 2008, the Pension Benefit Guaranty Corporation (PBGC), which takes over failed corporate pension programs and manages the funds on behalf of workers and retirees, announced that it had adopted a new investment allocation for its $55 billion portfolio. PBGC used to invest between 15 to 25 percent of its assets in stocks, with the rest in fixed-income investments. PBGC decided instead to allocate 45 percent of its portfolio into stocks, 45 percent into bonds, and the remaining 10 percent into alternative investments such as real estate and private equity. PBGC analysts belatedly discovered that by changing the allocation to more stocks and alternative investments, the organization improved the likelihood of fully funding its obligations within 10 years from 19 to 57 percent![90] A major lesson from this reallocation is that stocks, according to PBGC officers and other pension experts, even amid recent setbacks and volatility, remain one of the best ways to beat inflation over the long term. Additionally, unlike stocks, which benefit from rising dividends and corporate earnings, bond returns are typically fixed and are highly vulnerable to inflation.

Your investments would face taxable issues if they are placed outside of what the government considers "qualified accounts," such as IRAs, Roth IRAs, other retirement plans, education savings plans, certain life insurance policies and annuities. If you cannot invest in a qualified account or you have reached the maximum contribution limit(s), your investments will have to face the obstacle of tax.

Again, when investing, you must pay careful attention to the makeup of your portfolio. The mix of taxable and tax-deferred investments you choose can generally impact the overall performance of your portfolio and the amount you end up accumulating. As Figure 2.6 illustrates, the performance

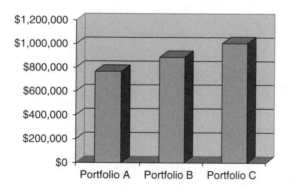

FIGURE 2.6 Tax-Deferred Investments Increase Portfolio Returns: Benefits of Tax Deferral 1983–2003[91]

Portfolio A: 80 percent Taxable + 20 percent Tax Deferred; Ending Value ($767,426)
Portfolio B: 50 percent Taxable + 50 percent Tax Deferred; Ending Value ($886,435)
Portfolio C: 20 percent Taxable + 80 percent Tax Deferred; Ending Value
    ($1,005,445)

of a portfolio that is heavily weighted in taxable investments can suffer from the effects of taxes.

Please note that with a tax-deferred investment, taxes are deferred until you begin withdrawing from your portfolio unless you invest in instruments such as education saving plans and Roth IRAs. With these investment instruments, your distributions are tax free, provided that, in the case of the education saving plans, the funds are used for their intended purpose—to pay for higher education. With regard to Roth IRAs, your distribution is tax free after meeting certain holding and age requirements. And, you can only use after-tax money to fund a Roth IRA.

When investing, it is crucial that you take into account the impact of taxes. For example, dividend income, long-term capital gains, and short-term capital gains are taxed at different levels. A capital gain is only realized (subject to taxes) when the investment changes hands or is sold. Taxable bonds usually pay higher interest than tax-free bonds. Depending on your tax bracket, your net returns from a taxable investment may not be greater, and may even be less, than the lower-paying tax-free bond investment.

Tax efficiency is an important contributor to potentially lowering your taxes. Passionate passive investors—those who believe primarily in investing in index funds—argue that since index funds typically buy and sell less often than actively managed portfolios, including mutual funds, index investing is more tax efficient. Actively managed funds can increase the likelihood of capital gains distributions. Mutual fund shareholders, for example, purchase and redeem shares from the fund, which may result in capital gains distributions to *all* shareholders. Also, exchange traded funds buy and sell shares on an exchange, which does not affect other shareholders.

Please consult with your tax advisor to help you evaluate whether tax-free investments are appropriate for you and whether certain investment vehicles such as index funds and exchange traded funds are more appropriate investment vehicles, given your tax situation.

In short, when investing, be mindful that inflation cuts into the value of your investments the way taxes cut into your investment returns.

Utilize Multiple Investment Vehicles and Products

Investing is the placement of money into a financial vehicle with the objective of making a profit. Investment can be achieved through ownership, loaning money, derivatives, and paying off costly debt. There are numerous financial instruments/vehicles that facilitate your investing. The most common of these are mutual funds (open- and closed-end funds), index funds, unit investment trusts, exchange trade-funds, and separately managed accounts.

The Six Ways to Achieve Investment

Investing can be achieved six ways:

1. **Ownership,** such as buying a stock or real estate
2. **Loaning money** to an entity such a corporation or the government
3. **Interest-bearing instruments**, such as checking and savings accounts, and certificates of deposit (CDs)
4. **Derivatives,** buying options or futures contracts
5. **Alternative investments**
6. **Paying off costly debt**

INVESTING THROUGH OWNERSHIP   Companies use stocks to raise capital to get started or help sustain the growth of a business through marketing, adding new products, or even acquiring new businesses. As a stockholder, you become one of the owners of that company, no matter how small your piece of the pie may be. This is the reason stocks are considered equity investments. **Common stocks** provide a share of ownership in a company and provide the shareholder with a right to vote in company issues. The price of a share of stock will vary dramatically among companies, from pennies to hundreds or thousands of dollars, depending on a large of number of factors such as held assets, market share, profitability, price to earnings ratio, and so on. Stocks, especially individually held stocks, are regarded as one of the riskiest investments. By comparison, **preferred stocks** often yield higher and more stable dividends. **Dividends** are the payments that a corporation makes to its stockowners and are based on the corporation's earnings and profits. If you own common stock in a growth company—a company that needs to reinvest its profits in the company itself—you probably will not be receiving dividends.

Real Estate Investment Trusts (REITs) were created by the U.S. Congress in 1960 to give anyone the ability to invest in large-scale commercial properties. At least 22 countries have approved the creation of REITs, and the global real estate securities market represents more than $900 billion of equity capitalization and is growing rapidly. The most compelling reason to invest in REITs within an investment portfolio is its low correlation to other asset classes and to stocks and bonds, which make REITs a great diversification tool and can serve to lower the risk of your overall portfolio. REITs are considered an alternative and separate asset class, which is highly desirable for investors who seek attractive investment opportunities outside the traditional stock/bond universe. U.S. and non-U.S. REITs have had attractive returns over the past 15 years and typically pay out a substantial percentage of their taxable income to shareholders annually in the form of dividends.[92]

INVESTING THROUGH LOANING   **Bonds** are a way to invest by loaning money to an entity whether it is a corporation (domestic or international) or the government, whether federal, state, or local. By borrowing your money, these entities promise to pay back the principal balance at a set date. When that time has come, the bond is said to have matured. In return for your loan, you are promised a certain amount of interest at a fixed rate for a fixed period of time. This period of time can range anywhere from a few months to over 20 years. With some bonds, such as U.S. savings bonds or zero coupon bonds, you get all your interest when the bond matures because you buy the bond at discounted prices and receive the full value when it matures. Bonds are generally considered conservative investment vehicles. You need to be aware that bond prices fluctuate because when interest rate goes up, bonds decrease in value, and, conversely, when interest rates go down, bonds are more valuable because their interest rate is higher that the interest rate available for other investments.

Bonds are not risk free. Investing in bonds carries varying risks depending on the type of bond you own (municipal, U.S. government, or corporate). Bonds also carry the risk of default, although this is much less likely if you own municipal bonds, unlikely if you own U.S. government bonds, and possible if you own corporate bonds. Bonds have ratings that determine, to a good measure, the reliability of receiving interest on time and principal when the bond matures. Your income tax situation may influence your bond investment decision because the interest from certain bonds (municipal bonds) is not taxed at the federal, state, or local level.

CASH OR CERTIFICATES OF DEPOSIT (CDS)   If you deposit your cash in a checking, savings, or money market account, you will most likely receive interest payments, usually credited to your account on a monthly basis. The interest rate differs from one financial institution to the other and depends often on the amount of cash you deposit and the prevailing interest rate environment. There is no risk in investing in a checking or a savings account since cash deposits are insured by the government, at least up to a certain level per account and per financial institution. This is not the way to get rich because in most cases, your interest payments are below the annual inflation rate meaning that your cash is losing its purchasing power over time.

In an environment where the Federal Reserve is slashing interest rates, billions of dollars of investor money flows into money market funds, which are the most rate-sensitive investments. The flight to safety, as some investors view it, is in reality turning from one form of risk to another due to inflation. As of February 2008, money-market mutual fund assets stood at a record $3.27 trillion. The money-market rates paid out are hardly attractive with a yield of 3.17 percent. With inflation standing at 4.1 percent as measured by the Consumer Price Index in 2007, the net-net effect adjusted for inflation for money market holders is negative.[93]

CDs differ from bonds in that they are debt instruments offered through banks. With CDs, you place certain amounts of money into a CD for a predetermined period of time ranging from several months to several years. In the exchange, the bank agrees to pay a predetermined amount of interest. CDs are generally insured, up to certain limits, by the Federal Depository Insurance Corporation (FDIC), in the unlikely event of the failure of a bank to pay you interest or your principal back. CDs are viewed as extremely conservative investment instruments.

DERIVATIVES—INVESTING WITHOUT BUYING THE UNDERLYING INVESTMENTS A derivative is a "risk-shifting agreement, the value of which is derived from the value of the underlying asset. The underlying asset could be a physical commodity, an interest rate, a company stock, a stock index, or virtually any other tradable instrument upon which two parties can agree."[94] With derivatives you are investing in the stock or commodities markets, for example, and not buying any stocks or commodities. The use of derivatives can be a risky and controversial strategy since most politicians, senior executives, regulators and even portfolio managers have limited knowledge of these complex products.[95] Derivatives include options or futures contracts. These enable you or obligate you to buy or sell stocks or commodities at a certain price.[96] Institutional investors have increasingly used derivatives to either hedge their existing positions, or to speculate on given markets or commodities. The growing use of these instruments is a double-edged sword because, although derivatives can be used to mitigate portfolio risk, institutions that are highly leveraged can suffer huge losses if their positions move against them.

A number of well-known hedge funds have suffered severe losses in recent years as their derivative positions declined in value, forcing them to sell off their securities at significantly lower prices to meet margin calls and customer redemptions. The 2008 turmoil in the financial markets affected negatively a wide spectrum of banks, investment banks as well as hedge funds. Many of the most well-known names in the financial industry either went bankrupt or were purchased at rock-bottom prices by larger financial entities. Still, one of the largest hedge funds to collapse in recent years as a result of adverse movements in its derivatives positions was the Long Term Capital Management (LTCM).[97]

Principal protection notes, another innovative investment vehicle, offer similar return potential as traditional investments, yet also provide protection against a market decline when held to maturity (subject to the credit risk of the issuer). Unlike traditional fixed-income investments that pay predetermined periodic interest, the return on principal protection notes

(PPNs), also known as structured products, is determined at maturity based on the performance of the underlying investment. PPNS can give you exposure to a wide variety of underlying investments or strategies, including benchmark indices, stocks, interest rates, and even commodities or currencies. Please note that investing in PPNs is not equivalent to investing directly in the underlying instruments. They are only sold by prospectus and involve many risks including illiquidity in the secondary market.

ALTERNATIVE INVESTMENTS   Alternative investments are not for everyone and are fraught with risks that go beyond those associated with investing in stocks, bonds, and cash. Alternative investment products are often speculative. Investors could lose all or a substantial portion of their investments. They are only suitable for long-term investors willing to forgo liquidity and put capital at risk for an indefinite period of time. They may be highly illiquid and have no regulated secondary market. They have higher fees than traditional investment vehicles and can engage in leverage and other speculative practices. They are not subject to the same regulatory requirements as mutual funds and provide limited transparency with respect to their holdings and investments. They involve complex tax structures and may be tax inefficient.

If you are turned off by all these warnings and risk potentials, you should not be. Alternatives have been used by endowments and high-net-worth individuals and, more recently, increasingly by average investors through alternative-like mutual funds. By adding a strategic mix of lower-correlating asset classes (such as real estate, global utilities, natural resources, other commodities, international real estate, currencies, and a long/short investment approach), you can potentially boost your diversification significantly, increase your growth potential and reduce your risk over time.[98]

Pete Seeley, the highly respected economist at the MSIM Institute, summarizes his views on alternatives by stating, "It may seem risky to invest in alternative strategies when they are new to us and have risks that we cannot fully understand. However, in my view, it may be more risky to restrict oneself to conventional stock and bond investments during the years ahead."[99]

INVESTING THROUGH PAYING OFF COSTLY DEBT   It is somewhat unconventional to address investing by looking at your debt. Even though debt, especially credit-card debt, affords a great convenience when shopping or paying bills, it is a "slow-acting poison for people that don't pay them off in full and on time every month."[100] Depending on your credit history and your credit card company, the total interest, late charges, finance charges, and penalties imposed on paying your credit card debt over time, or even skipping some monthly credit card payments, could range between 18 to 30 percent or even more. So, every dollar invested in reducing your credit card debt returns between 18 and 30 percent. Where can you find this type of guaranteed return or savings, in this case? This type of return pales in comparison to the average return over investing in the market over time. It is not taxable to you, it will improve your credit rating, help you begin building the wealth that you aspire for, and give you peace of mind. In short, if you have debt, especially crippling credit card debt, your best and guaranteed investment is to pay off these credit card debts.

Investment Vehicles and Products

As an investor, you can buy individual stocks and bonds. However, among individual investors, the five most common investment vehicles and products are:

1. Mutual funds, which include: open- and closed-ended funds, target-date funds, and index funds
2. Exchange traded funds
3. Unit investment trusts
4. Separately managed accounts
5. Alternative investments, which include hedge funds and private equity

This section will provide you with a brief overview of the existing and most commonly utilized investment vehicles and products. A more comprehensive discussion of this topic is beyond the scope of either this chapter or this book.

MUTUAL FUNDS   When investing, you cannot avoid risk, you can only manage it. For most investors, investing in securities is done through mutual funds. About 88 million Americans own mutual funds—by far, the most popular and common investment vehicle.[101] A mutual fund pools investors' money to invest in stocks, bonds, and cash. The two most important advantages to investing through mutual funds are diversification and professional management. Investors cut down on the risks associated with investing in securities by diversifying investments. Because your money is pooled with a large number of other investors' funds, you have the ability to invest in a huge range of securities that would be unavailable to you because the minimum cost of investing would be too high for an individual investor.[102]

Mutual funds are actively managed by a team of professionals using preset guidelines. By investing in mutual funds, you have the services of financial professionals who use information, often secured from first-hand sources and possibly hard to come by, to make decisions that further a mutual fund's objective. Mutual funds are fairly liquid in that you can buy and sell them on a daily basis. Mutual funds have fees associated with them to cover management, trading, and sales fees. Often, however, they do not charge fees and commissions for reinvesting dividends and gains or for transferring investments within a mutual fund family.

There are three main categories of mutual funds—stock funds (invest primarily in stocks); bond funds (invest primarily in corporate or government bonds); and money market funds (these make short-term investments in an effort to keep their share value fixed at $1). All mutual funds have investment objectives—growth, balanced growth, income, or capital preservation. Mutual funds invest in various sizes of security categories such as the size of the company, its total market value or its market capitalization. Mutual funds invest in domestic and international markets, in various sectors of the economy, in domestic and international bonds, in companies that pay increasing dividends, and in value versus growth stocks. The mixture among these categories is sometimes mind boggling:

1. *Open- and closed-end funds*—Most mutual funds are **open-end funds** meaning that the fund would sell as many shares as investors want. Sometimes open-end funds are closed to new investors when they grow too large to be managed effectively. **Closed-end funds** are similar to open-end funds except they raise money only once and offer only a fixed number of shares that are traded on an exchange or over the counter. The market price of a closed-end fund fluctuates in response to investor demand as well as to changes in the value of its holdings.
2. *Target-date funds, also known as lifecycle funds, are the latest mutual fund craze, especially inside retirement plans.* After a slow start in the 1990s, **lifecycle funds** have grown rapidly to over $200 billion in assets under management, thanks to the Department of Labor's approval of their use in qualified retirement plans as a Qualified Investment Alternative at the end of 2007. Retirement plans can now automatically enroll new participants in one of these investment vehicles if the participant declines to choose an investment option.[103] Fund managers allocate and manage a diversified portfolio, depending on the retirement age of the participant. The more years you have to retirement, the higher exposure you would normally have to domestic and international stocks. The closer you are to retirement; the fund tends to shift its asset allocation to more conservative instruments such as bonds and cash. Be careful, however, in selecting your target-date funds as their allocation, diversification, and investment style are highly dependent on the fund manager and do not necessarily follow a set formula.

3. *Index funds.* An index is a "selection of securities intended to represent various markets. The index representation can be as broad as the U.S. stock market (such as the Russell 3000) or as narrow as one country or industry (such as the MSCI Japan or NASDAQ Biotechnology). Each index has its own construction methodology, or rules of inclusion, established by its index provider. The companies that compose an index are commonly referred to as *constituents.*"[104]

With the proliferation of so many mutual funds, an investor is overwhelmed by trying to decide which fund to use. For many individual investors, the simple solution to this dilemma is to select an index fund. An index fund does not create itself. In 1896, Dow Jones launched what is now known as the Dow Jones Industrial Average, one of the most widely followed stock market indicators comprised of 30 blue chip U.S. stocks. Since then, there has been a proliferation of indexes measuring the performance of broad and narrow sectors of the financial markets. The S&P 500 Index was created in 1957. Its components are determined by an eight-person index committee.[105] The committee weighs individual stocks that might be eligible for inclusion based on certain criteria, while maintaining a balance among sectors and industries that aim to make the index representative of the U.S. domestic market.

Indexes are used in different ways, the most common of which are these:

- *Serve as an indicator of the market's health and direction.* The S&P 500 Index is commonly seen as a measure of the overall U.S. equity market.
- *Serve as a benchmark for an investment manager's performance.* Money managers are often evaluated on their ability to outperform the benchmark that most accurately reflects their style of investing.
- *Serve as the foundation for an investment product, such as an index mutual fund or an exchange traded fund (ETF).* The index fund manager's goal is to provide the investor with the return represented by the index since an investor cannot directly invest in the index itself.[106]

An index fund is tied to the performance of a stock market index, such as the S&P 500. These indexes attempt to gauge the performance of the market by tracking a certain number and variety of stocks. It is usually the goal of most mutual funds to beat the major index performance corresponding to the most appropriate and relevant index. Since there is no absolute measure of investment performance, comparing your investments to benchmarks is really the only way to evaluate your results. If your portfolio of large-cap stocks gained 8 percent in a particular year, that is a good average annual return. However, if during the same year, the S&P 500 Index gained

15 percent, that means that your portfolio of large-cap stocks significantly underperformed its benchmark by a wide margin.

Some investors and advisors opt to invest using index funds for two main reasons: About 80 percent of index funds have resulted in higher returns than actively managed mutual funds, and index funds have lower fees since they are not actively managed.[107]

You have to be careful to avoid measuring the performance of one asset class, let us say mid-cap company stocks, against the benchmark of another asset class such as large-cap stock companies. You need to compare apples to apples, as the saying goes, to accurately gauge the performance of your mutual fund compared to its corresponding index. At the same time, some funds take a much higher level of risk to achieve the same return as another fund that takes on a much more moderate risk in investing its assets. You simply cannot make comparisons solely based on returns. There are so many variables involved that need to be taken into consideration when comparing and evaluating mutual funds (in the same asset class) versus their benchmark index.

EXCHANGE TRADED FUNDS (ETFs)   Although ETFs have been around since the mid-1990s, their popularity has increased only in the past few years. ETFs are not mutual funds. They are baskets of stocks that track an index such as the S&P 500 Index. ETFs are an "excellent, low cost, tax efficient method of capturing the world's markets,"[108] and according to some advisors should be a component of every passive investor's portfolio. ETFs are traded on an exchange just like company shares. Unlike mutual funds, ETFs can be bought and sold throughout the day much like an individual stock. Also, many ETFs have options and futures and can be shorted and bought on margin. You can find ETFs for domestic and international, large, mid and small cap, growth and value funds as well as fixed income offerings. ETFs carry some risks. Among domestic ETFs, assets of sector funds have grown more rapidly in recent years than those of broad-market funds. These narrowly focused funds, if not used sparingly in a portfolio, could hurt inexperienced investors should the funds fall sharply.[109] Additionally, ETFs can be more expensive than traditional index funds for investors who buy ETFs in small quantities over time, because you pay a trading commission every time you buy and sell ETF shares.

As of March 2008, the Securities and Exchange Commission was inching closer toward a final green light to "active" ETFs that would not be required to track a set index. If active ETFs are eventually approved, they are not guaranteed to be a smashing success because they will be operating with no real-world track record and without investment managers who are known to most investors and wealth advisors.[110]

Morgan Stanley research predicts that global ETF assets under management will reach $2,000 billion by 2011 up from $604.2 billion in 2007. Deborah Fuhr, an analyst at Morgan Stanley, commented that as "the job of most portfolio managers has become broader and deeper... we have found that many are admitting that they do not have the time nor the resources to try to add value in all markets and are embracing the use of ETFs to gain international market exposure. This allows them to pick stocks in the markets that they feel they can add value in."[111]

UNIT INVESTMENT TRUSTS (UITs) A **unit investment trust (UIT)** is a registered investment company that buys and holds a generally fixed portfolio of stocks, bonds, or other securities. A UIT has a stated date for termination that varies according to the investments held in the portfolio. A UIT investing in long-term bonds may remain outstanding for 20 to 30 years. The securities in a UIT are professionally selected to meet a stated objective such as growth, income, or capital appreciation. UITs employ a "buy-and-hold" investment strategy—once the trust's portfolio is selected, its securities typically will not be sold or new ones bought. Historically, the majority of UIT assets have been invested in fixed-income investments, especially tax-free bonds. More recently, however, deposits in equity UITs have exceeded deposits in both taxable and tax-free debt. Many UITs are structured to mirror the composition of a particular stock index. UITs that concentrate on specific market segments, such as health care, energy, technology, real estate, telecommunications, or certain international markets seek to capitalize on the growing popularity of these sectors. As of the end of 2006, UITs held over $49.66 billion in assets—of these, 22 percent were in bond trusts.[112] In 2006, 858 new UITs were created—714 were new equity trusts and 144 were bond trusts. UITs, like mutual funds and closed-end funds, are subject to stringent federal laws and oversight by the U.S. Securities and Exchange Commission (SEC).

As an investment vehicle, UITs are most useful as part of an overall diversified portfolio. UITs allow exposure to both broad and highly specialized areas of the market. They are a great vehicle in a satellite account concentrating on opportunistic and sometimes often ignored areas of investing such as global infrastructure, water resources and certain alternative energy sources.

SEPARATELY MANAGED ACCOUNTS (SMAs) It was only in 1975 when Jim Lockwood, an E.F. Hutton broker, began charging clients a fee to have several managers oversee their portfolios.[113] Today, depending on the firm and the investment platform, it is possible to hire a world-class money manager with as little as $50,000. In the past and even today, if you go directly to these money management firms, the monetary threshold to become a client is significantly higher and beyond the reach of most individual investors.

Compared to investing in mutual funds, some of the advantages of investing in separately managed accounts include the following:[114]

- Tax-efficiency, either because of a manager's low turnover or because of the manager's ability to take on tax loss harvesting. **Tax loss harvesting** is a process of selling securities at a loss to offset any investments sold that incurred a capital gain. The client is then able to possibly minimize his/her annual tax bill.
- Transparency because, unlike a mutual fund, with SMAs you own stocks, bonds, or other investment instruments outright.
- Low turnover because redemptions will not force a manager to sell other shareholders' holdings, just the one whose account is being liquidated.
- Customization—a technology executive would request not to hold stock in his own company or sector since he/she might already be overly exposed to that sector. The investor might also request not to own "sin" stocks such as liquor, tobacco, or gambling stocks. You cannot make such a request if you own a mutual fund.
- Lower expenses because of the combination of low turnover, higher account minimums, and the sensitivity to tax efficient investing.
- Experienced managers—the average tenure of a mutual fund manager is 3 to 5 years while SMA managers have an average of 15 to 20 years of money management experience.

The major drawback of investing in SMAs is that frequently investors and their advisors do not take full advantage of the many features offered by this money management platform.

Monitor Your Plan and Make Necessary Changes

Even a thoroughly thought-out investment policy statement that sets out detailed, realistic personal and investment goals, that identifies your risk tolerance and time horizon, and that is properly diversified and asset allo- cated to various sectors of the market and regions of the world, has to be revisited at least once a year or as often the needs arise, to ensure that all components of your investment plan are working in sync to help you attain your desired goals. Portfolios are not static; they often change without us doing anything to them. Market forces will make some investments better than others, fund managers can veer off the stated path, the economy could fall into a recession, interest rates might spike, your source of income might increase or decrease, your family might expand, and your professional goals might change.

Once you construct an investment portfolio, no matter how carefully, you must monitor a number of factors to ensure that, through a changing world, you will ultimately reach your destination. When it comes to constructing an investment portfolio, you need to monitor the following basic building blocks:

- Your goals—personal, financial and professional.
- Your asset allocation and diversification—the building blocks of any portfolio.
- Your portfolio balance. Portfolios that are not rebalanced can be much more volatile over time compared to those that are periodically balanced.
- Your stock, bond, and other alternative investment holdings. Companies change over time and so does the economic cycle, which can drive your investment results.
- Your ultimate financial objectives. These will be affected by changes around you, which might force you to change the amount you save, and your time horizon. We live longer and we need to plan these days for at least 30 or so years in retirement.
- Your health and that of your family members can also change your future financials needs.

Given all these unknowns, you cannot afford to wait. The sooner you recognize your changing needs, the more able you are to adjust in order to meet your goals. This is why it is imperative to regularly or, at the very least, annually, review your investment portfolio with an eye on quickly adapting to the sea of change that surrounds you. If I were to leave you with three recommendations, they are: Regularly rebalance your portfolio; keep your plan up to date; and save more.

Seek Professional Advice

It is an understatement bordering on naiveté to think of investing as a simple, easy process. In the past, an investor would buy some blue chip stocks, some bonds, have some cash in the bank, own a house, and either have a steady lifetime job with a pension plan or run a business. Today's investing, however, has become as complicated as the world that we live in. The landscape is continuously shifting. We are living in a global world where events in China could very well affect our lives in rural America. Investing instruments and vehicles have grown in sophistication and, along with it, risk. We need to diversify our portfolios, properly asset allocate them among sectors and industries. We need to rebalance our portfolios, take advantage of new investment vehicles and structures, worry about taxes and inflation, not to mention going to work to earn a living and taking care of family affairs.

Few physicians would treat themselves if they fell ill, and few lawyers would defend themselves in a court of law. When it comes to investing, you should be well read, highly educated, aware of changes around you, but smart enough to realize that you need professional help to allow you to navigate through the complicated world of investing. Select someone whom you are compatible with, whom you trust, who understands your goals, fears, and emotions and who is reputable. The type of advice and guidance you can receive from a professional is well worth the extra cost to give you peace of mind and to help ensure your future financial well being.

Avoid the Most Common Investor Mistakes

I cannot think of a more fitting way to conclude this chapter than by summarizing 21 of the most common mistakes that investors make and that, in most cases, may be avoidable with the help of competent investment professionals.[115] These mistakes or investing pitfalls include the following:

1. *Procrastination*—The longer you wait to invest, the longer it will take you to reach your desired goal. Delaying will dilute the power of compounding that increases only with time.
2. *Greed*—Greed is the enemy of a good investor. It means taking on unnecessary risk with the hope of making a "killing." Most investors buy when the stock market is soaring, in other words when it is expensive. However, it is important to realize that investing entails risk, and without realistic and measured risk, you might not meet your desired goals.
3. *Fear*—In this case, either you are afraid to take risk by parking most of your funds in money market accounts and watching inflation erode your buying potential or, when volatility hits the market, you sell and lose out when recovery occurs.
4. *No planning*—Without creating a plan that helps you set your goals, time horizon, and risk tolerance so you can chart a course of action, how can you make any sound decisions? A well-conceived investment plan does not need frequent adjustments. Investment decisions should be made with that investment plan in mind.
5. *Not saving*—Unless you save, and save early, you will most likely not have enough to live through a comfortable retirement. Unless you save,

you will not be able to pay for emergency expenses. Unless you save, you might not be able to help your kids go to college. Unless you save, you might not be able to pay for increasingly outrageous medical bills.

6. *Chasing returns*—Investments go in cycles. Most investors want to buy the hot stock or the high performing mutual fund. Again and again, this strategy has failed. A disciplined approach to investing is the way to go. Construct, with the help of your wealth advisor, a well-diversified portfolio, monitor it, and rebalance it as needed. This is the way to make money over time.

7. *Turning down matching funds*—If your employer offers you matching funds through a retirement plan, this should never be passed up. It is not only free money but it is money that you have already earned and you are choosing not to collect it!

8. *Taking on too much debt*—Some form of debt, such as mortgage debt, as long as it is reasonable and affordable, is acceptable debt. Living off credit cards is not acceptable. Lower your standard of living or take on another job to make both ends meet.

9. *Having unrealistic expectations*—There are no "get rich quick" investments. Your investment goal should be to earn reasonable returns over the long term by investing in high-quality, diversified investments.

10. *Avoiding the sale of an investment with a loss*—Investors get attached to stocks because selling them means admitting making a mistake. When evaluating your investments, review objectively each investment and keep in mind that it is not the investment that matters but the end result of making money from that investment.

11. *Overdiversifying*—Diversification is good. It helps reduce your portfolio's volatility and works differently in varying market conditions. A common investor mistake is for investors to keep adding investments to their existing portfolios that are similar in nature to what they already have and that contributes no additional value to the diversification process.

12. *Not checking your portfolio and its performance*—You need the periodic check-up to make sure that you are on track and that your actual return is close to the target you set. If you are not achieving your targeted return, you risk not achieving your financial goals. Checking your portfolio's performance daily, weekly, or even monthly could be counterproductive and can potentially lead you to overreacting and making unwise and rash decisions. At the most, check your portfolio quarterly and, at the very least, annually.

13. *Expecting the market to continue either its upward or downward direction*—If the markets are gaining, investors expect that the trend will continue for an extended period of time. The same applies if the markets are retreating. History has taught us that when markets have an

extended period of above- or below-average returns, it is only a matter of time before the markets revert to the average mean.

14. *Buying low-priced stocks*—Many investors like to buy low-priced or "cheap" stocks because they can buy more of them, but "cheap" stocks are generally missing a key ingredient of past stock market winners—institutional sponsorship. Institutional investors account for 70 percent of the trading volume each day on the exchanges, and if they shun cheap stocks, there is usually a good reason.[116]

15. *Avoiding stocks with high P/E ratios*—Stocks with high price to earnings ratios are not necessarily expensive and should not be summarily avoided. Their performance usually demonstrates that there is plenty of bullishness about the company's future prospects.

16. *Letting small losses turn into big ones*—Cut your losses in any stock that falls below a certain level from where you bought it. This way, you limit your losses. A 50 percent loss on a stock would need to rise 100 percent to get back to the break-even point. Stocks are investment instruments; they are not your children. You can sell them if the fundamentals turn sour. Besides, stock picking should be left to the professionals, not individual investors.[117]

17. *Averaging down*—Averaging down means buying more of the stock that you hold as the price goes down. It is like placing your foot under a falling knife. If a stock falls significantly, there must be fundamentals that have caused this drop. Unless you are a professional or a money manager, leave those decisions to the experts.

18. *Considering only pretax returns*—Taxes can erode your portfolio's value. Thus, when investing and evaluating returns, do not just consider your pretax returns, look at your after-tax returns. If too much of your portfolio is going to pay taxes, look at investment strategies that can help reduce your taxes so that you can increase your net, after-tax, return.

19. *Forgetting to take profits*—Investors tend to fall in love with securities that rise in price and forget to take their profits, especially if the company was once their employer. Unless you sell, your gain is unrealized and not real. Sometimes, this is done out of devotion, other times, it is done because investors do not want to pay taxes. No matter how much you have made on a stock or how attached you are to it, do not forget the cardinal principle of diversification.

20. *Overdosing on information*—In this age of the Internet, information is abundant, redundant, and can blur your vision and drown you in useless details. You become paralyzed with information to the point of indecisiveness. Worst yet, you become confused between research and marketing materials. Focus your information-gathering process on a logical and well-documented investment strategy so you are more productive in your pursuit of facts.

21. *Not asking for help*—Do not dig yourself into deeper losses if you do not know what you are doing when it comes to investing. Investing has become complex, the array of investment vehicles have become extensive, and trends are moving quicker than ever before. Seek professional advice.

Concluding Remarks

Although what is certain in the world of investing is uncertainty itself, there are fundamental principles that provide the foundation for a successful investment strategy. Additionally, there are common and recurring mistakes that should be avoided. By implementing the successful investment principles and avoiding the most common mistakes, you can be more reasonably in control of your investment and financial destiny.

CHAPTER 3

Why Everyone Needs an Estate Plan

D on't die without an estate plan! The consequences for those you love could be dire and costly. Estate planning should be a central component of your wealth management plan. Setting up an estate plan is easy and relatively inexpensive compared to the substantial estate taxes that your family might incur in the absence of an estate plan, not to mention the lack of privacy that your estate would be subjected to and the possible disregard of your wishes after your death.

Estate planning is the strategy and the process designed to assist you in accumulating, conserving, and distributing your assets in the most efficient manner during your life and/or upon your death. However, estate planning is not just about tax planning. It also involves important issues such as naming a guardian for your minor children, deciding when and how your adult children are to inherit your wealth, and preparing for the possibility that you or your spouse may become physically or mentally disabled.

Estate planning allows you to do the following:

- Protect your estate from probate, a costly court process used in settling estates after an owner's death. If you do not decide in advance who will settle your financial affairs, the courts in your state will make this decision for you regardless of what your wishes might have been.
- Transfer assets to beneficiaries in the most tax-efficient manner with the goal minimizing federal estate taxes.
- Maximize the value of the assets passed to your beneficiaries.
- Provide income-tax-free benefits to your beneficiaries.
- Prepare for the orderly succession of a family business.
- Provide for guardianship and support of minors.
- Establish trusts to manage the inheritances of minors or other survivors who do not have the capacity or experience to handle substantial assets.

- Assure professional, prudent management of assets for your heirs (for example, by appointing a well-qualified trustee for a trust created in your will).
- Make provisions for incapacity.

Who Needs an Estate Plan?

Everyone needs an estate plan. A will alone may be adequate as an estate plan when you are young, have few assets and no children. Once you have children, the question of guardianship emerges, as well as the funds for the children's care in the event you die prematurely or become disabled.

As your investments and other assets grow over time, preserving your wealth and minimizing estate taxes become increasingly important. This is when you will need a plan to help minimize your estate taxes and provide for the continued management of your assets upon your death or incapacity.

Under current law, estate tax liability decreases each year. The estate tax exemption will be as high as $3.5 million in 2009, meaning that the first $3.5 million of someone's estate will be exempt from taxes. This is a fairly large sum, and more money than most Americans possess in their estates. In 2010, there will be no estate tax at all. Unfortunately, the current tax law includes a *sunset provision*. This means that, unless Congress enacts new legislation before 2010, estate taxes will revert to what they were in 2001—making 55 percent the highest estate tax rate and allowing only the first $1.0 million of someone's estate to be free from federal estate taxes. Given that your estate includes all of your assets—your home, savings, retirement assets, investments, and even your life insurance policies—many people may find that the issue of estate tax will affect them, and it is an issue that not only wealthy individuals should be concerned with. This makes it more pertinent for most people to consider ways to use their exclusion amounts to minimize estate taxes.

The Three Basic Estate Planning Documents

While the strategies that make up an individual's estate plan vary widely, all estate plans should contain three basic documents: a will, a trust, and a durable power of attorney.

The Will

A **will** is a formal legal document that establishes your intentions and provides direction for how your affairs should be handled and your estate distributed after your death. It also appoints those in charge of executing the tasks and responsibilities outlined in the will.

A will is one of the most important documents that you will ever sign. It allows you to decide who will receive your assets, as well as how and when they will receive them. Creating a will is simple and fairly inexpensive, but it must be done in writing and meet certain legal requirements.

A staggering 70 percent of Americans die without a will.[1] Dying intestate—without a will—has dire consequences especially for your heirs:

- Your wishes will be ignored in terms of who receives your assets and what portion. Outside of your wife and children, the law may not provide for a family member such as your parent, or a friend to receive any inheritance.
- In the absence of a will, state law dictates that a judge, a stranger, is to make all the pertinent decisions regarding your estate.
- Without a will, the court alone will decide who the executor or personal representative should be.
- A probate court will assign a guardian for your minor children. This guardian will care for your children and manage their inheritances.
- Your beneficiaries might receive less assets and property than you intended because you did not take some steps that could have minimized estate taxes.
- Your children will have control over their inheritance once they reach the age of majority. They will receive the inheritance even if they have no experience or maturity to manage their affairs.[2]

Although there are many ready-made kits that allow you to draft your own will, it is always more prudent to have a lawyer help you prepare your will. Wills are state specific, and you would want to select a lawyer who is familiar with your state law and who can execute an effective will.

Once you have a will, it is critical that you review it every two to four years and make any changes if necessary. A will should reflect your changing life circumstances. Your estate is affected by births, deaths, marriages, divorces, relocation to a different state, tax law changes, and the size of your estate, among other factors. A will can be changed, modified, or completely revoked before death.

One of the most important decisions that you have to make in preparing a will is naming an **executor**—the person or institution that will supervise the resolution of all issues regarding your estate. The person you name as your executor will have fiduciary responsibilities for handling your estate, including managing the assets in your estate, filing the appropriate tax returns, paying off the estate's debts, and distributing your assets to the beneficiaries in the manner you have designated.

The executor should be someone honest whom you trust and who is a capable individual. That person should have no conflicts of interest in executing your wishes, have the time to do it, and be willing to serve. A trusted friend or a family member can serve as the executor, or you can hire a professional such as the trust department of a financial institution. And, as a matter of precaution, you should designate an alternate executor in the event your first choice is unwilling or incapable of performing the responsibilities.

Even if you only have a will, your estate is subject to **probate**. Probate is the process of reviewing your will and estate by the court at your death, with the intention of transferring your assets. Based on the complexity of your estate and whether you owe taxes, probate can take several months to several years to complete, be costly, and is a matter of public record.[3] According to the American Association of Retired Persons (AARP), probate fees and settlement costs range from 3 to 8 percent of the estate.[4] Strangers will have access to the terms of your will and can find out your personal matters.

If you want to avoid the cost and delays of a probate and keep the process private, you should do three things:

1. Hold the title of properties in forms such as joint tenancy, community property with the right of survivorship, and transfer on death.
2. Name your beneficiary for assets such as life insurance or retirement plan accounts where property is transferred automatically by contract.
3. Consider creating a trust or trusts, depending on your needs and goals.

The Trust

Most people tend to leave assets to their heirs outright through a will, which is subject to probate. Two other tools commonly used to transfer assets include joint tenancy with right of survivorship (such as a joint bank account), or by beneficiary designation (being named as a beneficiary of a retirement plan or a life insurance policy). Even though these three methods represent the easiest way to bequeath assets, it might not be the wisest or best way, especially if the heirs are young children.

When a trust is created under your will, it is called a **testamentary trust**. Alternatively, you can establish a trust during your lifetime called a **living trust.** These trusts perform similarly in that they can help protect your beneficiaries and provide additional security for your family. With either trust, you can select a guardian for your children and a professional trustee who is experienced in managing assets for children.

Assets held in a living trust avoid probate and can provide substantial lifetime planning and asset management benefits for you. By establishing certain types of trusts, you can substantially reduce, and possibly eliminate, estate taxes.

The section titled "The Use of Trusts in Estate Planning Strategies" will deal with the various types of trusts available to help you in devising your most appropriate estate planning strategies.

The Durable Power of Attorney

Having a valid will, including the appropriate trusts, is not sufficient to legally communicate and protect your medical and financial decision-making ability in the event you become incapacitated.

A durable power of attorney allows you to assign someone to represent you in almost all business transactions if you become incapacitated. Unless the document says "durable" it may not be effective in the event you become mentally impaired. A **medical durable power of attorney**, also known as **health care proxy**, allows you to designate a person to make medical decisions on your behalf when you are unable to do so. A **living will**, by contrast, is a document that indicates your preferences for extraordinary treatment. The living will describes the kind of medical care you want under specific situations. You can request or refuse artificial respiration or feeding, especially when there is no chance you will ever regain consciousness or you have been diagnosed with a terminal illness.[5]

Even though a **letter of instruction** is not a legal document, it represents a list of commands and instructions that is prepared for people to follow when you are sick or have died.

The Use of Trusts in Estate Planning Strategies

Whether a trust is created within a will or as a separate legal entity, there exist different types of trusts to meet specific needs and address certain concerns. The most commonly used trusts are the revocable living trust, the credit shelter trust (also known as the bypass trust), the qualified terminable interest property trust, the generation-skipping transfer (GST), the irrevocable life insurance trust (ILIT), and the charitable remainder trust (CRT).

The following section lists the six uses of trusts in estate planning strategies.

Revocable Living Trust—To Maintain Control

A revocable living trust is the most basic of all trusts. It is a trust that you, the grantor, create during your lifetime that allows you to retain the right to change or revoke it at any time. Revocable trusts are an efficient and effective method of managing and transferring assets at death. They give you complete control during your lifetime and avoids probate, thus allowing property to be transferred to beneficiaries immediately.

An important advantage of a living trust is that after your death, it allows uninterrupted asset management of your assets to continue for your heirs. To arrange this, you use your will to direct that any of your assets not held in the trust be "poured over" to the trust. This allows your trustee to manage the added assets, along with the assets already in the trust. Assets that *pour over* into a trust have to be probated because they *pass through* your will, but the trust's other assets avoid probate.

A revocable living trust can provide confidentiality and privacy at the time of the estate settlement. However, it does allow creditors to make claims against the assets in the trust, even after the trust assets have been distributed to your beneficiaries. Additionally, this trust has no ability to lessen or avoid estate taxes.

Credit Shelter Trust—To Protect Your Individual Estate Tax Exemption

The entire estate of a husband and a wife can pass to each other free of income and estate taxes upon the first spouse's death. This is called the **unlimited marital deduction**. The marital deduction allows you to transfer to your spouse an unlimited amount of property during life and at death free of gift and estate taxes. Given that a significant percentage of residents in the United States are immigrants and many of them might not have acquired citizenship, it is important to note that if your spouse is not a U.S. citizen; your spouse is *not* entitled to the unlimited marital deduction. This means that transfers between you and your spouse above the limited exemption amount are subject to estate taxes. However, if you establish a **qualified domestic trust (QDOT)**, this trust will enable assets to pass from a decedent spouse to the surviving spouse as if both spouses were citizens.

Going back to the citizen spouse, you have to be aware that assets transferred to a spouse using the unlimited marital deduction are included in the surviving spouse's taxable estate when he or she dies. If the surviving spouse's assets at death exceed the $3.5 million tax-free estate limit for 2009, then any amount above that limit will be subject to estate taxes.

In this case, you and your spouse should set up the **credit shelter trust**, which is also known as the **bypass trust**, **A/B trust**, or **family trust**. It is an irrevocable trust that is funded at death from assets in a revocable living trust. The assets transferred to the trust should be equal to the estate tax-exemption amount, a number that changes almost every year.

By leaving property to each other in a credit shelter trust, a couple can guarantee that, if one spouse dies before the other, they can maintain their individual estate tax exemption, allowing them to pass up to $7 million in 2009 to their children or heirs.[6] Without the credit shelter trust and if all the assets were passed on to the surviving spouse, then the exemption of $3.5 million in 2009 and the assets above that amount will be subject to estate taxes. Because the tax laws after 2010 are uncertain, you will need to discuss with your wealth management team the correct amount to place in trust.

Those with large estates probably should not leave their entire estate to their spouse. By setting up a credit shelter trust, the surviving spouse can receive income from the trust and can even have access to the principal at the discretion of the trustee, but the trust will not be included in the surviving spouse's estate. Rather, it will pass tax free to your beneficiaries upon the surviving spouse's death.

Qualified Terminable Interest Property Trust—To Control the Ultimate Distribution of Assets

If your estate is larger in value than the assets placed in a credit shelter or bypass trust and you want to control the remainder of your estate, then leaving those assets to your spouse may mean that he or she will control the ultimate distribution of those assets. If your spouse remarries, the new spouse may end up inheriting some or all of those assets. Or, if you have children from a previous marriage, you may want to ensure that those children receive a portion of your estate. In this case, you may want to consider using a **qualified terminable interest property trust (QTIP)**. Thus, any assets not placed in the bypass/credit shelter trust can be placed in the QTIP trust while allowing for income to be distributed to your spouse during his or her lifetime. After your spouse's death, the principal is distributed to your designated beneficiaries.

The QTIP trust receives assets qualifying for the marital deduction. These assets are not subject to gift and estate taxes upon the death of the first spouse but are included in the estate of the surviving spouse. Nevertheless, they pass to beneficiaries originally named by the first spouse.

Generation-Skipping Trust—To Avoid Paying Estate Taxes Twice

Leaving assets to wealthy children often means that estate taxes will be paid when your children receive the assets and again when your grandchildren receive the assets. In this case, a **generation-skipping trust (GST)** is recommended. The GST is designed to pay income to more than one generation (spouse and/or children), and then the principal goes to the grandchildren, the beneficiaries. Thus, bequeathing the assets directly to the second or third generations can reduce estate taxes.

There is a GST tax, however, that is intended to prevent families from avoiding a generation's worth of estate taxes. This tax is set at the highest estate tax rate but will only apply to amounts transferred in excess of your GST exemption, which follows the estate tax exemption.

Note that there is no GST tax if you transfer assets to your grandchild whose father or mother has died.

Irrevocable Life Insurance Trust—To Provide Liquidity and Reduce Estate Tax Liability

A life insurance trust is established to accept life insurance death benefits upon the death of the insured. An irrevocable trust is a trust that cannot be altered by the grantor(s). Thus, an **irrevocable life insurance trust (ILIT)** is one that owns your life insurance policy and the trust itself is the beneficiary. When you die, the trustee collects the insurance money and manages it for the benefit of your heirs.

A properly set-up trust will keep the insurance proceeds out of your taxable estate unless you transfer the life insurance policy to the trust within three years of your death. If you are in bad health, do not transfer existing life insurance policies to the trust. Buy a new policy. Of course, if you are in poor health, it might be prohibitive to buy a life insurance policy.[7]

Charitable Remainder Trust—To Provide Lifetime Income with Tax Benefits

A **charitable remainder trust (CRT)** is a trust that provides payments to beneficiaries (usually the donor and/or family members) for a set period of time or for the donor's lifetime from assets contributed to a charity. A CRT is an ideal vehicle if you are charitably inclined, have a concentrated and highly appreciated position in stocks or other assets, and would like lifetime income generated to you from those assets, while eventually making substantial future contributions to charity.

If you own, for example, a large position in your company stock that was purchased with a low cost basis, you can donate the stock to a charity through a charitable remainder trust. You will receive current-year income tax deduction for the present value of the stock and avoid immediate capital gains on its sale. The trust can last a term of up to 20 years, your lifetime, the lifetimes of you and your spouse, or even longer.

The CRT immediately sells the concentrated position (appreciated stocks, real estate, or business interest) without any capital gain tax liability to you. The sale proceeds can be fully reinvested in a diversified portfolio to generate cash flow to you and reduce your investment risk. You have the option of receiving a fixed amount of lifetime annual income or a fixed annual percentage of the value of the portfolio.

Upon your death or those of the named income beneficiaries, the assets are then transferred outright to a qualified charity or charities, including your family foundation that you can name as beneficiary.

There are other types of trusts that exist to help you manage additional estate planning needs—such as a personal residence trust, a special needs trust, a standby trust, and gifting trusts, among others.

When Should You Review Your Estate Plan?

If you already have an estate plan or are now convinced to set one up, do not forget to go back on a regular basis to ensure that your estate plan is up to date. When your circumstances change, your plan may need to be changed as well. You should reexamine your estate plan for any of these events:[8]

- Births
- Deaths
- Marriages
- Divorces
- Inheritances
- Relocation between states
- Changes in your assets
- Business changes
- Tax law changes

A new birth in the family means that you will need to include the new child in your plan. A death of your spouse or any of your beneficiaries may require major changes or simple substitutions of named beneficiaries. If you or any of your beneficiaries get married, it might certainly require adjustments to your plan. If you get divorced, it is a must that you make necessary changes to your plan. Presumably, you would not want your ex-spouse to be the beneficiary of your life insurance policy. If any of your beneficiaries get divorced, you might want to ensure that none of your assets go to the ex-spouse. When one generation passes its wealth to the next, those who inherit often suddenly have radically different financial circumstances. A death of a spouse, for example, when insurance proceeds and employee benefits are involved, would require a reassessment of your increased assets.

Moving between states is a red flag because estate settlement is dictated by the laws of the state where you are a resident when you die. State laws are not uniform, and legal differences could invalidate the provisions of a plan designed in another state. If your assets increase or decrease substantially, your tax standing could change, requiring modifications to your estate plan. If you are involved in a business, you will be affected by the death of a partner or the existence of a buy–sell agreement.

Federal tax laws are constantly changing. A plan that is only a few years old could require modifications based on the changes in the tax laws.

With so many variables involved, it is prudent to review your estate plan and your strategy on a regular basis. It is best to make it a goal to review your plan at least annually or whenever any of these events occur.

How to Calculate Your Net Worth

Calculating your net worth is critical to determining whether your estate would be subject to estate taxes. Most people tend to underestimate their net worth because they tend to concentrate on their liquid or visible assets. If you adopt the prudent view and assume that the U.S. Congress will not amend existing legislation that repeals estate taxes in 2010 and reverts to the exemption amounts and estate tax rates that were in place in 2001, then in 2011, estate tax exemption will be a mere $1.0 million and the highest estate tax rate will be a staggering 55 percent. Given this assumption, an individual with a $1 million to $2 million life insurance policy or more will likely be subject to estate taxes.[9] Keep in mind that it would take a mere $2,330 a year in premiums to purchase a $2.0 million 20-year term life insurance policy for a healthy 40-year-old male who is a nonsmoker.[10] This type of policy guarantees that the premium paid will be the same for a 20-year period, after which the policy expires. Stated differently, you do not have to be millionaire during your lifetime for your estate to potentially owe estate taxes once the proceeds from a life insurance policy are paid out upon your death.

Please note that even though you should be able to estimate whether your estate would be subject to estate taxes, you should consult a certified public accountant or a tax lawyer to provide you with a fairly accurate estimate of what your estate might owe in taxes. Tax laws, amount of exemptions, credits, and deductions change making it difficult for you to make an accurate calculation.

This worksheet can help you estimate the actual value of your estate. This worksheet is not comprehensive, and you might have other assets or categories that are not listed.

ASSETS MARKET VALUE

Cash, certificates of deposit, money market accounts	$_____
Stocks, bonds, and mutual funds	$_____
Other investments	$_____
Individual retirement accounts	$_____
Employer-sponsored retirement plans	$_____
Equity in personal residences	$_____
Equity in vacation homes/time shares	$_____
Other real estate holdings/investments	$_____
Life insurance proceeds and annuities	$_____
Business or partnership interests	$_____
Debts owed to you	$_____
Automobiles and recreational vehicles	$_____
Jewelry and collectibles	$_____
Other (furniture, personal belongings, etc.)	$_____
Total Gross Assets	$_____

Liabilities

Residential mortgages	$_____
Personal debt (loans, credit cards, etc.)	$_____
Estate settlement costs (3–8 percent of estate)	$_____
Business-related debt	$_____
Total Liabilities	$_____

Net Worth (total assets minus liabilities) $_____

Your net worth is therefore the approximate value of your taxable estate. While estimating your net worth today is a critical first step to help you in determining whether you would be subject to estate taxes and to plan strategies to minimize those taxes, it is crucial to keep in mind the future growth of your assets. This is why it is important to regularly calculate your net worth, given the continual changes in estate tax exemptions and the potential growth of your net assets over time.

Concluding Remarks

In this chapter, we have outlined the reasons you should have an estate plan—the consequences could be dire in the event you do not have a plan, while the benefits of having a plan are many. Estate planning is an integral part of the wealth management process. A person's death is tragic and traumatizing to those left behind. Death presents a slew of problems and challenges to the survivors that can be avoided or minimized with proper planning during a person's lifetime. The types of problems that can be addressed by proper estate planning are financial burdens; complications in the transfer of assets; and care of minors. A well-thought-out and properly executed estate plan can do the following:

- Avoid the significant costs of probate.
- Help reduce, and sometimes eliminate, estate taxes.
- Provide liquidity (cash) to pay estate settlement costs.
- Provide cash and income to the loved ones left behind, such as a spouse or children.
- Avoid the delays of probating an estate.
- Seamlessly transfer assets to minor children through guardianship accounts.
- Avoid the immediate distribution of assets to children at the age of maturity to help preserve those assets to provide for the longer-term care of those children.
- Avoid paying unnecessary estate taxes with proper planning.
- Nominate a guardian for the minor children.
- Provide proper and uninterrupted asset management left to minors or inexperienced adults.

Take time to work with your tax lawyer, accountant, and wealth advisor to plan out your estate issues. Even though both death and taxes are certain, we know when taxes are due; we have no idea when we will confront death.

CHAPTER 4

Learn to Save and Properly Manage Your Debt

Americans are digging themselves into deeper trouble when it comes to saving and piling on debt. This is illustrated by a disturbing fact: There are more people in the United States declaring bankruptcy every year than there are graduating from college![1] In 2007, consumer bankruptcy filings climbed 40 percent, according to the American Bankruptcy Institute. It increased from 563,203 bankruptcy filings in 2006 to 801,840 filings in 2007.[2]

Financial security and peace of mind go hand in hand. Overspending and going into debt are dangers to financial stability and a source of stress for just about everyone. Unfortunately, as a society we have a tendency to save very little, if at all, and spend a lot, usually at the expense of increasingly going into debt. Saving money and managing your debt are the two most important elements of your financial security, and yet they seem to be the most elusive of financial goals.

Consider the following:

- Seven out of 10 Americans report living paycheck to paycheck.[3]
- In 1985, Americans were saving $11 for every $100 they brought home.[4] In May 2007, the savings rate was at a negative 1.4 percent of personal income. In fact, since the second quarter of 2005, the nation's savings rate has been negative. In other words, people are spending more than they earn, either by digging into their savings or building up debt.[5]
- In 2006, individuals went deeper into debt as personal savings dropped by $68 billion.[6]
- By August 2007, consumer credit outstanding grew to $2.470 trillion (mind you, not billion), while revolving credit, reflecting primarily credit card debt, grew to $915.5 billion.[7]

- From 2000 to 2006, the average credit card debt carried by Americans grew from \$7,842 to \$9,659, according to CardTrack.com. An estimated 88 million Americans had credit card debt.[8]
- In the first five months of 2007, credit-card delinquency was 3.77 percent higher than a year earlier, and late payments surged 30 percent higher during that period, according to Moody's, the credit-rating agency.[9]
- More than one-third of credit card holders acknowledge using their cards for purchases they cannot afford, according to a report issued by CreditCards.com.[10]
- Since 2001, more than \$350 billion in credit card debt has been shifted into home-equity loans or into mortgages refinanced by homeowners.[11]
- From 2001 through 2006, Americans pulled \$6.1 trillion of cash from the value of their appreciated homes, more than \$1 trillion per year on average.[12]
- The total value of home mortgage debt (including home equity loans) held by Americans increased by 53 percent in the last four years. The amount owed nationwide is \$10.5 trillion.[13]
- Consumer debt has grown faster than many families' financial assets have.[14]
- Less American households are currently saving for retirement (66 percent) than they were in the year 2000 (78 percent).[15]
- 69 percent of older workers (ages 55 to 64) participating in 401(k) plans do *not* feel that they are saving enough to retire "on time" and live comfortably.[16]
- 49 percent of workers have not even begun to save.[17]

Are we, then, worried or stressed out? The answer is a resounding yes:

- When asked what their biggest source of financial stress was, *Men's Health* readers responded overwhelmingly (70 percent) that it is living beyond their means.[18]
- In a recent survey conducted by the Gallup Organization for *USA Today* and the National Endowment for Financial Education, 60 percent of respondents said that they felt they faced more financial pressures than the generations before; 30 percent worried "frequently" about what they owe; and fewer than 45 percent had either an IRA or participated in a 401(k) plan.[19]

The purpose of this chapter is to alarm you (I am referring here to the average American) and to force you to recognize and admit that you are not saving enough and that you are slowly drowning into debt. Even though it is difficult to separate saving from debt management, the section on saving will deal with the benefits of saving and will explore saving strategies. It will compare the benefits of saving versus borrowing. Finally, the section on managing your debt will identify 14 steps to help you better manage your debt. The goal is to provide you with data, analysis, and actionable ideas to help you get into the habit of saving and to better manage your liabilities.

Why Save

There are many reasons why you should save beginning today and on a regular basis. When you save, it is not about depriving yourself. It is about managing your spending. You save for a future purpose and to attain a number of important goals. Most commonly, people save to accomplish the following:

- Set up an emergency or a rainy-day fund.
- Fund your children's education.
- Ensure a comfortable retirement and pay for future health care expenses.
- Make a major purchase or pay for a major event.
- Start a new business.
- Accumulate wealth for enjoyment during your lifetime.
- Leave an inheritance to your loved ones or charity.

The reasons to save are innumerable and varied. They depend on your own personal circumstances, your age and stage in life, your family size and dynamics, your values, your engrained or newly acquired habits, and your financial goals. Why we save is as personal and specific as who we are. The key to your success in saving is to plan, act, and be disciplined.

1. *Set up an emergency or rainy-day fund.* Most wealth advisors counsel their clients to have at least six months' worth of emergency funding set aside in liquid assets to cover living expenses and meet unexpected developments such as the loss of a job, an accident, a short-term disability, a prolonged illness, large medical bills, or the replacement of a major appliance in the house. If you do not have those emergency funds saved and readily available, you might then be forced to borrow money, resort to using your credit card, tap into your retirement funds, or liquidate investments at an inopportune time. Otherwise, the consequences of late or no payments on your mortgage, credit card, and other bills could be devastating on your credit history and your ability to borrow money in the future. Since 7 out 10 Americans live

paycheck to paycheck, a vast majority therefore needs to begin saving for an emergency or rainy-day fund.

A good alternative to having cash on hand for emergencies is to apply for a home equity line of credit *before* the need arises to tap into it. This would allow you to have access to the equity built-up in your house at a competitive interest rate, which, in most cases, could be tax-deductible as well.

2. *Fund your children's education.* Although you might hope that your children receive a grant or a scholarship when they go to college, don't count on it. In 2004 to 2005, 70 percent of all financial aid was awarded in the form of loans.[20] A survey by AllianceBernstein Investments of college graduates with student debt found that nearly 40 percent expect to take more than 10 years to pay it off.[21] And, even though there are 73.5 million children under age 18 in the United States, there are only 7.2 million college savings plan accounts.[22] This means that only 10 percent of children under 18 have a college savings plan. If you are in the market for student and parent loans with competitive interest rates, you might want to visit www.findaid.org. The Web site has a good tutorial on college financing. Later in the chapter, we will discuss and compare features of the various investment vehicles available to save for your children.

According to Babycenter.com, if you are a parent of a baby who was born in 2007, you will spend $322,000 (on a present value basis, or 2007 dollar value) to raise that child. The estimate includes projections for housing, food, clothing, healthcare and a four-year college education at, mind you, a public university.[23]

For those parents whose children are not necessarily convinced of the value of education, let them know that the level of their formal education is tied directly to their future potential earning power (see Table 4.1).

TABLE 4.1   The More You Learn, the More You Earn

Level of education	Median annual income
No high school diploma	$26,456
High school diploma	$33,294
Associate's degree	$41,240
Bachelor's degree	$60,662
Master's degree	$69,441
Doctoral degree	$99,880
Professional degree	$125,753

Source: U.S. Census Bureau[24]

3. *Ensure a comfortable retirement and pay for future health care expenses.*
It has long been assumed that if you save 10 percent of your gross income through your working life, you will have plenty of money for
a comfortable retirement.[25] If you begin saving when you are in your
thirties, you should consider increasing the amount you save from 10 to
15 percent of your gross income, while if you begin saving at age
40, you will probably need to set aside at least 20 percent of your
gross income, and that percentage will need to be increased to
35 percent if you are beginning to save at age 50.[26] Those who save
the 10 percent of their gross income throughout their working careers
ought to congratulate themselves because they are in the minority; they
are doing the right thing; they are disciplined; and they are more likely
to retire comfortably if they begin putting money away in their early
twenties and never waiver. Unfortunately, financial experts are now
suggesting that a higher percentage is needed because of the following
factors:

- Inflation keeps nibbling away at spending power. An individual living
  on a fixed income for the last 20 years would have 54 percent of the
  purchasing power today that he/she had in 1987.[27]
- Over the last two decades, the number of defined-benefit pension
  plans has declined dramatically (covering about one-third of American workers). The responsibility of providing lifetime income in retirement has shifted mostly to the retiree from the employer.[28] This
  means that individuals need to save more themselves to meet their
  own retirement needs.
- Americans are living much longer, and the money that they have
  saved for retirement needs to last just as long.
- About 50 percent of people live beyond the average age of life expectancy. The average life expectancy of an American male has increased significantly in the twentieth century, and by two more years
  for women.[29]
- In 1960, the likelihood that a 65-year-old living to age 90 was
  10 percent. In 2000, the likelihood increased to 23 percent.[30]
- Only 1 percent of Americans who were able to retire early did so
  because they achieved their accumulation goals sooner than they
  expected. 40 percent retired early because of an illness or disability.[31]
- Health care costs, including out-of-pocket costs, have soared and
  have increased on average at twice the rate of inflation. According to
  the Benefit Research Institute (2006), a typical retired couple would
  need roughly $300,000 to pay anticipated health expenses over aver-
  age life expectancies.
- Despite Medicare, Americans who are at least 65 are responsible for
  33 percent of all health care spending.[32]

- Because Americans live longer, they have a greater need for long-term care, which is not covered by Medicare.

    The case is clear that American workers need to save as early as possible and much more than the 10 percent many felt was adequate to meet the needs for a comfortable retirement.[33] You certainly do not want to be one of the 64 percent of American workers who expect a total depletion of their life savings during retirement.[34]

4. *Make a major purchase or pay for a major event.* It is quite probable that the most common American dream is to own your own home. When you are a teenager, it is usually a car that you want. Up until the 2008 credit crisis, most lenders required a down payment, usually 20 percent of the purchase value of a home, to qualify you to borrow the remaining 80 percent. In today's tight credit environment, the lending requirements have become more stringent. The majority of lenders now require a higher down payment and an impeccable credit history to lend funds to buy a home, especially in the nontraditional jumbo loan market—anything above the FHA limit of $417,000. If you are fortunate, your parents might provide you with the down payment. Most people, however, will have to rent first and save in the meantime for a down payment on a home. Parents might pass on the old family car to their teenage drivers. But, if those teenagers want a newer car, they would have to work and save for a down payment on such a car.

    Weddings have become elaborate and tend to be expensive. Even taking a weeklong vacation requires planning and saving. These are major events that require planning and if your financial means are modest, you will have to plan and save over time to pay for these events.

5. *Start a new business.* Even though the vast majority of aspiring business owners resort to borrowing to fund a new business, rarely does a lender provide 100 percent of the funds needed to finance a new business. Any lender would want the borrower to have a significant financial stake in the business. In addition, planning to either purchase a business or start a new one requires a business plan and a projected a budget. These are three minimal requirements if you are seeking a loan from a bank. Family and friends might loan you the necessary funds based on different criteria such as your relationship to them; your character; your reliability; and your current assets. In any case, your likelihood of success increases if you save your own funds for a significant down payment or, preferably, have additional reserves to overcome those tough periods when business growth does not mirror your business plan.

6. *Accumulate wealth for enjoyment during your lifetime.* If you are fortunate to earn enough money to take care of your basic financial

obligations—partially listed here—then you have excess funds that you should not squander but accumulate for your enjoyment throughout your life. Whether to trot the globe, buy exotic jewelry, sail in your yacht, or donate to charity, you have properly managed your income, expenses, and assets to allow you to accumulate wealth to enjoy throughout your life.

7. *Leave an inheritance to your loved ones or favorite charity.* Those who work hard, meet their daily needs, and are able to accumulate wealth end up leaving most of their wealth to their loved ones: 92 percent of high-net-worth individuals indicated in a 2006 survey that they expect to transfer their wealth to immediate and extended family members.[35] Substantial amounts are also left in bequests to charities. In 2006, U.S. charitable giving reached an estimated $295 billion. Of that amount, individuals contributed 75.6 percent, and an additional 7.8 percent was donated through charitable bequests.[36]

It is a different story for the mass affluent baby boomers, whose net worth is around a few million dollars and who are starting to turn 65. Forecasts and patterns suggest that many of them may leave little or no substantial wealth to their children.[37] Having financed their children's education and early adulthood, these boomers are realizing that the burden of a long and active retirement might leave very little for their children to inherit. If these baby boomers intend to leave a substantial inheritance for their children, they will have to plan early, possibly through the financing of life insurance policies, to ensure that their children receive the desired inheritance.

No matter what the reasons are that compel you to save, it is considerably much less expensive to save and pay in cash for what you want than to have to borrow.

Saving Strategies

Saving is not easy. It requires you to be disciplined, to control your spending, to live within a budget, and to recognize and appreciate the benefits of saving and the value of such savings to meet your future needs and goals. Saving is an indispensable component of a sound financial plan. Once you overcome the psychological hurdle and decide to save, you can maximize the impact of your savings by following these nine saving strategies:

1. Benefit from compounding.
2. Start saving early.
3. Save as much as you can.

4. Use an automatic deduction plan to save.
5. Save in tax-deferred accounts.
6. Save in tax-free accounts—Roth IRAs and college saving plans.
7. Save in accounts that provide you a tax deduction.
8. Save in accounts that match your contributions.
9. Save for others, especially your children and spouse.

Benefit from Compounding

Albert Einstein reportedly stated that the power of compounding is deemed as the "eight wonder of the world."[38] **Compounding** is the ability of an asset to generate earnings, which are then reinvested to generate their own earnings. With compounding, you earn returns on your original contribution. These earnings, if reinvested, will then earn their own returns. In a hypothetical scenario, if you invest $10,000 and earned a 20 percent return, over a 25-year-period, this investment will grow to $1 million without adding any more money to your investment. This compounding effect significantly accelerates the growth of your investment. Compound interest may be contrasted with simple interest, where interest is not added to the principal; therefore, there is no compounding. The frequency of compounding, or adding the interest earned to your original investment, is usually annual, semiannual, quarterly, monthly, or even daily. Compounding works in your favor and allows your investment to grow at an accelerated rate.

Start Saving Early

To demonstrate the value of time and the effect of compounding, we are going to look at three individuals who decide to save for their retirement at different intervals of their life. The first person will begin saving for retirement at the age of 25. The second person will save for retirement at the age of 35. The third person will begin saving at the age of 50.[39]

Each of these individuals will contribute to their IRA accounts for seven years only. In 2007, the 25-year-old puts away $4,000 in an IRA—the maximum allowable for that year—then adds a hypothetical $5,000 for each of the following 6 years. By year seven or in 2013, this 25-year-old ends up contributing a total of $34,000.

The 35-year-old contributes $5,000 each year for seven years to his IRA, for a total of $35,000. Finally, the 50-year-old contributes $6,000 each year for seven years, for a total of $42,000.

An IRA was selected as the investment vehicle to eliminate the impact that taxes would have on a regular checking or retail investment account. These accounts are normally taxed on annual basis. Traditional IRA accounts, by comparison, grow on a tax-deferred basis and are not subject to taxes until they are withdrawn.

Assume that that these investments are left until each individual reaches the age of 70. We are also assuming that the contributions are made on January 1 of each year and grow at an annual pretax rate of 6 percent.

At the age of 70, the retirement value of each of the three participants will be as follows:

- The 25-year-old will see his IRA contributions of $34,000 grow to $417,093.
- The 35-year-old will see his IRA contributions of $35,000 grow to $241,050.
- The 50-year-old will see his IRA contributions of $42,000 grow to $120,698.

What this tells us is that the earlier you save, the more your funds will grow. This is a function of time. With investing, time is on your side. It is also a function of compounding, because you earn returns on both your original contributions as well as the growth in your account. Therefore, begin saving early.

Save as Much as You Can

You might scoff at the idea of saving a small amount of money and wonder what difference it would make over time. Let us assume that you are a smoker and you pay an average of $5 for a pack of cigarettes. If you quit smoking, you will live a healthier and longer life. If you save the $5 that you would have spent daily on your cigarettes, you will end up with about $150 a month. Now, if you invest this $150 a month and receive an annual return of 10 percent, here is how much money you will end up with over time:[40]

1 year	= $	1,885
2 years	= $	3,967
5 years	= $	11,616
10 years	= $	30,727
15 years	= $	62,171
30 years	= $	339,073
40 years	= $	948,611

By saving $5 a day, investing it at a hypothetical return of 10 percent and ignoring the effect of taxes, you will save close to $1 million over a

40-year-period. You can only imagine what your savings/investment account would like if you decided to save $10 or $20 a day instead.

Use an Automatic Deduction Plan to Save Regularly

Be disciplined. If you depend on yourself to write that monthly check to move funds to your investment or savings account, you are putting your savings plan in jeopardy. One month you might forget to do so. Another month, you might have unexpected expenses. A third month, you could be tempted to spend the money on something else. Why take a chance? Set up an automatic deduction plan that transfers funds from your checking account to your savings or retirement accounts. After a while, you will not miss those funds and you will learn to live with the reduced budget.

Automatic monthly contributions, especially if they go into an investment account, take advantage of the normal fluctuations of the underlying investments. Your monthly automatic contributions are invested whether your investment is up and down. Over time, this tends to enhance your investment return by injecting dollar cost averaging into your investment plan.[41]

Save in Tax-Deferred Accounts

Tax deferral or deferring taxes until money is withdrawn can help you accumulate more assets. This is because you only pay taxes on money you withdraw, allowing all of your invested money to work for you. Thus, you earn returns on (1) your invested capital; (2) your earnings; and (3) funds that remain in the account (because of tax deferral) that would have been paid out in taxes.

If you invest $100,000 in both a taxable and tax-deferred account and if each gains 8 percent annually, then after 20 years, your tax-deferred account will grow to $446,096. If your investment account was taxable at a 35 percent rate, after 20 years, your account value will be $275,623—a difference in return of $171,000. The lower your tax rate, the more of the growth you will end up keeping and your account will be larger.[42]

If it is possible to invest in a tax-deferred vehicle that meets your liquidity needs and satisfies other investment requirements, then you should do so, given the substantial difference in returns between a taxable and a tax-deferred account. Examples of tax-deferred accounts include retirement plans such as a 401(k) plan and a traditional IRA, as well as annuities.

Save in Tax-Free Accounts—Roth IRAs and Education Savings Plans

If there is the opportunity to invest in a tax-free account, why would not anyone do so? These accounts will grow tax-deferred but, more importantly, the earnings are withdrawn tax free. The government is not prone to offer many of these tax-free accounts, as it relies on taxes to cover its expenses and budget. Examples of tax-free accounts include a Roth IRA, a 529 higher-education account, and a Coverdell Education Savings Account (ESA).[43]

The limitations that accompany some tax-free accounts tend to discourage people from using them:

- *A limit on the amount of funds that you can invest in them.* For example, if you are 50 or older, you can only invest $5,000 plus a $1000 catch up contribution because you are over 50 in 2008. For 2009 and after, Roth IRA contributions are $5,000 (and a catch up contribution of $1,000 if you are over 50) plus a cost of living adjustment. As of the writing of this book, the 2009 numbers have not been released by the IRS, however, they are most likely to increase to $5,500 plus the $1,000 catch up contribution if you are over 50. By comparison, other retirement accounts such as a 401(k) allow investing much larger amounts.
- *An income limit.* For 2008, you can qualify to contribute to a Roth IRA if you are single and your adjusted gross income is up to $100,999. Your eligibility would phase out if your adjusted gross income is between $101,000 and $115,999 for single filers and $159,000 to $168,999 for joint filers. As of the time of the writing of this book, the IRS had not released the 2009 phase out amounts. This income limit, however, does not affect 529 college savings accounts. For more information, see *2008 Pocket Tables*, www.kaplanfinancial.com; *2008 IRA and Tax Planning Reference Guide*, OppenheimerFunds, January 30, 2008.
- *Time restrictions on availability of funds.* A Roth IRA is a retirement vehicle and is intended primarily for use in retirement. Although under certain circumstances you can access the cash in a Roth IRA, there are time limitations and penalties if you access your Roth IRA either too soon, within five years from opening the account, or prior to age $59^1/_2$.
- *Use restrictions.* A 529 college savings plan is intended to pay for college or higher education. If you use those funds for other reasons, your earnings might be subject to a 10 percent penalty and tax on the growth.

Please refer to Chapter 5 on how to plan for a comfortable retirement for an in-depth and more exhaustive discussion on the benefits and limitations of investing in a Roth IRA. In the next section, we will highlight the benefits, limitations, and tax advantages of saving in education plans.

529 COLLEGE SAVINGS PLANS[44]   To encourage individuals to save for college education, states in collaboration with various investment companies have developed Section 529 college savings plans, named after a part of the Internal Revenue tax code that allows earnings to accumulate free of federal and state income tax and to be withdrawn tax free to pay for college costs. Newly introduced and slow to acceptance, these plans are gaining in popularity. By the end of 2002, all states had such plans in operation, and by 2007, there were over 100 such 529 savings plans.[45] According to the National Association of State Treasurers, there were 9.3 million 529 plan accounts in 2006, compared with 4.4 million in 2002.[46] A total of $105.69 billion was invested in 529 plan accounts by the end of 2006.[47] Plan assets are managed either by the state's treasurer or an outside investment company. There are two types of 529 plans: savings and prepaid tuition.

Most *prepaid plans* are limited to state residents. The state allows you to buy tomorrow's tuition at today's prices. Contribution limits depend on plan rules, but typically range from $15,000 to $30,000.[48] When your child reaches college age, the state will pay tuition and fees at any state college or university. Withdrawals are federal-income-tax free if used for qualified higher education expenses, and the adult in whose name the account is registered is the account owner. Contributions to prepaid plans are not subject to family income limits, and adults other than parents can make contributions.

Even though you can use your savings at an out-of-state or private college, you will lose the guarantee. If the cost of an out-of-state or private college exceeds the value of your account, you will have to make up the difference. You can contact the prepaid tuition plan for your state through the College Savings Plan Network at www.collegesavings.org. You can invest in the prepaid plan by paying cash up front or through a series of payments over time. By selecting this option, you do not have to worry about the performance of your investments or any larger-than-usual increases in the cost of college education. Your state plan effectively guarantees that your agreed-upon investment will be sufficient to pay for college expenses at the designated state college.[49] Please note that public universities can only offer the prepaid plans.[50]

By comparison, if you elect to save in any of the 50 states' regular 529 college savings plan, not the prepaid plan, you are responsible for the performance of your investments inside that plan. You chose how much you want to invest and over whatever period that you select. When the time comes to withdraw funds to pay for college expenses, you may end up with enough funds to pay for college expenses or you may end up short depending on the performance of your underlying investments and the amount of money that you have contributed into the plan from the very beginning.

There are several reasons to consider investing in a 529 college savings plan:

- *Tax advantages*—Investments in 529 college savings plans grow tax deferred, and qualified distributions for college expenses[51] are now permanently tax free. However, contributions to educational savings accounts are funded with after-tax money. They are not tax-deductible in general although some states offer a limited income tax deduction.
- *Tax deductibility*—There are 34 states (including Washington, D.C.) that allow a state income tax-deduction for residents contributing to their 529 college savings plans. Eight states lack a deduction and nine states have no personal income tax. There are four states—Arizona, Kansas, Maine and Pennsylvania—that allow residents to take a deduction for contributions made to any college savings plan. Arizona, for example, features an annual deduction of $1,500 for married couples and a $750 deduction for singles and heads of household who invest at least that amount beginning in 2008 tax year and extend for five years. Another added bonus is that this benefit can be taken by grandparents or other family members who invest, not just parents.[52]
- *Ability to withdraw funds*—If you are faced with a financial crisis after you have contributed to a 529 plan, you can withdraw the money and use it for whatever purpose you choose. You should not exercise this option lightly because you will have to pay taxes on earnings and a 10 percent penalty. This ability to withdraw funds compares positively to funds contributed to custodial accounts, such as Uniform Gift to Minors Act accounts (UGMAs), which are irrevocable.
- *Retain control*—With custodial accounts, such as UGMAs, when a child reaches the age of majority, either 18 or 21 depending on the state, the child becomes the legal owner of the account and can do whatever he or she chooses with the money. With 529 accounts, you remain the owner of the account, you can change the beneficiary, and you can ensure that the funds are used only for college expenses. You can even assign a contingent owner in the event that you no longer wish to control the fund or in the event of your death.
- *Completed gift*—Contributions to 529 accounts are treated as completed gifts from the donor to the beneficiary "despite the fact that the account owner retains all incidents of ownership and control over the account, including the ability to withdraw from the account at any time, for any purpose, subject to the rules of the particular 529 program."[53] Such contributions, and their earnings, would not be included in the taxable estate of the donor, or the 529 account owner (which may be different from the donor), but rather, would be included in the estate of the beneficiary.[54]

- *High contribution limits*—Multiple donors may contribute to the same 529 account and fund it to its maximum plan limit of $325,000 without incurring a gift tax.[55] However, since contributions are treated as a completed gift, they are subject to the gift tax rules. Each donor may gift up to $12,000 to any beneficiary each calendar year using the annual exclusion. 529 plans allow the donor to utilize four future years of annual exclusions at the same time and thus contribute up to $60,000 individually, or $120,000 if married, tax free. To fully utilize this application of the annual gift exclusion, the donor must be living at least to the first day of the year utilized for the exclusion. The multiple donor approach makes it possible to fund the maximum plan limit of $325,000 while avoiding paying any gift tax.[56] Front loading, or gifting to the account up front, will give the money contributed more time to compound and grow.
- *Estate planning tool*—If a set of grandparents each contributes $60,000 to a 529 account in 2008 ($12,000 for 2008 and four future years of annual exclusions [4 × $12,000 = $48,000] thus totaling $60,000) and then each contributes $102,500 applying it from their Lifetime Gift Tax Credit that allows gifts by each individual of up to $1 million during their lifetime, then a set of grandparents is able to single-handedly fund the maximum of $325,000, without any gift tax paid. Assuming that in 5 years the account earns an average of 7 percent each year, the 529 plan would grow to $455,829.[57] This amount will be completely outside the taxable estate of the grandparents and should the owner (the grandparent) die after five years, the resulting estate tax on this 529 account will be zero. The heirs (or successor account owner) would inherit the entire $455,829. This is also an exceptional estate planning tool for donors who wish to reduce the size of their estate tax liability.
- *Child may still qualify for financial aid*—Your child may still be eligible for financial aid. Under federal rules, a 529 plan has a minimal effect on financial aid. If the parent owns the account, only 5.6 percent of the assets are included in the amount the family is expected to contribute toward the child's education. And, if the 529 plan is owned by a grandparent, none of the assets are included in the financial aid formula.[58]
- *Low minimums*—Some plans, such as Van Kampen's Higher Education 529 Fund, allow you to establish an account for as little as $1,000, or if you set up an automatic investment plan, you can begin investment with as little as $25 a month.[59] This is a valuable and affordable feature, especially for parents with limited incomes. It allows them to begin the process of saving for their child's college education.
- *Professional management*—Most 529 plans give you the option of investing the funds that you contribute based on your child's age and

how many years they have before they go to college. You do not have to worry about asset allocation or rebalancing. These plans do the investing for you and reallocate the investment (more conservatively) as your child gets closer to college age. Not all plans, however, are equal in terms of performance and fees. You should carefully research plans that you might be interested in or ask your wealth advisor to help you make the appropriate selection. You can research 529 plans by visiting the Web site for the College Savings Plans Network at www.collegesavings.org. As a general rule, look at your own state's plan first, especially if your state allows you to take a tax deduction for your contributions to your state's 529 plans. Note, however, that once you have invested in a plan, you are usually restricted to making investment changes or change the investment strategy to once per calendar year.[60]

Coverdell Education Savings Accounts

The Coverdell Education Savings Account (Coverdell ESA) was formerly known as the Education IRA. The Coverdell ESA has more flexibility and many more restrictions than a 529 plan. The main point of flexibility is that Coverdell ESA funds can be used to fund a child's elementary and secondary education (K–12), as well as post-secondary education (college, graduate school, vocational school, etc.).

Other than this major variance in benefit, the Coverdell has many more restrictions:

- The account must be opened for the benefit of a child (designated beneficiary) under the age of 18. Contributions to the account will not be accepted after the designated beneficiary reaches the age of 18, unless the child is a special needs beneficiary.
- You are limited to a $2,000 maximum contribution per year and only if your modified adjusted gross income is less than $95,000 as a single tax filer, or $190,000 as a married couple filing jointly in the tax year in which you contribute. The $2,000 maximum contribution limit is gradually reduced if your modified adjusted gross income exceeds these limits.
- Anyone, including the child, may contribute to a Coverdell ESA as long as the income of those who contribute falls within the income guidelines and the total of all contributions for one beneficiary does not exceed the $2,000 annual limit.
- Distributions must not exceed the amount of qualified education expenses for the year in which they are taken. Otherwise, earnings might be subject to taxes and penalties.

- All funds in the account must be distributed to the designated beneficiary one month after her thirtieth birthday (unless she is a special
needs beneficiary). After age 30, the balance of the account can be
rolled over to a Coverdell ESA for another designated beneficiary who
is also a qualified family member under the age of 30.[61]

Although many states offer a limited income-tax deduction to those
of you who contribute to a 529 college savings plan, no such income-
tax deductions are available to those who contribute to a Coverdell ESA.
However, all earnings in the account accumulate on a tax-deferred basis
and can be withdrawn from the account tax-free if used to pay for qualified
education expenses.

Given the many restrictions imposed on Coverdell ESA, its main advantage over contributing to a 529 college plan is that distributions from
Coverdell ESA may also be used for elementary and secondary education.
Unfortunately, unlike the provisions of 529 plans, which were made permanent when President Bush signed the Pension Protection Act of 2006 into
law, this and other improvements to the ESA are set to expire at the end
of 2010. Your best alternatives are then to either use up the Coverdell ESA
funds by 2010 or roll over funds—tax-free—from the Coverdell ESAs to 529
plans by the end of 2010.[62]

Funds from custodial accounts, such as UGMAs and UTMAs, to benefit
your minor can be used, with little or no tax advantages, to help fund your
child's education. There is a more extensive discussion later in this chapter.

Save in Accounts that Provide You a Tax Deduction

Most retirement plans such as a 401(k), a traditional IRA, a SIMPLE IRA,
or a defined benefit plan—with the stark exception of a Roth IRA—are
funded with pretax contributions. Because your gross salary is reduced
by the amount of your contribution to your retirement plan, your taxable
income is lowered for the year in which you make your contribution. That
means that more goes into your plan than comes out of your paycheck, and
that your money will grow tax deferred for many years—presumably until
you decide to retire or begin taking out withdrawals. At that point in time,
your retirement withdrawals are then subject to income and other taxes.

Save in Accounts that Match Your Contributions

Many, but not all, retirement plans offer an employee contribution or a
match. Although the match is free to you, you have earned it and it is
considered part of your overall compensation package. Unfortunately, many
employees, especially younger ones, tend to leave this benefit on the table

and not take advantage of it. If you are young, your rationale is most likely something like this:

- I am too young to worry about retirement.
- I need the money instead to pay for day-to-day expenses, and given my age and experience, I am one of the lowest paid employees.
- I am unsure how long I will be working with this employer, either because it is one of my first jobs or I am unhappy with my current employer.

This logic is flawed. You are never too young to start saving for retirement. The earlier you start, the more you will end up with at retirement. Even when you live on a tight budget, you should get into the habit of saving even as little as $25 or $50 a month. Finally, if you decide to leave your employer and you have already vested in their retirement plan, you are able to roll over the retirement funds from your existing retirement plan to your new employer's retirement plan or to an individual IRA.

What you are doing is leaving behind the opportunity to earn extra money from your employer—money that you have earned and to which you are entitled. Many retirement plans that match employee contributions offer, in some cases, a matching contribution equal to 25 percent of the employee's eligible contributions, up to 8 percent of their compensation. If your match is only $1,000 and you receive that match each year, after a 30-year period, assuming that your investment grows at 8 percent and because it is in a retirement plan it grows tax-deferred, you would have missed out on $119,708 in additional retirement income.[63]

Look at the after-tax cost of your contribution to a 401(k) plan. Assume that you earn $50,000 a year and your employer matches 50 cents for every dollar you contribute to your 401(k) plan, up to 6 percent of your pay. If you contribute 6 percent of your pay, or $3,000, in the plan and your employer matches 3 percent, or $1,500, your contribution will cost you less than 6 percent because the funds are taken out before income taxes. If you are in the 25 percent tax bracket, your $3,000 contribution will save you $750 in taxes, or 1.5 percent of your pay. So, between your contribution and your employer's match, you will contribute 9 percent of your salary to your retirement but, in reality, it will only cost you 4.5 percent of your pay—you are already growing your retirement fund just by contributing on pretax basis and taking advantage of your employer match.[64]

There are no investment accounts that will guarantee you a return such as the 25 percent match and that is even before accounting for the projected returns on your contribution and your company's match. There is no reason why you should leave your company match unused or why you should not begin investing as early as possible in your company's retirement plan.

Save for Others Especially Your Children and Spouse

If your children, spouse, or other loved ones do not have the financial means or the discipline to save, you can proactively save on their behalf and not give them cash that they would go out and spend. The following are the most common saving vehicles available: custodial accounts; funding your working children's Roth IRA; funding a spousal IRA; and purchasing U.S. savings bonds. Each vehicle comes with its set own of restrictions and limitations, as well as valuable benefits.

CUSTODIAL ACCOUNTS   You can save money for your children in custodial savings accounts established under the Uniform Transfers to Minors Act (UTMA) or the Uniform Gifts to Minor Act (UGMA). There are a number of reasons why parents opt to invest in an UTMA or an UGMA for their children:

- Children, as minors, cannot legally control their own investment or savings accounts. They have to have an adult or a custodian to act on their behalf until they reach the age of maturity (18 or 21, depending on the state where they reside).
- Gifts to custodial accounts are irrevocable and may only be used for the benefit of the child. They are therefore not part of a parent's net worth or estate and are considered an asset-protected investment (from lawsuits, liabilities, or bankruptcy filings of either parent or custodian). The assets are to be used for the sole benefit of the child or beneficiary.
- Adults, other than a parent, can make contributions to these custodial accounts.
- Reduced taxes—For 2008, Congress raised the "kiddie tax" threshold so that income above $1,800 of children 18 and under, or under 24 if they are full-time students and dependent on their parents, is taxed at the parent's marginal tax rate.[65] In comparison, for 2007, annual earnings on investments held in UTMA/UGMA accounts for a child under age 18 were taxed as follows: The first $850 was tax free; the next $850 was taxed at the child's rate (presumably lower than the parents') and anything over $1,700 was taxed at the parents' rate.[66]

    Contributions to trust accounts do not grow on a tax-deferred basis, nor are the contributions tax-deductible. Furthermore, unlike a 529 college plan, your child gains control of assets at the age of maturity—18 or 21, depending on the state where you reside.

    A benefit or a loophole, depending whether you are a parent or the IRS, was eliminated in May 2006 when legislation was passed that altered the tax structure for a child from 14 to 18. In the past, once your child reached 14, all earnings on savings and investments were to be taxed at the child's rate—usually a very low rate. This, of course, allowed wealthier families to reduce their overall income tax bill by gifting money and other investments to preteens, who, upon turning 14, would pay lower taxes on the investment earnings. In fact, parents in the upper-income tax brackets could assign highly appreciated assets to children going to college. These children could then sell the investments themselves, which could put them in a lower tax bracket and thus reduce significantly the family's capital tax bill.[67]

From a financial-aid perspective, it is better to save for your child in a 529 college plan than it is in custodial accounts. Schools can use up to 35 percent of the value of a custodial account each year in advance of any need-based grants, loans, or scholarships. So, if your child has a custodial account with $100,000 in it, then $35,000 has to come out before any aid is given. By comparison, only $5,600 would be come out of a $100,000 parent-owned account, including a 529 college plan. In May 2006, the Department of Education changed the financial aid treatment of child-owned 529s. The new rule treats these accounts as "invisible" when deciding how much aid should be given to your child.[68]

If you have custodial accounts, do not necessarily rush to liquidate them or convert them to UTMA/UGMA 529 accounts, for the following reasons:

- You should not tie up all the funds you save for your children in 529 accounts, since these can only be used for qualifying higher education expenses. You might need to buy your child a car to go to work or school, or you might want to save money to help your child with the purchase of a first home.
- 529 plans have to be funded with cash. This means that liquidating investments in an UTMA/UGMA account to fund a 529 may trigger a capital gains tax. If you wait until your child is 18, this may mean that the gain could be taxed at a lower rate—your child's rate as opposed to yours.
- If you plan on selling UTMA/UGMA assets to fund a 529 and you are likely to apply for financial aid, try to complete the sale at least two calendar years before your child applies for financial aid. Otherwise, the sales proceeds will show as your child's assets, and thus substantially reduce the financial aid package that would have been awarded for the first year of college.
- You have the option of transferring the UTMA/UGMA into a child-owned 529, which could increase the eventual financial-aid package offered by a college (the funds in a 529 plan do not count as your child's assets, will grow tax-deferred, and are withdrawn tax-free for qualified higher education expenses). However, since it is a "child-owned" 529, it would be difficult to transfer this type of 529 to another family member. Also, if your child decides to spend his 529 proceeds

on nonqualified expenses, then taxes and penalties will be imposed on the earnings portion of the withdrawals. Finally, some colleges might count a child-owned 529 more heavily in awarding school-based financial aid.

- Given these complexities, you need to evaluate your course of action based on you and your child's specific needs. There is no one formula that provides the appropriate solution to everyone. Consult your wealth and tax advisors.

FUNDING YOUR WORKING CHILDREN'S ROTH IRA ACCOUNTS In Chapter 5, the Roth IRA is discussed in detail. In this section on saving strategies, it is worth noting that those of you who are parents tend to overlook encouraging your children to open Roth IRA accounts, even if you have to fund these Roth IRAs yourselves. If your child works and earns income, he/she can open a Roth IRA for their distant retirement—this would represent years of tax-deferred growth, and those funds can be withdrawn tax free in retirement. Five years after opening the Roth IRA account, your child can even withdraw some of these funds, without penalty, for a down payment on their first home (up to $10,000) or use the funds to pay for qualified college expenses. In both these cases, your child would still owe taxes on the earnings, but the penalty is waived.[69] This is not necessarily the ideal way to save for college, but it illustrates the flexibility of having a Roth IRA.

FUNDING A SPOUSAL IRA Many people are unaware that a nonworking spouse can make a deductible IRA contribution of up to $5,000 for 2008 ($6,000 if age 50 or older), as long as the couple files a joint return, and the *working* spouse has enough earned income to cover the contribution. Whether this IRA contribution is deductible or not depends on the adjusted gross income of the couple. The deductibility of the nonworking spouse's contribution is phased out for couples with adjusted gross income between $159,000 and $169,000,[70] provided that the working spouse is covered by a qualified retirement plan whether through an employer or self-employment.[71]

Whether you are a stay-at-home mom or taking time off to care for children or whatever other reason (there is no discrimination whether you are a man or a woman), generous federal guidelines encourage you to continue saving for retirement even if you are not working outside of the home and earning money. If you are a nonworking spouse, and as long as your household meets the conditions already listed, you should contribute annually to your IRA. Your contribution could be tax-deductible, your retirement plan will grow tax deferred, and you will have your own retirement funds in your older age.

PURCHASING U.S. SAVINGS BONDS   U.S. savings bonds can be bought for you or for others. They pay tax-deferred interest, and some bonds pay tax-free interest if the proceeds are used for college expenses. You are limited, however, to buying up to $60,000 of bonds annually, and you are not allowed to change the beneficiary of these bonds.[72] You have to be at least 24 years old to buy these bonds. The tax-free interest begins to phase out for singles with income over $63,100 and joint filers with income over $94,700. If you are applying for federal financial aid, the bonds count as assets of the bond owner. Series-EE bonds pay straight interest, while Series-I bonds pay inflation-adjusted rates.[73] The interest tax-deferral, the potential tax-free interest, and the safety of bonds backed by the federal government make these bonds an attractive investment vehicle for particularly conservative investors.

The saving strategies discussed in this chapter are easy to implement. Your wealth and tax advisors can discuss the best strategies for your particular situation as there is no formula that fits all. What you need to do is realize the benefits of saving, be disciplined in your approach, and act.

The Benefits of Saving versus Borrowing

Quite often, you might be tempted not to save and choose to borrow, especially for your children's college education. After all, student loans are abundant, and fairly easy to secure. The repayment of student loans is generally the responsibility of your graduating children to pay back. So, why would you want to deprive yourself from spending what you earn to save for your child's education?

Aside from the sense of responsibility parents feel toward paying for their children's education and allowing your children to graduate without the burden of loan paybacks, we are going to illustrate the monetary and economic benefits of saving versus borrowing.

Assume that your goal is to save $200,000 for your child's college education for a four-year college.[74] If you save $394 a month for 20 years and earn a 7 percent rate of return, you will save a total of $200,000—your total contributions amount to $94,575, while your accumulated investment earnings total $105,425.[75]

If you were to borrow the $200,000 needed for your child's college education and pay it off over 20 years at an 8.5 percent interest rate, your total cost to repay the loan will be $407,059. Of that amount, the cost of interest payments amount to $207,059.[76]

This scenario shows that in lieu of total contributions of $94,575 that you would have made over a 20-year period; your total cost to borrow and repay this loan to fund your child's education would have cost you $407,059.

Some parents might be tempted to tap into their 401(k) plans and borrow money to fund their children's education expenses. This is made easy because 85 percent of 401(k) plans allow for such loans.[77] This temptation should be resisted because you or your child can readily borrow money for college education, but you cannot borrow money for your retirement.[78] In this case, it is better to borrow money, even if it means that your child ends up with some debt after college.

Students have a variety of loan options at their disposal. Those who file a Free Application for Federal Student Aid, or FAFSA, and who are eligible for financial aid, often can take Stafford loans. These can be subsidized or unsubsidized, and they traditionally carry lower interest rates than private loans. With subsidized loans, the federal government picks up the interest tab while students remain in college. Furthermore, the federal financial aid formula does not consider your retirement accounts, including 401(k) plans and individual retirement accounts (IRAs), when calculating your expected family contribution. 5.6 percent of other parental assets and 20 percent of your student's assets are calculated as available funds to help pay for college. Thus, if you save as much as you can in your retirement plans, the chances of your child receiving financial aid award increases.[79]

Save, if you can, instead of borrowing. It is less expensive over time. And, leave your 401(k) and retirement plans alone. You need them because you cannot borrow to fund your retirement while your children have access to loans to fund their education.

14 Steps to Help You Manage Your Debt

"It is as important to manage what you own as it is to manage what you owe," a lending specialist once told me. Although the difference between "own" and "owe" is one letter of the alphabet, this statement represents one of the basic tenets of good wealth management.

Not all people with debt are those with low incomes unable to make both ends meet, borrowing to put food on the table. It is surprising how many people with hefty salaries and stable jobs are in debt. Whether their rationale represents overconfidence about their future ability to earn money and repay the debt sometime in the future or they are living in a mental state of self-denial regarding their monetary capabilities is irrelevant. This behavior is irresponsible and fraught with dangers. Saving and managing your debt go hand in hand and are critical components of a sound financial and wealth management plan. You need to save, but it would virtually be impossible to save if you are drowning in debt.

In this section, we will discuss ways to help you manage your debt and provide a balance between your income, saving strategy, and debt management. Ideally, most people would want to live debt-free. Realistically, most of us can only hope to live with manageable debt. Here are some suggestions to help you manage your debt.

Step 1: Have a Budget

Having a budget is one of the simplest ways to manage your income and liabilities. On the income side, list all sources of your income. On the expense side, list all your monthly liabilities, including saving for emergencies. Tweak your budget so you can balance your income and expenses and end with a balanced budget. Avoid being in a bind when you are faced with large unexpected expenses. Create a savings category for these types of unforeseen, large expenses. This way, you would not have to borrow to pay for these large unexpected expenses. Look at ways in which you can reduce your small daily expenses, especially if they are not essential—such as taking a lunch box to the office as opposed to buying lunch.

Step 2: Adopt Good Habits

Having a budget and living within that budget is a great habit to adopt. Set aside extra cash for emergencies or unexpected large purchases. Do not buy that $5 a day cup of fancy coffee. Grind your own beans and take the coffee in a thermos to the office. Add the earnings to your $5 a day saving, and over a 40-year period, this change of habit resulting in daily savings could become *your million dollar cup of coffee.* Carpool if you can, and tell your kids to do the same. Turn off the lights when you leave the room. Simple day-to-day changes in your behavior with a little bit of discipline are a great starting point to managing your budget.

Step 3: Spend Less

This is a simple concept, but a critical one. If your income is $100,000, then base your budget and spending habits on an assumed income of $80,000. Admittedly, this could be difficult to attain with all the demands on your income from your spouse, children, and the new toys—whether it is a GPS system or a fancy gadget. Just remember, they did not exist a few years ago and you were able to live without them. Alternatively, set aside a monthly goal to save and make it the first bill you pay out of your salary. Then, spend the rest.

Step 4: Aim to Retire Debt-Free

Your goal should be to have all your debt—including the mortgage—paid off before you retire. In most cases, you will be living on a fixed budget from a combination of sources—Social Security (38 percent), part-time work

(27 percent), assets (13 percent), private pensions (10 percent), government pensions (9 percent), and other sources (3 percent).[80] In reality, according to the U.S. Census Bureau (2000), 45 percent of individuals in their sixties had a mortgage on their home, and 20 percent of these had a second mortgage as well.[81] Mortgage obligations represented in 2000 21 percent of household income for individuals in their sixties and 24 percent of individuals in their seventies.[82] Why not enjoy peace of mind, extra spending money in retirement, by paying off your mortgage by the time you retire?

Step 5: Pay Down Your Mortgage

Mortgage debt is acceptable, and in the vast majority of cases is unavoidable. Houses tend to be our largest and most expensive investments. Mortgage debt is acceptable as long as you can readily afford your home. Make as large a down payment as you can and consider a shorter loan period, even though your payment will be higher. Manage your expectations and living standards. Shop for the best rates, and when you find them lock them in. Make the equivalent of an extra mortgage payment a year. If you have a 30-year $400,000 mortgage and start making the extra payment from the beginning, you pay off the mortgage seven years early and save $100,000 in interest payments.[83]

Step 6: Use Home-Equity Loans Sparingly

You might want to set up a home-equity line of credit (HELOC) for emergency use only. It is probably one of the least expensive ways to secure access to funds at favorable rates (because it is backed by the equity in your house and your good credit). Depending on your particular tax situation, the interest on a home-equity line of credit could be tax-deductible as well.[84] If you have a HELOC and you are careful not to use it for impulsive purchases, you are providing yourself with a security blanket in the event of an emergency. It makes sense to use your HELOC to consolidate your high-interest debt, especially credit card debt, provided you do not resort to using paid-up credit cards to pile on additional debt.

Step 7: Be Careful with Credit Cards

About 6.8 percent of outstanding consumer debt in the U.S. is credit card debt, while approximately 73 percent is mortgage debt.[85]

Credit cards are addictive and, in most cases, carry high interest rates. If you are an average American, your credit card debt is about $9,900, and it carries an average interest rate of 15 percent. If you pay $250 a month, it will take you 55 months to pay off your credit card debt.[86] Do not use credit cards to purchase items that you do not need. If you cannot pay with cash or know that you will be unable to pay off your credit balance at the end of the month, that is your clue not to buy that item, whether it is clothing, entertainment, or a vacation.

Most credit cards with introductory teaser rates, such as zero percent, come with hefty penalties and higher rates if you do not meticulously follow the terms of the credit card issuer—usually written in small type on many pages. These offers appear as maxed-out lines of credits and negatively affect your credit score. Also, if a teaser-rate loan is not paid off by the maturity date, you could owe not only the unpaid balance but also backdated interest.[87] Credit card issuers will quickly raise rates and shut down a line of credit if there is any late payment or signs of a problem. In 2007, punitive rates charged by the major issuers have reached nearly 33 percent—an all-time high, according to CardWeb.com.[88] Avoid the temptation. You do not need more than one or two credit cards. Multiple credit cards are viewed as easy access to credit and negatively affect your credit score. In weak moments, it is easy to charge up your credit cards without recognizing the dire consequences of this type of debt. You need to monitor your monthly bills, especially credit cards, and make spending adjustments accordingly. Avoid spending the maximum limit on your credit cards, because it is a good idea to have credit available for emergency uses.

Step 8: Compare Lenders and Rates

If you need to borrow to purchase a house, a car, or any other large purchase, compare lenders in terms of their reputation, their size, their customer service, and the complaints lodged against them with the Better Business Bureau. Compare the terms of any loan that you might seek. Be wary of prepayment penalties on any loan that you take. Avoid these. You are usually locked-in with a lender, not necessarily for your benefit. *Review your debt regularly* to find out if less expensive options are available. Be careful not to refinance your debt too often; the cost of refinancing could easily negate your benefits. Consult with your tax and wealth advisor before you make these decisions.

Step 9: Ask for Discounts

The key to receiving is asking, and the worst answer is a no. Ask your phone, cable, and other providers for a "loyal" client discount. You will be surprised how many of those would rather give you a discount than lose your business. It will cost them a lot more to secure another customer like you than to accommodate you with a courtesy- or a loyal-customer discount. When you buy a car, you rarely pay its sticker price. You would negotiate until the price comes down. You can do so the same for other products, especially those with a high sticker price. Keep in mind that many items are not subject to negotiations but you will be surprised how merchants will accommodate a courteous request for a discount.

Step 10: Teach Your Children

According to a nationwide survey conducted in April of 2007 by Harris Interactive, about one-third of parents have not discussed saving or investing with their children. Parents believed that their children were too young to worry about saving and investing, but the truth is that parents admitted that they did not know much about the topic themselves. The study concludes that "kids of all ages learn most of what they know about money from their parents. And, that's the way kids prefer it."[89] In 2006, 180,000 young adults between the ages of 18 and 25 declared bankruptcy. You do not want your child to be one of them.[90] A whopping 76 percent of all incoming freshmen will already have a credit card when they arrive on campus, and most undergraduate students will have four or more cards by the time they graduate. In fact, most students carry an average credit balance of nearly $3,000 during their final year in college.[91] An individual's credit history begins usually with their first credit card, and most young people are surprised to learn that their credit history will affect them for the rest of their lives. Their credit history could affect their ability to rent a condo, finance the purchase of a car or even get a job.[92] Keep in mind that your kids are watching and learning from your actions. Help them learn by being a good example.

Step 11: Pay Bills on Time

Promptly paying all your bills, including payments due on loans and credit cards, is critical. It is a good habit to get into, and it affects significantly your credit history and rating. On-time payments count for 35 percent of your FICO score, so even if you pay only the minimum due, a timely payment is crucial. A pattern of late payments not only lowers your credit and insurance scores, but late fees and interest payments can add up and your interest rates could be increased as a result.

Step 12: Keep in Touch with Creditors

If you are moving, do not forget to notify your financial institutions. If you lose bills in the mail and pay late or not pay at all, it could place a black mark on your credit report no matter what your reasons might be. One way of avoiding this potential problem is by taking advantage of electronic billing and payment.

Step 13: Monitor Your Credit Score

A low credit score could cost you, even if you are a high earner, thousands of dollars in additional finance charges. It could prevent your access to credit, insurance, and even a job. Credit scores are "not just about credit," says Travis B. Plunkett, legislative director for the Consumer Federation of America in Washington, D.C. "They affect your ability to get many services and employment."[93] According to Steven Katz, a spokesman for TransUnion's Truecredit.com, "The score is a numerical representation of what's contained in an individual's credit report. The lenders provide credit reports on payment habits of those consumers, and that's how a credit file is formed."[94]

Undeniably, your credit score is one of the most important scores that affect many aspects of your life, throughout your life. Surprisingly, according to a recent survey, only 37 percent of respondents nationwide have ordered their credit reports within the past 12 months.[95] To help you better understand your credit score, here are some highlights:[96]

- Scores typically range from 300 points to 850 points. Most of you will not find out your number until you apply for a loan.
- Fair Isaac Corp (FIC) developed what is viewed as the "traditional" credit score, which it calls FICO. This is used by more than 90 percent of the largest lenders.
- About 40 percent of the population has a FICO score of 750 or higher; 27 percent have scores between 600 and 699; and 15 percent have scores below 600.
- The score weighting is based on the following criteria: **35 percent** for your payment history—this includes whether you pay on time and whether you have adverse records such as a lien or bankruptcy; **30 percent** for the amount you owe—if you borrow the maximum on a credit card, it will lower your score compared to someone who has borrowed less than what is available on their card; **15 percent** for your credit history—the older your accounts, the better; **10 percent** for type of credit on your record—it makes a difference whether you have credit card debt, installment loans and mortgages, or just credit card debt.
- Raising your score could save you a lot of money, especially on mortgages. If you raise your score of 580–619 to 660–699, it could save you $5,148 in one year if you have a $300,000 fixed mortgage, according to Fair Isaac's Web site, www.myfico.com. Unfortunately, given the turbulence in the credit and financial markets beginning in the latter part of 2007, it has become extremely difficult for someone with a moderate credit rating let alone a low credit rating to secure a loan. Many people have been frozen out of the credit markets and only those with

high credit scores are able to access the credit markets; however, with much more stringent requirements that usually includes a larger down payment than in previous years.

- In a historically normal economic and lending environment, a score of 720 or higher could earn you the best rates. With the deepening of the subprime crisis that started to boil over in the second half of 2007, you needed a score in the high 700s to get the same benefits.

How can you improve your credit score? Take the following steps:

1. *First, you need to know what your score is.* Reports are available to you free once a year from each of the three major credit reporting agencies. However, you must use the Web site, www.annualcreditreport.com, rather than individual Web sites, to get the free reports.
2. *Check your credit scores for errors, omissions, and potential identity theft.* If an error exists, go to the agency's Web site to get forms to file a complaint. You should consider sending a written complaint as well via certified mail. The agency has 30 days to verify your complaint. It must remove the contentious item if it cannot verify that is correct. If the agency discovers the information is wrong, it must notify the other two agencies. If after 30 days the dispute has not been resolved, experts recommend that you call a lawyer.
3. *Pay off your debt.* It is just as simple as that.
4. *Do not sign up for a store credit card to get the 10 percent discount.* A few new cards in a short period of time will lower your score.
5. *Do not cancel old cards that you do not use.* "Closing an account eliminates a positive reference," according to Katz of TransUnion.
6. *Keep your balances low on your credit cards and other revolving credit.*
7. *If you plan to apply in the near future for credit, do not use your credit cards for groceries and other payments.* Credit-rating companies only see the balance on the day they check your credit.
8. *Always pay your bills on time.* All your bills—not just the credit cards but also the utilities, the cell phone, the parking ticket, and even your library card. Missing one single payment that you owe could lower your score by 100 points![97]

A July 2007 report by the Consumer Federation of America and Washington Mutual found that if consumers with an average score improved their credit score by only 30 points, they would save $76 a year in finance charges. Apply this to the entire country; it would represent $20 billion in savings.[98]

It is crucial to note that even if you are wealthy both in terms of cash and assets, your wealth is not calculated in your score, nor does it affect it. Your income and savings history are separate items that do not affect your credit score. You can, therefore, be very wealthy with a low credit score![99]

Step 14: Beware of Identity Theft Fraud and Scams

In 2007, 8.4 million Americans were victims of identity theft. Identity theft is the number one crime in the United States, and it is spreading worldwide.[100] Through 2006, the Federal Trade Commission's database contained a whopping 3.5 million consumer fraud and identity theft complaints that have been filed with federal, state and local law enforcement agencies and private organizations. Identity theft fraud includes credit card fraud (25 percent), other identity theft (24 percent), phone or utilities fraud (16 percent), bank fraud (16 percent), government documents and benefits fraud (10 percent), attempted identity fraud (6 percent), and loan fraud (5 percent). About 18 percent of victims have experienced more than one type of fraud.[101] Residents in Arizona, Nevada, California, Texas, and Florida—in that order—were victimized the most, based on the number of cases and the size of each state's population.[102]

These fraudulent actions can potentially ruin your credit, rob you of your hard-earned money, and scam you into giving to or "investing" in nonexistent businesses or ventures. All sectors of the population are targets—the elderly, college kids, and even illegal immigrants. Often, it is dumbfounding how easy it is to access people's sensitive information. For example, 49 percent of college students receive credit-card applications on a daily or weekly basis. A casual attitude toward credit could mean graduating with massive debt and bad credit. And, if these offers are not immediately shredded, predators could have access to them by rummaging through garbage cans. Forty-eight percent of students have had grades posted by Social Security number, making the students' personal identities too accessible.[103] This should be an easy fix by school administrations, especially if they issue instead nonidentifying codes and/or numbers for each student.

The schemes employed vary in range, style, approach, and sophistication. Someone could call and claim to be a law enforcement officer, a jury coordinator, a bank teller, or a credit card company and intimidate victims into giving out sensitive data such as their Social Security numbers, dates of birth, and credit card numbers. Get-rich schemes prey on people's greed, gullibility, or kind-heartedness and promise to quickly make a lot of money in return for a fee to be paid in advance. Whether it is through the phone, face-to-face, cell phone text messaging, mail, and, increasingly, the Internet, the approaches are getting more sophisticated and relentless. Even though some victims—for example, credit card victims—may not suffer financial harm because charges on their cards were fraudulent, they may still have to spend many hours attempting to correct their personal records and prove that those charges were not theirs.

If you suspect that you are a victim of identity theft or a scam, call the police immediately and file a complaint with the Federal Trade Commission Consumer Response Center at 1-877-438-4338 or www.ftc.gov. Here are some tips to help you fend off potential scammers and protect your identity:[104]

- Review your bank and credit-card statements monthly.
- Notify banks or credit card companies immediately of any unauthorized activity.
- Do not sign the back of your credit cards. Instead, write "Ask for photo ID."
- Ask your credit-card companies to stop sending you blank checks in the mail.
- Carefully review your credit reports. All three major credit bureaus must provide you with a free copy once every 12 months. Do not order all three at the same time. Stagger them throughout the year to keep a constant eye on your credit. You can get the free credit reports at www.annualcreditreport.com.
- Keep documents with personal information and PIN numbers in a safe place.
- Use your credit card, not your debit card, when ordering by phone or mail. Credit cards generally offer greater protection.
- Do not carry your Social Security card with you.
- Do not give out your Social Security number unless it is required for a legitimate purpose, such as opening a bank account or filling out an employment application.
- Do not use your Social Security number on your driver's license.
- Do not respond to e-mails that claim to be urgent and confidential and that promise riches to help transfer cash out of a country into the United States in return for a promised share of the cash. Often, unsuspecting recipients receive a check in the mail and are asked to deposit the check and send part of the money back to the sender. The check ends up bouncing and the victim ends up sending money to a scam artist, losing an average of $3,000 to $4,000 each. In 2007, the U.S. Postal Inspection Service started an international crackdown that resulted in arrests in the Netherlands, Nigeria, and Canada. More than 540,000 fake checks with a face value of $2.1 billion were seized.[105]
- Do not sign checks that come in the mail that are tied to offers. Once you sign the back of the check, you are agreeing to the terms of the

offer, which are usually listed in the back of the check. Although most of these are legitimate, you might not be fully aware what you are signing up for or buying. If you are unsure, call and request further details. Better yet, request that additional information be sent to you in writing. In any case, it is better to err on the side of caution. The only times these checks should be cashed is when you have established that the offer and the company offering it are legitimate and you are firmly convinced that the product being offered is something that is of either benefit or interest to you. When in doubt, shred the offer.

These are but a few of the steps that you can take to prevent being a victim to identity theft and scams. When in doubt, listen to your instincts. Follow the age-old edict, "If it seems too good to be true, it is."

Concluding Remarks

No matter how much you earn or what you own, your net worth is determined by what you own (your assets) minus what you owe (your liabilities). You might own a lot, but if what you owe is more, it could mean that you are poorly managing your resources and taking on more debt than what you need.

Learning to save and properly managing your debt are critical components of good financial planning. We normally save for a variety of reasons. These include setting up an emergency or rainy-day fund, funding your children's education, ensuring a comfortable retirement, paying for future health care expenses, making a major purchase, paying for a major event, starting a new business, accumulating wealth for enjoyment during your lifetime, or leaving an inheritance to your loved ones or favorite charity.

You need to be systematic in your saving strategies—benefit from compounding, start saving early, save as much or as little as you can, use an automatic deduction plan, save in tax-deferred accounts, save in tax-free accounts, whether it is a Roth IRA or college saving plans, save in accounts that provide you with a tax deduction, save in accounts that match your contributions, and save to meet your loved ones' needs, such as your children and spouse.

Saving for your children's education, one of the largest expenses during your lifetime, is particularly important, given the tax-advantaged and valuable investment vehicles available to you such as 529 college plans and Coverdell educational savings accounts. These allow you to enjoy tax-free growth and distribution so long as the funds are used for educational purposes and meet certain criteria.

If you have ever wondered whether you should save now or borrow later to fund a major purchase or your children's education, always chose to save—it is far less expensive over time, and there is no price to your satisfaction and peace of mind.

Managing your debt is difficult and challenging. Often, there is no alternative to borrowing, especially when it comes to making major purchases such as a home or a car. The 14 steps outlined in the chapter are important guidelines that can help you manage your debt. These include having a budget, adopting good habits, spending less, retiring debt-free, paying down your mortgage, using home-equity loans sparingly, being extra careful with your credit cards, shopping around for lenders and rates if you have to borrow, asking for discounts, teaching your children good saving and debt management habits, paying bills on time, keeping in touch with your creditors, monitoring your credit score, and being alert to scams and identity theft.

These are valuable tools that can help you learn to save and properly manage your debt. It is now up to you to act, irrespective of your existing habits. You are, or at least should be, in control. If you need help, seek the advice of your tax and wealth advisors.

Finally, on the bright side, the Federal Reserve reported in September 2007 that U.S. households' net worth rose 2.1 percent to $57.86 trillion in the second quarter of 2007. Household net worth is a measure of total assets, such as houses and pensions, minus total liabilities such as mortgages and credit card debts.[106] U.S. home prices, however, which peaked in July 2006, were down 20 percent as of the third quarter of 2008 and the expectation is that they will continue to spiral down for much of 2009. Roughly, one in eight U.S. jobs is dependent on the housing market directly or indirectly. And, since housing traditionally leads the economy through a recovery, tough times might be ahead.[107] Be mindful, however, that the increase in net worth relates mostly to nonliquid assets such as the value of your home and pensions—assets that are not readily available for spending and are long-term in nature. Although the gross value of the average American's primary residence makes up 29 percent of a household's total assets, the value of the actual home equity is equal to only 19 percent of the household's net worth. This is because home mortgage debt has almost doubled (up 91 percent) since the end of 2001.[108] Americans aggressively took out cash out of the equity in their homes. Following the turmoil that was precipitated by the subprime debacle, the credit crunch, and the ensuing turmoil in the financial markets, foreclosures skyrocketed, especially among homeowners with adjustable-interest-only rates and those with shaky credit history. Lending came to a freeze and most banks even froze existing lines of credit that had been taken out on homes primarily because of the slump in home values and the reluctance of financial institutions to lend whatever cash they might have had given the lack of liquidity in the markets and the freezing of most loans among banks. Getting a mortgage loan has become tough except for those with sterling credit.

CHAPTER 5

How to Plan for a Comfortable Retirement

The twentieth century witnessed the evolution of the modern world like no other era in history. We marvel at our ability to have created the automobile, the airplane, nuclear power, and the computer, let alone the miraculous landing on the moon. In reality, the most important development of the twentieth century has been our ability to extend the span of human life more so than at any other time since the creation of the world.[1]

Consider this: On the first day of the twentieth century, the average life expectancy in the United States was 47. On the last day of the twentieth century, it was 76. What would you guess life expectancy will be on the last day of the twenty-first century? No one can answer this question; however, if you were a 65-year-old male in 2006, your life expectancy would have been 83 years—85 if you were a female.[2] The fastest-growing age group in America today is those over 100 years old.[3]

Given that few of us want to die, this news is elating. We get to be alive longer to enjoy the finest things in life—be with our families, attend our grandchildren's weddings, travel the world, pursue our hobbies, be healthy, and retire in comfort. As much as you are entitled to a longer life, you have the responsibility, no matter how old you are now, to plan for your future retirement if you want to live a long, happy, productive, and healthy life.

Within the space of only one generation, four major changes have made the process of retirement planning more urgent and, certainly, more challenging:

- We live longer—much longer.
- The responsibility for saving for retirement has shifted to you individually away from your employer and the government.
- Almost 60 percent of women are working outside the home. Couples are planning and coordinating two retirements, not just one.

■ The accelerating cost of health- and long-term care, at least twice that of the overall inflation, is a new major strain on the retirees' budget.

The 10 Most Common Retirement Worries

Preparing for retirement can be stressful, emotionally charged, full of uncertainty, and sometimes daunting—not so much for those who plan for retirement, however. Here are the top 10 worries of someone nearing retirement or has reached the retirement age:

1. How to make it to age $59^1/_2$—the age when funds can be withdrawn from retirement accounts without the IRS-imposed 10 percent penalty and whether to begin relying on these retirement funds.
2. How to make it to age 62—the age you can begin accessing your Social Security benefits, and whether to wait until age 65 to 67.
3. How do you pay for your retirement? What sources of income are available and have you saved enough to last you through your retirement?
4. Will you have enough funds to live a longer life and meeting the increasingly expensive health care costs?
5. Will you lose your independence because of failing health and the need for long-term care?
6. How can you reduce taxes? When it comes to taxes, the IRS does not distinguish between a retiree and a nonretiree. As long as you make money, you will be liable to pay taxes.
7. When should you access your Social Security benefits? There is a lot of uncertainty surrounding the survivability of Social Security.
8. Will I need to work? Many are looking at part-time work to supplement living expenses.[4]
9. Will you find it difficult to adjust to a new lifestyle and enjoy the freedom offered by retirement?
10. Should you continue to live in your same house, or should you downsize to save on money and maintenance? Should you continue to live near family and friends, or move to retirement friendly states such as Florida and Arizona?

This chapter's goal is to help you plan for your retirement, no matter how old you are. We will discuss the life stages of retirement, help you evaluate whether your nest egg is sufficient to retire in comfort, when should you retire, and how to calculate your retirement needs. This chapter will also analyze the four main sources of income in retirement—Social Security, employer-sponsored retirement plans, your IRAs, and your other personal investments. We will explore the common mistakes the average individual makes in planning for their retirement, which of your retirement funds you should spend first in retirement, and the most common risks that you face once you have retired. The hope is to provide you with a roadmap for a comfortable retirement.

Six Life Stages of Retirement Planning

Planning for retirement is not a one-time or an annual event. It is a process that needs to be well thought out and properly planned. The most frequently asked questions pertaining to retirement planning are:

- When should I begin saving for my retirement?
- How much do I need to put away?
- When should I retire?

You should begin saving for your retirement as early in your life as you can and, definitely, whenever you begin earning reportable income. A much longer life span requires that you save more funds now compared to what you would have only a decade ago. The amount you save during your teenage years and how you invest those funds is clearly different from later stages of your life. The urgency and the pressure peak in the years immediately preceding your target retirement date. This section will identify the six life stages of retirement planning and how they differ in terms of your goals, earning potential, what you need to do, and your investment allocation.[5]

Stage 1: The Teenage Years (13–19)

These are the years when you are mowing lawns, working in an ice cream parlor, or helping out dad at his office or job site. It would be close to a miracle to convince a teenager to save his/her hard earned money for retirement. If you are a parent, however, you can offer your child an added incentive for working on the side, by offering to match whatever they earn (up to $5,000 in 2008) and placing those funds in a retirement account. This way the child would not have to give up their earned income, but the parent can help instill the value of working and saving in their children.

The more you save at an earlier age, the more you will accumulate over time, thanks to the power of compounding, and the less you might need to put away at a later stage in your life. A Roth IRA is an ideal retirement vehicle for this age group because your savings will grow tax free, and funds from a Roth IRA can be withdrawn, without penalty, for the purchase of a first home or to fund college education. Your portfolio allocation should be of a long-term, aggressive nature as you have the time to withstand volatility in the market—100 percent in stocks with up to 40 percent in international and emerging markets, 40 percent in domestic stocks, and 10 percent in alternative investments.

Stage 2: Young Adults (20–29)

At this point in your life, you are young, starting a career, and possibly burdened with college debt. If your job offers a 401(k), particularly if there is any company matching involved, participate to the extent that it allows you to maximize on the matching offered. Matched 401(k) funds are benefits provided to you by your firm that are often left unutilized because of the excuse that you are too young, broke, and do not have a need for a retirement plan yet.

If your firm offers a 401(k) that is not being matched, consider opening a Roth IRA instead. Better yet, contribute to both if you can. Start an emergency fund to save for a rainy day. Otherwise, you might have to borrow to fund an emergency or even liquidate your retirement fund. Make a living will so your family will know your wishes in case of a health emergency. Your portfolio allocation should be 40 percent international stock funds, 40 percent domestic stock funds, 10 percent bonds, and 10 percent in alternative investments.

Stage 3: Adults (30–39)

You are now starting a family, your income has increased, and so have your expenses—a wedding, a house, and children. You are thinking about saving for the kids' education, and you would like to take a vacation or two. Keep saving in your 401(k), both for the tax-deferral benefits (you pay less taxes on your income now and allow your investments to grow tax deferred until withdrawal at retirement) and for the company matching—a benefit or free money that many employees often leave at the table because it requires them to set money aside for retirement and decreases their current income.

Write your will and, if you get married, have children, or have amassed some wealth, get a trust. Do not ignore the need of getting a life insurance policy. Even if you are a skilled surgeon with high income potential, unless you have life insurance, your family will be left high and dry without the means to survive. When you are young and healthy, your cost of life insurance should be minimal given the large death benefit paid to your family in the event of your untimely death. You might consider a portfolio with a 35 percent allocation to international and emerging markets, 10 percent to foreign bonds, 35 percent to domestic funds including large, mid, and small cap stocks, 10 percent to domestic bonds, and 10 percent to alternative investments.

Stage 4: Middle Age (40–49)

There is little doubt that you are now either concerned about or looking forward to retirement. In either case, make sure that you are maximizing your 401(k) contributions, saving for your wealth accumulation fund, and setting aside emergency funds to cover your expenses for up to six months. Your home will most likely be your biggest investment. Review and update your will and trust. Consider leaving your allocation from Stage 3 the way it is and, if your investable net worth qualifies you, invest about 10 to 15 percent of your assets in alternative investments. You still have some 15 years or more to retirement, so you can withstand market volatility in pursuit of higher returns.

Stage 5: The Prime Income Age (50–59)

You are probably at the peak of your earning potential. Your kids are out of college and getting married. Take full advantage of the catch-up provisions of your 401(k)s and IRAs, which raises the maximum amount you are permitted to set aside for retirement. Continue saving in your wealth accumulation fund. Your portfolio should be reallocated to allow for a 20 to 25 percent exposure in domestic and international bonds and increase your allocation to alternative investments to 15 percent of your holdings. Review your will and trust and begin thinking about wealth transfer strategies. Get estimates of your Social Security and pension funds.

Stage 6: The Home Stretch (60–67)

The best advice is not to retire before the age of 67. That is when Social Security benefits will kick in at the highest rate (if born after 1954), and by that time you would have already qualified for Medicare (at age 65) and have reached the normal retirement age at work. Given that at, 67, you are expected to live another 20 years, continue to save aggressively. Review your will and trust annually and begin implementing your estate planning strategy including your wealth transfer strategies. This will help you decide how and to whom your assets should be transferred during your life and at death in the most tax-efficient manner. Review your Social Security and pension benefits annually and reallocate your portfolio by increasing your fixed income exposure to 25 to 30 percent or more based on your time horizon, objectives, and risk tolerance. Then get set for a comfortable retirement.

According to a 2007 study conducted by Harris interactive, here are the top five most important financial goals for mature adults (age 61 and over):

1. 98 percent want to protect assets to ensure against loss.
2. 97 percent want to ensure having enough income for life.
3. 94 percent are concerned about their ability to cover health-care costs.
4. 93 percent want to always have an adequate emergency fund.
5. 91 percent want the ability to have a steady income during retirement.[6]

The six stages of planning for retirement are mere guidelines and are intended to give you ideas on how to plan for retirement over time. Retirement planning is a lifelong process and not a one-time annual event.

Is Your Nest Egg Sufficient to Retire in Comfort?

Are you aware of the following?

- On January 1, 2006, the first baby boomers turned 60 years old. The U.S. Census Bureau estimates that there are a whopping 78.2 million of those baby boomers.
- A 2004 survey conducted by Prudential Financial indicated that the two most important goals of recent retirees are to maintain their standard of living (45 percent) and to avoid being a financial burden (40 percent).[7]
- A recent survey of retirees found that 38 percent are concerned that they will deplete their savings and be left with only Social Security.[8]
- A 2006 survey about how confident Americans were in having enough money for retirement, 24 percent responded that they were very confident, 44 percent were somewhat confident, 17 percent were not too confident, and 14 percent were not all confident.[9]
- With increased longevity, retirement often accounts for 25 to 30 percent of a person's life.[10]
- 36 percent of high-income American families (defined as having household income of at least $117,000) will have to lower their standard of living during their retirement years.[11]
- About 35 percent of Americans believe that they need at least $3 million to retire.[12]

Not every retiree will need $3 million to retire. The amount needed at hand for retirement depends on a number of factors: Will you be receiving funds from a pension plan? Do you have debt, including a mortgage on your house? Are you in good health? Have you purchased a long-term care plan?

How much have you budgeted to spend annually in retirement? How much have you already saved in your retirement and other savings accounts?

One of the easiest methods to calculate how much you will need in savings to retire was developed by Charles J. Farrell, a tax attorney. The **replacement ratio** method assumes that a retiree will need 80 percent of his/her gross income. To calculate the size of the nest egg needed to have on hand at the time of retirement, multiply your current gross income by 12.[13]

If your current gross salary is $100,000, then you will need 80 percent or $80,000 in retirement. The amount of savings needed for retirement will be your gross income of $100,000 × 12, or $1.2 million. The income for retirement will then come from earnings of about 4 to 5 percent (net of inflation) generated from your retirement savings. You can then safely withdraw 5 percent, or $60,000 a year. The balance of your $80,000 annual income in retirement will come from Social Security and your pension, if you are lucky to have one.

Salary Needed in Retirement	Savings Needed for Retirement
$100,000 (current gross income)	$100,000
× 0.8	× 12
$80,000	$1,200,000

It has been widely accepted that retirees will need less income in retirement than they would have while working. This is because retirees will pay less in taxes, transportation, mortgage, and savings once they retire. Financial planners, however, tend to argue these days that a retiree might actually need 100 percent or more of preretirement income because of increased health care cost, leisure activities such as travel, and home improvements. Whether you believe that you will spend more or less in retirement than your preretirement income, the range of what you need in retirement is between 75 to 100 percent of your preretirement income, and you should plan accordingly.[14]

Another simple tool to gauge where you are and where you need to be in your quest to save the necessary funds for your retirement was published in an article in the *Journal of Financial Planning* in 2006 by Charles Farrell. The tool factors your age, your savings-to-income ratio and your debt-to-income ratio.[15] The goal assumes that you will retire at age 65 with no debt and with a nest egg equals to 12 times your annual salary.

To find out where you need to be if you are 50 years old, multiply your salary of $100,000 by the savings-to-income ratio of 4.5. This will give you a total of $450,000—the savings you need to have on hand to meet your retirement goal. If you have more savings (excluding the equity in your

TABLE 5.1   Planning for Retirement Using Savings-to-Income
and Debt-to-Savings Ratios

Age	Savings-to-Income	Debt-to-Savings
35	0.9	1.50
40	1.7	1.25
45	3.0	1.00
50	4.5	0.75
55	6.5	0.50
60	8.8	0.20
65	12.0	0.00

home), then you are in good shape. Otherwise, you need to increase your retirement savings.

The same 50-year-old should have no more in debt than $75,000. You calculate this by multiplying your salary of $100,000 by 0.75 from Table 5.1. If your debt is higher, then you will need to decrease your debt. At the age of 65, if that is when you decide to retire, you should be debt free and have saved for your retirement 12 times your most recent annual income.

When Should You Retire?

Unless you are in poor health or are caring for someone who needs your full-time attention, or absolutely hate your job (a better option would be to find a different job that you like), you should not retire before the age of 65 to 67. Ironically, the retirement age of 65 was chosen randomly, based on prevailing retirement standards in 1935.[16] In 2006, about 40 percent of current retirees had no choice and had to retire earlier than planned due to layoffs or poor health.[17]

If you are under age $59^1/_2$ and have to retire, you may make penalty-free withdrawals from your IRA under **rule 72(t)**. In this case, you must receive substantially equal periodic payments at least annually and must continue for at least five years or until age $59^1/_2$, whichever is later. You may then choose one of three standard formulas to calculate the withdrawal amount: life expectancy, annuity, or amortization. Once chosen, you have to use the same formula as long as withdrawals continue. There is one exception allowed. If you initially choose the amortization or annuity formula, you can reduce the amount of the annual withdrawal and have a one-time option to switch to the life expectancy formula without incurring penalties. Otherwise, changes in the formula or dollar amount, or stopping withdrawals early, may trigger a 10 percent penalty on all money withdrawn.[18] As with all tax-related issues, consult with a tax advisor when choosing the 72(t) formula.

Astonishingly, a staggering 72 percent of current retirees receive reduced Social Security benefits because they started them before they were eligible for full retirement benefits.[19]

Here are the reasons why you should *not* retire early:

- If you were 62 years old in 2006, you could expect to live another 23.5 years, and if you were 67 years old, then you could expect to live another 19.4 years. That is a long time to live in retirement.[20] And if you rely solely on your average life expectancy to determine how long retirement savings need to last, be careful. About 50 percent of people live beyond the average life expectancy.[21] The big risk here is that you might outlive your retirement savings.
- If you retire at age 62, your Social Security benefits will be reduced by 30 percent for the rest of your life! If you were born between 1943 and 1954, you would not be eligible for full Social Security benefits until you turn 66. And, if you were born in 1960 and after, your full Social Security benefits will not kick in until you reach age 67.[22] If you are the primary breadwinner, and unless neither you nor your spouse needs your Social Security income, it would be double jeopardy for you to take early retirement. If you retire at age 62, your Social Security benefits will be reduced by 30 percent, and when you die 20 years or so later, your surviving spouse will receive the same "reduced" annual benefit for the rest of his/her life.
- You should pay off as much of your debt as you can before you retire or tap your nest egg.
- Medicare, unlike Social Security, is not available until age 65. If you retire early, you would have to worry about providing for your own health insurance in the interim—a costly process at that age and prohibitive if you or any covered members of your family have medical issues.
- If your nest egg stood at $1 million at age 62 and you delayed your retirement to age 67, then at an 8 percent annual return, your nest egg will grow to $1,469,328 by the time you turn 67. At a withdrawal rate of 5 percent, this would mean taking out $73,466 instead of $50,000 annually—a 46.9 percent increase.
- Do not discount the dangers to your nest egg from taxes and inflation. If you add up Social Security benefits, pensions, and withdrawals from a 401(k) or other savings accounts, you might discover that your tax bracket has not decreased compared to when you were employed. Even when factoring a modest inflation rate of 3 percent, a $1 million nest egg will have a reduced purchasing power value of $737,000 after

10 years. You somehow need to make up for the reduced value of your purchasing power.

■ In your later years, health care and long-term care costs can be the biggest threats to your nest egg. For a 65-year-old couple, all cumulative health care expenses, including health insurance premiums and out-of-pocket expenses, may cost as much as $550,000 by age 95.[23] Even though Medicare will cover most of your health care costs, your dental, vision, and hearing expenses are your sole responsibility in retirement. Neither Medicare nor your private health insurance, if you have one, will pay for much of your long-term care.

■ Beware of boredom and depression in retirement. Drastic changes in lifestyle, particularly for active individuals, whether socially or at work, could have serious psychological effects. Retirement ushers in a new phase in life and is not the beginning of the end.

In 2005, about 5.3 million people age 65 or older were working in the United States, according to the Bureau of Labor Statistics. It makes you wonder how many of these individuals are working because they want to be engaged in society and productive or how many are working because they realized a little too late in their lives that they needed to work to make both ends meet and provide for their retirement.[24] In any case, the decision to continue working through at least the age of full Social Security retirement benefits is a wise one indeed.[25]

What Are the Sources of Your Retirement Income?

Americans have begun to quickly recognize that in order to meet their retirement needs, they have to depend on themselves—not the government or their companies. In a 1999 study published by AARP, over 80 percent of adults surveyed indicated that they have to be self-dependent to meet their retirement needs, relying less on Social Security and other sources and placing the onus of responsibility on themselves.[26] Fortunately, Americans over 65 are healthier (measured by their longevity) and wealthier. The U.S. Census Bureau reported that the poverty rate among Americans over age 65 has declined from 35 percent in 1960 to just 10.2 percent in 2000—a more than two-thirds decline. For the population as a whole and over the same period, poverty rates declined from 22 percent to 11 percent.[27]

Most people draw on *four main sources* of income during retirement:

1. Social Security retirement benefits
2. Employer-sponsored plans: qualified or nonqualified
3. Individual qualified retirement plans
4. Personal savings, part-time work, and other sources of income

According to the Social Security Administration (2004), the breakdown of the typical income sources of a current retiree are:[28]

- 39 percent, Social Security
- 19 percent, Qualified retirement plans, including 401(k)s and IRAs
- 25 percent, Earnings
- 14 percent, Other assets
- 3 percent, Other

Social Security Retirement Benefits

The Social Security system was started in 1935 and was enacted as a broad program of social and welfare benefits including aid to families with dependent children, food stamps, survivors and disability insurance, and old age. No one knew then that old age would be redefined by the impressive increase in life expectancy. Traditionally, unreduced or full retirement benefits begin at age 65 for those born before 1937. Beginning in 2000, the government, recognizing that we live longer and to rein in the cost of retirement benefits, has gradually moved the benchmark to 67 for people born in or after 1960.

Social Security retirement benefits are intended to provide you with only a portion of your retirement income. The funding for Social Security comes from you and your employer through payroll taxes. The monthly benefits you receive are based on the income you earned over the course of your life, subject to a maximum amount and adjusted for inflation on annual basis. The maximum Social Security benefit for a person who retires in 2007 at full retirement age is $2,116 per month and considerably less for a nonworking spouse. Although this maximum amount might not seem like much money, at a 4 percent annual withdrawal rate, you would need a total of $635,000 to generate this monthly income.[29] Social Security benefits are a very valuable benefit, since benefits are adjusted for inflation annually and the value of this benefit becomes apparent when you realize how much is needed to generate that income.

About 20 percent of Americans age 65 or more rely on their Social Security income as their sole source of income, while two-thirds of beneficiaries rely on Social Security income for more than half their income.[30]

Here are some helpful tips when considering your Social Security retirement benefits:[31]

- Review your annual Social Security statement. Because your benefits are based on your earning record, ensure that all earnings are accurately recorded. If you are at least 25 or older, the Social Security

Administration will send you an annual Social Security statement one month before your birthday.

- For general planning purposes, regularly review your retirement benefit estimates. These are included in your annual Social Security statement or can be requested from the Social Security Administration.
- Delay as much as possible drawing on your Social Security retirement benefits until you qualify for full retirement benefits. If you can wait beyond your full retirement age to access your benefits, you can collect more than 100 percent of your full retirement benefits. After age 70, your monthly benefit will no longer increase by postponing benefits. For someone retiring in 2008, based on a typical retiree who has paid into the Social Security system over his or her entire career, your maximum monthly benefit will be:

Age 62	$1,682
Age 65	$2,030
Age 70	$2,794[32]

- If you are the primary breadwinner, think about your spouse. A spouse with low income or who has not worked is entitled to as much as half of the higher-earning spouse's Social Security benefits. If you take out Social Security benefits early, the benefits will be reduced for both you and your spouse permanently.
- If you are among the 50 percent or so of American couples who are divorced, you can collect Social Security benefits based on your former spouse's work record if the two of you were married for at least 10 years and you are currently 62 years old and unmarried. The amount you collect has no bearing on what your former spouse collects.
- If you are a widow or widower, you can switch from your own benefit to your deceased spouse's benefit, the survivor's benefit, taking the one that provides you with the bigger benefit.
- Consider the impact of taxes and the benefit of delaying Social Security benefits. By delaying Social Security benefits until your full retirement age or, preferably, to age 70, you will end up with a higher Social Security benefit and you could end up paying fewer taxes over time. Generally, Social Security benefits are not taxed. However, up to 85 percent of your benefits could be taxable if a combination of your other income plus 50 percent of your Social Security adds up to more than $32,000 if you are married and filing jointly. If you can afford to delay your Social Security benefits from age 62 to 70, and live off your other retirement funds, your total tax bill should be lower. This is

TABLE 5.2   Tax Effects on Social Security

	Approach A	Approach B
IRA income	$45,000	$20,000
Social Security	$45,000	$70,000
Total pretax income	$90,000	$90,000
Taxable income	$70,975	$35,350

because, at most, 85 percent of your Social Security income is taxable compared to 100 percent of your other retirement income.[33] Table 5.2 shows how it works.

Approach A: Take reduced Social Security early and supplement it with higher IRA withdrawals.

Approach B: Delay Social Security.

By delaying Social Security income, a married couple filing jointly, will reduce their income subject to taxes by almost 50 percent.[34]

- Evaluate how working in retirement affects your Social Security retirement benefits. A survey by AARP revealed that 7 out of 10 retirees plan to work in retirement.[35] If you collect early retirement benefits and work, your retirement benefits will be smaller (if you do not wait until your full retirement age) and your added income could boost you to a higher tax bracket.[36] Also, if you work and collect Social Security benefits between age 62 and your full retirement age, you lose $1 of every $2 in benefits—a 50 percent marginal tax rate—if you made more than $12,480 in 2006. By comparison, if you reach your full retirement age, the government eliminates this penalty and you would be able to make as much as $33,240 without losing any Social Security benefits.[37]

The viability and future existence of the Social Security system is a major worry for retirees and those planning for their retirement. Social Security Trustees announced in 2006 that the trust fund backing the payment of Social Security benefits would be zero in 2040. In April 2007, the annual report determined the trust fund will be gone in 2041, an additional one year. The March 2008 Social Security annual report stated that the trust worth $2.0 trillion at the end of 2007, will be gone in 2041. A zero trust fund does not mean the payment of Social Security benefits would also go to zero, but rather, would drop to 78 percent of their originally promised levels.[38] It is no surprise that, in a June 2006 U.S. Trust survey, 48 percent of respondents stated that they were more concerned that Social Security will run out.[39] This increasing concern is not without reason and is based on 11 troubling signs:

1. In 1935, 40 worker wages supported one retiree receiving Social Security. In 2006, 3.3 worker wages supported one retiree receiving Social Security. By 2030, only 2 workers will bear the same burden.[40]
2. In 1940, 220,000 people received Social Security benefits. This represents a mere 1 percent of today's benefit recipients.
3. Today, one-third of Americans over age 65 receive 90 percent of their income from Social Security.
4. In 2007, Social Security and Medicare expenses made up 34 percent of the federal budget and are expected to rise to 39 percent by 2012.[41]
5. In 2017, Social Security will begin paying more in benefits than is collected in taxes.
6. By the year 2028, the entire baby boom generation of 78 million will be eligible for Social Security benefits.
7. In 2040, without changes, the Social Security Trust Fund will be exhausted and if Social Security is still around, it is anticipated that in 2040, Social Security benefits for new retirees at age 60 may be reduced by 26 percent from currently scheduled levels unless changes are implemented.[42] In reality, the Social Security Trust Fund is "merely an accounting device filled with IOUs that future taxpayers must repay." In fact, no money ever goes into the trust fund. The trust fund balance is the result of two accounting entries by the U.S. Treasury Department: First, the Treasury Department estimates how much of the taxes collected are Social Security taxes and then credits the Social Security Trust Fund with that amount. Second, the Treasury then subtracts the total amount paid in monthly Social Security benefits from the trust balance.[43]
8. America's total liabilities and unfunded commitments for pension and health programs for the elderly (Social Security and Medicare) have increased from about $20,000 billion to about $50,000 billion in the six-year period ending in fiscal 2006.[44]
9. A September 2007 U.S. Department of Treasury report revealed that Social Security faces a shortfall over the indefinite future of $13.6 trillion in present value terms—equal to 3.5 percent of future taxable payrolls.[45]
10. We are living longer, and a larger number of Americans are eligible for Social Security benefits. The percentage of Americans age 65 or older has increased over time:
    - 1946—8 percent, or 11 million people
    - 1999—13 percent, or 35 million people
    - 2030—20 percent, or 70 million people[46]

11. Former Federal Reserve Chairman Alan Greenspan once characterized the rising Medicare expenses as the number one threat to our economy, greater than the current mortgage/housing crisis. In the chaotic credit and markets beginning with the last quarter of 2007, I am sure his assessment would have been revised to reflect the gravity of those crises including the serious slump in housing prices in a short two- to three-year period. Nevertheless, Medicare expenses are expected to be $396 billion during the 2008 fiscal year, or 14 percent of total government spending.[47]

Although it is highly unlikely that any elected politician will dare allow the extinction of the Social Security system, it is clear that reforms to the system are needed to meet the needs of an aging population and the increased demand and reliance on the Social Security system. Any future changes or reforms might not be favorable to the American retiree. It would, therefore, be prudent to plan for your retirement with caution and with an eye on being less dependent on Social Security benefits and significantly more on your own resources.

For the foreseeable future, Social Security retirement benefits should be an integral part of your retirement planning. It is money that you have earned and that you and your employer have contributed to the system over the years. When accessing these benefits, you need to consider carefully those strategies that will provide you with the most benefits. We have highlighted some of those strategies and the pitfalls that you might face and can avoid.

Employer-Sponsored Retirement Plans

The bulk of retirement income for most Americans will come from employer-sponsored retirement plans. These can be classified as follows:

- Defined benefit plans
- Defined contribution plans
- Nonqualified plans

DEFINED BENEFIT PLANS (TRADITIONAL PENSION)   With a defined benefit plan, retirement benefits are generally based on a variety of factors, including salary, length of service, and a benefit formula that averages the employee's earnings over a number of specified years. A defined benefit plan derives its name from the fact that benefits are specified or defined under a definite formula. It is not dependent, for example, on the performance of the stock market or the returns of the underlying investment. An actuary estimates how much must be contributed each year to fund the anticipated benefit.

The investment risk rests with the employer and benefits are generally taxable. The amount of the employer contributions to a defined benefit plan is determined annually by an actuary. This ensures that the plan is adequately funded to provide the benefits promised by the plan. In some instances, an employee may make additional contributions but, generally, the cost of the plan is borne by the employer.

If you are entitled to a defined benefit plan, you must wait to reach the normal retirement age, typically 65, and be vested in the plan. Upon retiring, you may have the options as to how and when you collect your benefits, in monthly installments or as a lump sum. And, if you are married, you are required to make a choice if you opt for the monthly payments—take the maximum monthly income for the life of the retiring employee or take a reduced pension for the lifetime of both the retiring employee and the spouse.

Defined benefit plans are dwindling in numbers. Beginning in the early 1990s, companies began getting out of the business of providing for their employees in retirement. Only about one in three Americans is covered by a defined benefit pension plan.[48] About 31,000 pension programs remain in force today, and the financial health of an increasing number of these plans is in question. The Pension Benefit Guaranty Corporation, a federal agency that guarantees the payment of pension benefits, estimates that insured pension plans in the United States are underfunded by a total of $350 billion—only those companies whose funding deficits exceed $50 million are required to file reports.[49] In other words, the extent of the underfunding could be worse.

Do not panic! Defined benefit plans are the only retirement plans required to carry insurance with the Pension Benefit Guaranty Corporation. The provider of your pension is required to give you written notice annually if the plan has been less than 80 percent funded for the past year or two and less than 90 percent funded for several years.[50]

DEFINED CONTRIBUTION PLANS—YOUR 401(K)   Unlike defined benefit plans which specify the amount of benefits the retiree receives and is primarily funded by the employer, defined contribution plans, such as a 401(k), 403(b), or SEP plans, are funded by employee contributions, in the form of a percentage of the employee's salary. Sometimes, and at the sole discretion of the employer, the corporation matches the employee contribution up to a certain limit, from 0 to 25 percent of the employee's salary,[51] up to a maximum dollar amount not to exceed government-imposed limits. As an employee, your retirement benefit will depend on the amount contributed by you and your employer, your investment return, and the number of years until you retire and have contributed to the plan. The investment risk rests on you—the participant, and not the employer, and benefits are generally taxable.

Defined contribution plans have grown rapidly in popularity. 401(k) plans, which were introduced in 1981, are rapidly assuming the top role in retirement planning for Americans. As of November 2006, 90 percent of 401(k) plans are the only retirement plan offered by employers, according to the Investment Company Institute. 47 million workers participate in 401(k) plans, compared with 21 million covered by traditional employer-sponsored defined benefit plans.[52] According to the Employee Benefit Research Institute, small employers and younger firms are much more likely to offer a 401(k) plan than a traditional pension. There was $2.7 trillion in 401(k) plans as of December 31, 2006, an increase of $1 trillion in the last 5 years. The average 401(k) balance was $58,328.[53]

Nevertheless, about 30 percent of eligible workers do not sign up for their employer-offered 401(k) plans and that number is even higher for people earning $10,000 to $25,000—half of those do not participate in their available 401(k) plans.[54]

The most commonly used defined contribution plans are:

- **401(k) plans**—The 401(k) plan is an option in a profit sharing plan. It is offered by many private employers, and allows employees to defer up to 100 percent of compensation ($15,500 maximum for 2007, and if you are over 50, you can contribute an additional $5,000) on a pretax basis. You employer may voluntarily match your contribution; however, the combined total of contributions total of all contributions cannot exceed $45,000. Earnings are tax deferred, and employee contributions are always 100 percent vested. If you withdraw money from your 401(k) before age $59^1/_2$, you will be subject to a 10 percent federal income tax penalty, except under certain circumstances such as hardship, purchase of your first home, or to pay for educational expenses. However, if you retire at age 55, you can take withdrawals from your 401(k) plan without incurring the 10 percent early withdrawal penalty. Of course, you will still have to pay income taxes on any withdrawal. If, by contrast, you roll your 401(k) into an IRA, you will have to wait until you are $59^1/_2$ to take penalty-free withdrawals.[55]

  Profit sharing plans, which include 401(k) plans, are the most popular qualified retirement plans because of their flexibility. They are available to self-employed individuals (such an **individual 401(k) plan**) as well as to large corporations and must include all employees age 21 and above who have at least two years of service. Employers may make discretionary annual contributions of 0 to 25 percent of compensation, up to $46,000 (in 2008) per employee.[56] **403(b)** and **457 plans** are similar to 401(k) plans. The difference is that 403(b) plans are for people who work for nonprofit organizations such as schools and hospitals and 457 plans are for state and municipal employees.

- **Roth 401(k) plans**—Beginning in 2006, employers were able to offer a Roth 401(k) in addition to a traditional 401(k). This new plan incorporates elements of a traditional 401(k) and a Roth IRA. It allows employees to make *after-tax* contributions according to the same limits as a traditional 401(k). Earnings grow tax free and distributions at retirement are tax free provided the employee is at least $59^1/_2$ years old and has owned the account for five years. An employee may contribute a maximum of $15,500 per year in 2008 ($20,500 for those age 50 and older), inclusive of the contributions made to a traditional 401(k). Matching contributions made by an employer must be invested in a separate traditional 401(k), not a Roth. You are required to take out the required minimum distribution (RMD) from a Roth 401(k) at age $70^1/_2$, much like a traditional 401(k) and unlike an individual Roth IRA, which has no age distribution requirement. To avoid having to take out the required minimum distribution, you may roll over the Roth 401(k) funds into an individual Roth IRA.
- **SIMPLEs (Savings Incentive Match Plans for Employees)**—SIMPLEs are used by small businesses with 100 or fewer employees who earned at least $5,000 in any prior two years. In 2007, eligible employees may elect to contribute 100 percent of compensation up to $10,500 per year. The catch up provision for employees 50 or older is $2,500. The employer *must* match contributions dollar-for-dollar up to 3 percent of pay or contribute 2 percent of pay for all eligible employees. Your contributions are pretax and you are 100 percent vested immediately. Withdrawals, however, during the first two years of employee participation are subject to a 25 percent penalty tax if the participant is under age $59^1/_2$.

NONQUALIFIED RETIREMENT PLANS   An employer may set up a plan, often in the form of a deferred compensation plan, which does not meet federal requirements to be considered "qualified." Benefits are generally taxable when received. Such plans are often used as a supplement to qualified retirement plans.

In a nonqualified deferred compensation plan, the deferral of benefits is generally agreed upon before the compensation is earned. The corporation agrees to pay compensation for a set period after a stated date or death. In return, the key employee agrees to continue service until a specified date—for example, normal retirement age—and, sometimes, agrees that after separation not to compete and/or to provide consultative services.

There are several other employer-sponsored plans that are less utilized such as money purchase pension plans, target benefit plans, stock bonus plans, ESOPs, age-weighted profit sharing plans, thrift plans, simplified employee pension plans (SEPs), 412(i) plans, Keogh plans for self-employed, and cash balance plans.[57] These plans are designed to meet the specific requirements of employers and how they chose to provide the retirement investment vehicles to their employees.

Individual Qualified/Retirement Plans—Your Traditional and Roth IRAs

Individual retirement arrangements—not "accounts," as they are commonly misnamed—or IRAs are becoming increasingly important and may hold the key to achieving your retirement goals. They represent about 26 percent of the $14.5 trillion U.S. retirement market. Assets in IRAs are increasing on average 13 percent a year and are expected to continue accelerating.[58] IRAs are intended to complement your income from Social Security, your employer-sponsored plans and your personal savings. The most common individual retirement arrangements are traditional IRAs and Roth IRAs.

The positive features of IRAs are as follows:

- *Tax deferral*—All IRAs enable investment earnings to grow tax-deferred as the long as the money stays in the account.
- *Tax-free withdrawals*—Money can be taken out of a Roth IRA tax-free if you are at least $59^1/_2$ and have had the account for at least 5 years.
- *Tax deductions*—Your traditional IRA contributions can be fully tax deductible if neither you nor your spouse participates in an employer-sponsored retirement plan. If you participate in an employer-sponsored plan yet your income is sufficiently low as defined by the IRS, then a portion of your contribution might be tax deductible. For higher income individuals, contributing to a non-deductible IRA is still an excellent option because of the tax-deferred growth feature of the IRA.
- *Flexibility*—You can open an IRA with any financial institution; invest in stocks, bonds, CDs and even tangible assets. You can contribute all or a portion of your allowable limit. You can make your contribution on January 1st or up to April 15th (the tax filing deadline) of the following year. You can contribute to both traditional and Roth IRAs during the same year; however, the combined annual contributions cannot exceed the allowable IRA limit.[59]
- *Higher limits*—Initially, the annual contribution limit to IRAs was $2,000. This amount has increased over time. For 2008, the annual contribution base limit was $5,000, with an extra $1,000 for people age 50 or older. *Exceptions*—Prior to age $59^1/_2$, taking money out of an IRA comes with a 10 percent penalty tax. However, in certain circumstances, such as buying a first home, incurring heavy medical expenses, or disability, the 10 percent penalty is waived.

- *Asset protection*—The 2005 bankruptcy act clarified and expanded the rules pertaining to retirement funds. In the past, credit protection applied only to 401(k)-style plans, but the new legislation included IRAs, both traditional as well as Roth IRAs. While federal bankruptcy protection is limited to $1 million, adjusted for inflation, this ceiling does not apply to IRA rollovers, thereby putting much higher IRA balances out of the reach of creditors.[60]
- *Spousal IRAs*—If you are a nonworking spouse or a working spouse who does not participate in an employer-sponsored retirement plan, you can open up your own spousal traditional (deductible or non-deductible) or Roth IRA and contribute up to $5,000 per year in 2008, with an additional $1,000 if you are 50 years or older, and you need not have earned those funds yourself. A husband and wife may contribute up to a total of $10,000 or $12,000 if they are 50 years or older, as long as their combined compensation is at least that amount.[61]

TRADITIONAL IRAS VERSUS ROTH IRAS   This is a list of similar and dissimilar features of traditional IRAs and Roth IRAs.

Six Similar Features:
1. *Tax deferral*—Both types of IRAs allow you to set aside money for retirement in a tax-deferred account.
2. *Contribution limits*—The contribution limits for both IRAs are the same $5,000 for 2008 with a $1,000 catch-up provision for those ages 50 or older.
3. *Asset protection*—The assets in both IRAs are protected from creditors.
4. *Deadline*—Contributions, whether whole or partial, must be made by the tax filing deadline, usually April 15th.
5. *Access provisions*—Both can be accessed for a first-home purchase, educational and health expenses, as well as disability.
6. *Contractual inheritance*—IRAs are contracts and the designated beneficiaries inherit them without regard to the terms of the owner's will or trust.

Five Dissimilar Features:
1. *Tax deductibility*—Traditional IRAs may be tax deductible. Depending on your income and whether you participate in an employer-sponsored retirement plan, you may be eligible to take an income tax deduction. Contributions to Roth IRAs are not tax deductible. They are made with after-tax money.
2. *Taxability of distributions*—Traditional IRAs grow tax deferred but you must pay taxes upon making a withdrawal, avoiding the 10 percent

penalty only if you do so after age $59^1/_2$. Withdrawals from traditional IRAs are taxed as ordinary income tax. Roth IRAs grow tax deferred as well. Roth *contributions* may be withdrawn anytime free of taxes or penalties regardless of age. Withdrawals of Roth *earnings,* however, are taken out tax free, provided you have owned the account for five years and are at least $59^1/_2$.[62]

3. *Eligibility*—Anyone with earned income is eligible to open a traditional IRA. Whether it is fully, partially or not tax deductible is dependent on whether the tax filer participates in an employer-sponsored plan and on income level. By comparison, eligibility to contribute to a Roth IRA is restrictive. If you are single and making more than $116,000 in 2008, or married and making more than $169,000 in adjusted gross income, you are *not* eligible to contribute after-tax dollars to a Roth IRA. Congress did not want the rich to get richer by taking advantage of the central Roth IRA feature, the ability to withdraw money invested in Roth IRAs tax free.

4. *Required distributions*—Upon reaching age $70^1/_2$, a traditional IRA owner must start withdrawing minimum amounts by December 31st of each year. These are known as required minimum distributions (RMDs). By comparison, Roth IRA withdrawals are not required upon reaching age $70^1/_2$.

5. *Conversion*—Traditional, SEP, and/or SIMPLE IRAs (after the two-year withholding period) may be converted into a Roth IRA. There is one caveat—if your income is above $100,000, whether you are married or single, you cannot do the conversion. Luckily, changes made to the 2006 Tax Increase Prevention and Reconciliation Act enacted by Congress will permit anyone, regardless of their income, beginning in 2010, to convert their traditional deductible and nondeductible IRAs into Roth IRAs. On tax-deductible traditional IRAs, when you convert, you will pay taxes on your original investments and the accrued earnings. On nondeductible IRAs (ones opened with after tax money), you will pay taxes on your earnings only. And, in another unusual nice gesture by Congress, if you convert a traditional IRA in 2010 into a Roth, you can delay tax payments, paying half in 2011 and the rest in 2012. Even though contributions to Roth IRAs are still restricted, the new conversion rules will make Roth IRAs available to anyone that chooses to convert his/her existing traditional IRAs.[63]

IRAs play an increasingly important role in preparing for your retirement planning. They are retirement accounts that you control. It is your sole responsibility and not anyone else's to fund these IRAs and to invest them in a prudent yet intelligent manner. Even before 401(k) assets are rolled over into IRAs, IRAs are emerging as the largest source of retirement funding. How early you begin to invest in IRAs, the extent to which you fund these IRAs, the type of IRAs that you invest in, and the nature of the investment strategy that you pursue, are all factors that will determine how much money is available to you in your retirement and thus the quality of your lifestyle in retirement.

Personal Savings, Part-Time Work, and Other Sources of Income

Personal savings should be an integral part of your retirement pool of assets: 32 percent of retirees admit that the "biggest financial mistake" they have ever made was not beginning to save earlier in their lives for their retirement years.[64]

Unlike your pension plan, your Social Security benefits, your employer-sponsored 401(k) plan, and even your individual IRAs, your personal savings and assets, including the equity in your home, come with no restrictions in terms of how much you can invest in them, when you can access them, and, more importantly, how much you can take out of them.

Those of you who were fortunate enough to have been able to contribute the maximum to your retirement plans and had the wisdom to save and save early should have accumulated sufficient wealth to meet your future needs and to eventually provide for your heirs. Additional sources of income include revenue from your investment portfolio and, possibly, rental income or funds generated from a buy-sell agreement of your business. A whopping 66 percent of affluent baby boomers plan to help pay for retirement by selling their home, unlocking what is normally the largest asset base that most people own.[65] Of course, many retirees are electing to work part time in retirement to supplement their retirement income and to keep active. You need to be careful and evaluate the effect of working on your Social Security benefits.[66]

ANNUITIES   Annuities are a unique financial product that, along with your other sources of retirement income can enhance your retirement income. An annuity is an agreement, usually between an individual and a life insurance company, designed to help you grow your retirement assets and provide regular withdrawals/income when you are in retirement. Fixed annuities provide you with a specified percentage return on your investment. This rate of return could be linked to many indicators such as the five-year U.S. treasuries. Variable annuities can be immediate or deferred. With a deferred annuity the account grows until you decide to make withdrawals (you have to be $59^1/_2$ to avoid the 10 percent penalty). You can either annuitize your payments, thus receive regular payments over a set of time, or you can withdraw money as you need it.

Annuities have at least 11 attractive features:[67]

1. *Earnings are tax deferred.* Many investments are taxed annually such as your money market account. With annuities, investment earnings, both capital gains and dividends, are not taxed until you withdraw money. Your money, therefore, grows faster because the funds that would have been withdrawn to pay taxes stay in the account and grow tax deferred until they are withdrawn. If you are in the high income bracket and have maxed out your 401(k) and IRA, a variable annuity might make sense especially if you have 20 or more years to retirement. You may need more than 20 years for the benefit of an annuity's tax deferral to exceed the benefit of the 15 percent long-term capital gains rate on profits from selling your mutual funds. Keep in mind that annuities are taxed at ordinary income tax rates, which run as high as 35 percent at the federal level.[68]

2. *Annuities are protected from creditors.* If you own an immediate annuity that allows you to receive a stream of income from the insurance company, the funds belong to the company and the most that creditors can access is the payments as they are made. However, some state statutes and court decisions also protect some or all of the payments from those annuities. As of August 2004, 40 states had laws fully protecting insurance and annuities in addition to 401(k) plans, IRAs, and other such vehicles from lawsuits.[69]

   As of May 2007, only two states—Arkansas and New Hampshire—along with the U.S. Virgin Islands provided no protection in place for either life insurance policies or annuities; all other states provided either full or partial protection to either life insurance policies or annuities and even both. In each state, "there are likely cases that carve out exceptions to these exemptions, such as for alimony, proceeds of crime, and child support, etc. Federal tax liens are often not subject to state exemptions."[70]

3. *There are diverse investment options.* You have the option of investing in a fixed annuity that offers a specified interest rate or a variable annuity that allows you to invest in stocks, bonds, or cash. You and your wealth advisor can determine the appropriate allocation, or you may select from prepackaged and diversified portfolios offered by the annuity company.

4. *The principal is protected.* Annuity companies have created various types of "floors" that limit the extent of your investment decline and guarantee your principal. For example, the annuity might offer a feature that guarantees that your investment will never fall below its value set on an anniversary date.

5. *Transfers among investment options are tax free.* Unlike mutual funds and other investment made with "after-tax money," with annuities there are no tax consequences if you sell funds and replace them with different ones because these transactions occur within the annuity structure. This is valuable when you rebalance your portfolio, as you should, on a regular basis. Rebalancing entails selling portions of those funds that have outperformed over time and buying ones that have underperformed. By rebalancing to your desired allocation among assets, you potentially increase your returns over time and, at the same time, lower your risk.

6. *It pays a lifetime income.* Because your life expectancy has increased and you are likely to spend more time in retirement than you would have a generation ago, annuities with lifetime income riders guarantee that you will receive a specified stream of income for the rest of your life even if your annuity runs out of funds. This is possible because income from annuities is generated by the investment earnings and funds from a pool of people in your group who do not live as long as their life expectancy. This pooling is unique to annuities, and it is what enables annuity companies to guarantee your lifetime income. All insurance companies including annuity companies are required to have reserves set aside to counter the risk of extended longevity. Many of them reinsure their insurance policies to spread out their risk. All insurance companies are overseen by the state insurance commissioners. The state commissioners would step in if there was an insurance company that failed and find a buyer of the assets. The buyer, usually another insurance company, would be required to keep the terms of the policies the same or even make them better.

7. *You can structure the annuity to pay benefits to your heirs.* People who invest in immediate lifetime annuities fear that if the annuitant dies shortly thereafter then the insurance company gets to keep all of the investment in the annuity. Although this can happen, it can be avoided if you buy a "guaranteed period" with your immediate annuity. The insurance company will then have to continue payments after you die to your designated beneficiaries, depending on the guaranteed period that you select—usually 10 or 20 years after you started receiving your annuity payments. Much like life insurance, IRAs, and 401(k) plans, benefits pass to your heirs without going to probate and are unaffected by your will.

8. *You can purchase a death benefit rider.* If you are in bad health, you can purchase an annuity and add an enhanced death benefit rider that will pay your beneficiaries an additional 40 percent or so of the value of the annuity upon death. Since the purchase of the annuity is more controlled by the age of the annuitant than his/her health, it is an indirect way of purchasing additional life insurance.

9. *It offers some protection against life insurance losses.* If you own an underwater universal life insurance policy, a policy that has cash value less than the accumulated premiums that you have paid into it, you may want to transfer the assets to an annuity. Life insurance losses are not tax deductible. However, if you move the money into an annuity, the losses can be used to offset the annuity's gains.[71]

10. *You can make money in a down year.* Some income annuities that guarantee a 5 or 6 percent growth irrespective of market performance should be left alone during a down year in the market. If the market declines by 10 percent during a specific year, the terms of some annuities will still credit your annuity a specified percentage. This is an attractive feature of some but not all annuities.

11. *There is no limit on the amount you can invest.* Unlike the income that you would receive from Social Security, which is tabulated and limited, and/or the earnings from your other retirement plans, which are limited by the amount of funds you can contribute to them, annuities have no limit. You can invest as much as you want in an annuity, usually subject to the constraints of the life insurance company from whom you are purchasing the annuity. Therefore, annuities can be a substantial income source.

Here are five negative features of annuities:

1. *There are surrender charges.* Annuities have surrender charges ranging usually ranging from five to seven years. Although most annuities allow for penalty free withdrawals on annual basis, if you decide to cash out your annuity prior to the end of the surrender period or if you withdraw more than the allowable limit, you will be hit with surrender charges.

2. *Annuities have higher expenses than many other investment vehicles.* The benefits you receive from annuities are not free of charge. You pay for those benefits. The costs vary, depending on the annuity and include the cost of issuing and maintaining the contract, base death benefit and investment management expenses. Optional riders, which have additional fees tagged to them and vary among issuers, include the lifetime income guarantee, the step up guarantee, the spousal protection guarantee, and the enhanced death benefit just to name a few.

3. *There are possible tax penalties.* Even though annuities grow tax deferred, earnings on gains from your annuity are taxed as ordinary income when withdrawn unlike income from dividends and capital gains. The highest income tax bracket is 35 percent while the highest capital gains rate is 15 percent. And, if you die with money remaining in your annuity, your beneficiaries will inherit all the taxes that you have

deferred and are liable for federal estate taxes on anything over the federal estate tax exemption of $3.5 million for 2009.[72]

4. *There are penalties for early withdrawal.* Once you buy an annuity, you are more or less stuck with it. Withdrawal of earnings from annuity are levied a 10 percent penalty if taken out before age $59^{1}/_{2}$.

5. *Annuities are complicated and confusing.* The fee structure is complicated by the features and all the available riders and, in turn, the benefits are determined by these riders, the payment options and, for the variable annuities, by the performance of the stock market.

Social Security pays retirement income for as long as you live and so do defined-benefit pension plans. The only other source of income that may continue for the rest of your life is an annuity.[73]

The quality of your life in retirement is dependent to a good extent on the actions you take when you are younger. With the decline in the employer-sponsored pension plans and the uncertainty surrounding Social Security retirement benefits, Americans are realizing quickly that to meet their retirement needs they have to rely on themselves to provide for their own retirement. This is why we have seen the mushrooming of the 401(k) plans and the various individual retirement plans. Because of the limitations on how much a person can put away in these retirement plans, Americans are recognizing the need to supplement these traditional sources of income for retirement with their own personal savings.

The Most Common IRA and 401(k) Mistakes

With the shifting of responsibility for meeting your retirement needs from Social Security and pensions to plans controlled by you—most commonly the 401(k) and the IRA—it is critical to be aware of and avoid the most common 401(k) and IRA mistakes.[74] These retirement plans are innovative products with many benefits and lots of flexibility. However, they have rules and regulations that need to be followed properly otherwise the consequences could be dire. Here is an outline of the 10 most common mistakes and how to avoid them:

1. *Keeping your assets in your employer-sponsored plan after retirement.* Once you retire or leave your current employer, you have three options when it comes to what to do with the assets in your 401(k) plan. You can leave it with your former employer; you can roll it over to your new employer's 401(k) plan; and you can roll it over into an IRA. If you leave the assets in your 401(k) with the old employer or roll to the new employer's 401(k) plan, you may be missing out on some key planning opportunities. Your investment options within 401(k) plans are usually

limited, few 401(k) plans offer customized individual advice and your flexibility for estate planning purposes might be constrained. Moving retirement assets to an IRA may result in significant tax savings, better investment options and increased estate planning flexibility. IRAs offer "stretch" capabilities whereby whoever inherits your IRA would be able to take gradual payouts over his or her lifetime thus taking advantage of the growth in the IRA on a tax-deferred basis. By comparison, if someone inherits your 401(k), he/she would have to take the assets out within five years and pay taxes on that amount. Additionally, the option to convert to a Roth IRA is only possible if the 401(k) had been converted to an IRA. A Roth IRA grows tax deferred and withdrawals are tax free and a Roth has no mandatory withdrawal requirements.

2. *Not taking advantage of the "net unrealized appreciation" tax break.* If you have company stock in your 401(k) plan, be careful before you roll it into an IRA or before you make any withdrawal, at any age, of any assets from the plan. A little-known tax break, known as net unrealized appreciation (NUA), allows you to pull out some or all of your company stock into a retail account, while you roll the rest of your 401(k) funds into an IRA. When you use this strategy, any increase in the price of the stock after you originally purchased it inside the 401(k) plan would be subject to long-term capital gains (with a maximum rate of 15 percent), rather than ordinary income tax which can be as high as 35 percent. You will still have to pay income taxes on the cost basis of the company stock purchased but you would not owe any capital gains until you sell your company stock in the new retail account (provided you hold the company stock for at least 12 months post-distribution). If, for example, you accumulated 10,000 shares of your company stock over the years at a cost basis of $20 per share, your cumulative cost basis will be $200,000. Once you retire, if the share price of your company stock rose to $40, and you opted to roll over the entire 401(k) into an IRA, then the entire $400,000 (the total value of your company stock) would be subject to income taxes upon withdrawal and the rate could be as high as 35 percent. However, if you take advantage of the net unrealized appreciation, your cost basis of $200,000 would be subject to the higher income tax rate, while your additional $200,000 would be subject to long-term capital gains, which are capped at 15 percent.

To take advantage of the net unrealized appreciation, you have only one chance to do this. You cannot take any distributions from your company retirement plan, including required minimum distributions; otherwise, you would no longer be eligible. Also, carry out both parts of the transaction—the withdrawal of the stock and the rollover of any remaining assets into an IRA—during the same year. The IRS, otherwise, could deny the tax break.[75]

3. *Failing to name a beneficiary, a contingent beneficiary, and a successor beneficiary, or to review and update your beneficiaries.* You cannot afford to be negligent or lazy. IRAs and 401(k)s do not pass to your beneficiaries by a will; they are contracts and pass to your beneficiaries by designation. Outside of the equity in your home, your IRA and 401(k) could be your second largest asset. If you do not name a beneficiary or a contingent beneficiary in the event of the death of the original beneficiary, the default beneficiary will generally be the owner's estate. This will then require that distributions from the IRA be made as a lump sum or within five years after the death of the IRA owner. Without a named beneficiary or a contingent, your IRA will be subject to the costly and time-consuming process of probate and the income tax rate tends to be higher when IRAs are paid to an estate rather than individual beneficiaries. If you get divorced and do not change your IRA beneficiary, your ex-spouse will inherit your IRA. Make it a habit to conduct an annual review of your IRA beneficiaries to ensure that they go to the intended heirs. Finally, if you inherit an IRA, do not forget to name a successor beneficiary that would inherit the IRA in the event of your death.

4. *Beneficiaries' failure to "stretch" their IRA distributions.* When beneficiaries inherit an IRA, they often tend to quickly liquidate the inherited IRA and income taxes are due immediately. As a beneficiary, you have the option of stretching your inherited IRA or taking distributions from the IRA over an extended period of time. This "stretching" of the inherited IRA provides you with the following advantages: Your tax liability could be spread over your lifetime; the assets that remain in the IRA and remain undistributed continue to be invested in a tax-deferred manner, even as withdrawals are being taken; and additional IRA assets can be accessed when needed.[76] Stretching an IRA may not be suitable for everyone. It is designed for people who have other resources of income.

5. *Naming trusts as beneficiaries.* Be careful about naming a trust as an IRA beneficiary. Trusts are taxed at a 35 percent tax rate on any income over $10,450 for 2007 that is earned or distributed into the trust and not distributed form the trust to the trust beneficiaries during the same year. If the trust does not qualify as a "look through trust," the IRA assets will be paid out within five years after the owner passes away which will eliminate the "stretch" option for beneficiaries and results in immediate taxation.

6. *Failing to complete an indirect rollover within 60 days and not arranging for a trustee-to-trustee rollover.* If you chose to roll over the assets in your 401(k) to an IRA, arrange for a "direct" transfer between financial

institutions or a trustee-to-trustee rollover. Do not have the rollover funds be written out in your name. Your company will automatically withhold 20 percent of your check, which goes directly to the IRS. You can only get back this money if you roll over the funds into an IRA within 60 days and only in the form of a refund from the IRS in the next tax year. And, if you fail to roll over the funds into a qualified IRA within 60 days, you risk losing the tax-deferred status of your IRA funds and you will have to pay income tax on the entire amount. Always arrange for any rollover to be transferred directly, or "trustee-to-trustee."

7. *Spousal continuation mistakes.* When a spouse inherits an IRA, the surviving spouse has the option to treat the inherited IRA as his/her own, or roll the IRA assets into his/her own IRA. However, this might not be the wise course of action in every case. If the surviving spouse is under $59^1/_2$ and needs income, there is no 10 percent penalty on distributions from an IRA kept in the deceased spouse's name. If the surviving spouse is older than $70^1/_2$, does not need income now, and his/her late spouse was younger than $70^1/_2$, he/she may keep the IRA in the late spouse's name because this allows the surviving spouse to delay distributions from the IRA until the deceased spouse would have turned $70^1/_2$ had he/she not died. And, if the applicable federal estate tax exemption has not been fully used, the surviving spouse may want to "disclaim" rights to a portion of the IRA up to the amount of the applicable exemption.

8. *Transferring inherited IRAs to nonspousal beneficiaries.* If a nonspouse inherits an IRA, he/she should not take actual receipt of the IRA assets if they will be transferred to another IRA. This would result in an immediate taxable distribution. The 60-day rollover rules do not apply to nonspousal beneficiary. Simply put—if you inherit an IRA and you are not the spouse, transfer the inherited IRA assets directly to a beneficiary IRA at another financial institution in a direct trustee-to-trustee transfer. You may be able to stretch the IRA distributions over your lifetime unless you inherit the IRA through the estate. Then you are subject to the five-year rule, which requires that the entire distribution of the IRA is completed by the fifth year following the original IRA owner's death.[77]

9. *Overlooking income-tax deductions with respect to inherited IRAs.* IRAs are generally included in the owner's estate for federal estate tax purposes. If estate taxes were paid, the beneficiary may have a right to take an income tax deduction equal to the amount of estate taxes attributable to the inherited IRA. This deduction is large but is often overlooked.[78]

10. *Not educating yourself.* Are you one of those individuals who spend more time planning for a vacation than learning and planning your

finances? If so, you are not alone. Nearly 7 out of every 10 participants in 401(k) plans (69 percent) do not know as much about investments as they would like to know.[79] Also, 57 percent of working Americans are concerned, as they should be, that they may become too conservative with their investment allocation during their retirement years.[80] The investment allocation of your retirement funds is one of the most important decisions that you can make and one that can directly affect the growth/performance of your retirement assets. Make it a point to read, learn, and ask questions of your 401(k) provider and your personal wealth advisor. The Pension Protection Act of 2006 has a provision that makes third-party investment guidance more readily available.[81] Prior to that, 401(k) providers were not required to give you advice. You were, more or less, on your own. Take advantage of this new change in the law, demand to learn and be educated. Some financial advisors offer their clients *shadow investing* services. If you provide them with the investment options your 401(k) offers, they can help you make the appropriate investment selections based on your age, goals, and risk tolerance even though the assets are not under their control.

When dealing with your 401(k)s and IRAs, it is your responsibility to pay special attention to the rules, implement them properly, and avoid the most common mistakes. Otherwise, the consequences might include leaving assets to unintended individuals or entities; incurring unnecessary taxes; and hindering your beneficiaries' tax-saving flexibility.

Which Retirement Assets Should You Use First, and at What Rate of Withdrawal?

When you begin your retirement, shifting from accumulation to the distribution phase, you will be faced with key issues that will affect your ability to retire in comfort:

- Your asset allocation will determine the average return on your investment.[82]
- The sequence of your investment returns—especially how the market performs in the early years of your retirement. Significant losses in the initial years of your retirement could force you to liquidate more assets than you should have to produce the annual income stream that you will need.[83]
- The consistency of your investment returns—a more volatile experience magnifies investor losses.

- Your selected distribution rate (i.e., if you opt to take out 7 percent a year to fund your retirement instead of the recommended 4 to 5 percent, you are more likely to run out of money sooner than later).
- Your method of distribution.[84]

Clearly, your goal is to have your assets last your entire lifetime and, if possible, pass as much as possible to your heirs. If at retirement you have the following resources available to you: a 401(k), traditional IRAs, Social Security benefits, a pension, an annuity, a savings account including investments, then a common sense strategy would be to do the following:

- *Leave your Social Security benefits alone until you qualify to receive full benefits.* If you are in bad health or need the benefits to survive, waiting would not be the most beneficial approach.
- *Draw down your taxable accounts first, since there is no tax incentive to keep them in your accounts.* In the meantime, allow your tax-deferred accounts such as your traditional and Roth IRAs, your 401(k), and your annuity to grow.
- *Use your tax-deferred accounts next.* By that time, your accounts such as IRAs and annuities have had time to grow at a faster rate than your taxable accounts because of the advantage of tax deferral. Of course, if you turn $70^1/_2$, you are required to take out required minimum distributions irrespective of whether your taxable accounts have been drawn down or not.
- *Use your Roth IRA last.* Roth IRAs grow tax deferred, and distributions are tax free and would make a great legacy gift because they will keep growing on a tax-deferred basis and withdrawals are tax free for your heirs after your death. Of all your retirement and investment vehicles, Roth IRAs offer the most advantageous terms.

These are general guidelines and not ideal for every situation. Consult your tax and wealth advisors to determine your best withdrawal strategy. The strategy should be one that meets your needs, reduces your tax liability, and allows for the most growth of your assets.

How much you should take out of your retirement funds to meet your needs will depend on your budget, first and foremost, and your total sources of income. Your sources of retirement income include your Social Security, your pension (if you were fortunate to have one), rental income (if you own rental property), a buy-sell agreement (if you had sold a business), income from dividends and investments, and annuity income (if you had purchased an annuity). The income from these will determine how much you will need to draw from your 401(k)s and your IRAs. In general, you can pull a fixed percentage of all available resources, say 4 or 5 percent no matter what the inflation rate might be. Another approach is to set an initial withdrawal rate then adjust it to inflation from year to year; this way you maintain your purchasing power. A third approach would be to withdraw a higher percentage of available assets early in your retirement and then reduce it over time. The rationale behind this approach is that you are more active in your early years of retirement traveling and maintaining your hobbies and, as you age, you will slow down and thus need to spend less. A fourth approach is to have a varying rate of withdrawal, depending on market performance. If the market rises, you take more, and if they decline, you take less.

There is no right or wrong approach. There is complexity because your needs change, inflation varies, stock performance is inconsistent, and to figure this out, you will need help. This is why it is critical that you regularly evaluate your strategy with your team of advisors—your financial advisor and your tax consultant. Choosing a rate of withdrawal from retirement sources is one of the most important decisions you need to make in retirement.

Concluding Remarks

Ready or not, the time will come and you will retire. Over the past few decades, so much about retirement has drastically changed. We are living longer, we are healthier, and we have opted for a more active lifestyle. Instead of spending endless hours in front of a television or sitting on a porch in a rocking chair, retirees are choosing to travel, volunteer, go to school, and even pursue a different career. Keep in mind that the three most important risks to a retiree's standard of living in retirement are: market risk, inflation risk, and the risk of living too long.[85]

Income from Social Security and the employer-sponsored pension plans used to meet many retirees' financial needs. Today, pension plans are dwindling and cover only about one in three retirees, while income from Social Security covers only a fraction of a retiree's needs.

Here are some suggestions in planning for a comfortable retirement:

- **Plan early.** The key to a comfortable retirement is planning and saving early in your life. Even if you are older, it is not late to begin planning. You are better off going into retirement with a plan than no plan.
- **Come up with a budget.** Figure out how many years you have for retirement, the lifestyle you expect to pursue in retirement, your

various sources of retirement funding, your retirement needs and plan as early as possible to achieve those goals.

- **Depend on yourself.** Pension plans are dwindling in numbers, Social Security's future is dependent on many variables, do not leave your fate in someone's hands. Save and plan for your own retirement.
- **Work longer.** If you retire at age 65, you can expect to be in retirement for 25 to 30 years. Work longer to accumulate the necessary funds to support you in retirement.
- **Access Social Security when you are entitled to take full benefits.** Drawing Social Security benefits early at age 62 means that your benefits will be reduced by 30 percent for the rest of your life. Unless you are in bad health or dire need, leave Social Security income until you are entitled to the maximum benefits.
- **Diversify your portfolio.** The key to successful investing is diversification. Do not chase returns, do not try to beat the market. Set a plan and follow it. Construct a budget that will give you an average of 8 percent return while you are working and an average of 7 percent in retirement. Beware of large concentrations in your company stock.
- **Maximize your 401(k) and IRA contributions.** The more you save in these tax-advantaged accounts, the more you will have for retirement.
- **Draw down on your retirement funds wisely.** You need those funds to last you for your entire retirement. Whether you take a set percentage annually or index it to inflation or vary your withdrawal rate based on your needs, you risk running out of money if you take out too much money early on in your retirement.
- **Properly select which retirement funds to take out first.** Leave the funds that grow tax deferred or tax free last. Use your taxable funds first when in retirement.
- **Do not retire before your Medicare benefits kick in.** Health care costs have skyrocketed and you will not be eligible for Medicare till age 65. Do not take a chance and be without health care before age 65.
- **Review your retirement plan regularly.** Find out whether you are saving enough, whether your portfolio allocation is where it should be, the accuracy of your Social Security estimated benefits, and act on the changes that need to be made.
- **Have in place an estate plan.** An estate plan will ensure that your loved ones are taken care of, will help you minimize estate taxes, will provide for a living will and a durable power of attorney, and will avoid the cost and delays of probate. Consider buying life

insurance to help meet your heirs' needs, provide liquidity to your estate, and possibly decrease your estate taxes.

- **Get help.** It is wise to seek the assistance of an attorney to draw your estate plan, a CPA to help you navigate the tax issues, and a wealth advisor to provide you with financial advice and be the coach of your retirement planning team.

These are general guidelines; they are not comprehensive, and their implementation is different from one person to the next. Be mindful of your personal circumstances and plan according to your own needs. In the end, retirement success rests on good planning.

CHAPTER 6

Why Insurance Is a Must in Your Wealth Management Plan

L et us be candid. You might have felt sometimes that insurance companies are pushy and are intent on selling you a product that you might or might not ever need. Insurance policies often have to be sold to people rather than people willingly buying them. This is probably the case because the purchase of an insurance policy does not have an immediate gratification. You do not come away with a shiny product in a fancy shopping bag. You usually go away with a stack of documents that promise to compensate you for a future loss. The promise is usually as good as the company that sells you the policy. If the company goes bankrupt, you could be out of luck. And, if you have the energy and the time to read the policy, it is usually written in small type with what seems to be an endless number of pages and words so big that you should have been offered, as a courtesy, a dictionary to go along with it.

Now, let us be realistic. You need insurance. Insurance is a vital financial product, and a central component of your wealth management plan. It is quite common for just about everyone to have different types and layers of insurance. Insurance, after all, is intended for unforeseen and unpredictable events in the future. Insurance manages the future risk of financial disaster due to a serious illness, accident, liability, disability, and death. Any and all of these events can spell financial ruin even to those with sound financial plans, including those of you with cash reserves for emergencies. Insurance is generally intended to protect you against catastrophes that few of us can withstand on our own. It safeguards your assets, the policyholder, by transferring risk from you, individually, or your business onto an insurance company.

To gauge whether you are underinsured or need insurance, how much of it, and what type, consider the following statistics:

Life Insurance

- 56 percent of married couples believe that their current life insurance coverage is inadequate.[1]
- 22 percent of families with dependent children will have immediate trouble meeting everyday living expenses, and another 26 percent can cover expenses for only a few months if a primary wage earner dies.[2]
- Insured husbands carry enough life insurance to replace their income for 4.2 years, and wives for 4.9 years instead of the expert-recommended 7 to 10 years of income replacement.[3]
- The average amount of life insurance coverage on insured husbands is a mere $235,600 and insured wives average $147,800 of life insurance.[4]
- Insured adults are more likely to have *only* group life insurance obtained at work. Adults with *only* group coverage carry the smallest amounts of life insurance.[5] If you leave your job and are in poor health, most likely your coverage will cease. You might be uninsurable, or the cost of insurance could be prohibitively expensive.

Disability Insurance

- 42 percent of full-time workers have no short- or long-term disability insurance.[6]
- 33 percent of 20-year-old workers are likely to be disabled for an extended period of time before they reach retirement age at 67, according to the Social Security Administration.[7]
- The primary cause of disability is chronic disease rather than work- or non-work-related accidents, according to a 2007 study for Life and Health Insurance Foundation for Education.[8]
- Two out of three older people with disabilities relied solely on family caregivers as of 1999, up from 57 percent in 1994, and these numbers are on the rise.[9]
- 43 percent of all people age 40 will have a long-term-care disability event (lasting 90 days or more) by age 65.[10]

Long-Term-Care Insurance

- Only 6 percent of Americans buy long-term-care insurance.[11]
- Medicare does not pay for custodial care, and private health insurance rarely pays any of the cost of long-term care.
- More than 33 percent of Americans older than 65 will spend time in a nursing home. About half of those will spend more than a year there.[12]
- Even if you want to buy a long-term-care policy, you might not be able to do so. In 2003–2004, 11 percent of applicants in their fifties, 19 percent in their sixties and 43 percent in their seventies were rejected when applying for long-term-care insurance.[13]

- The 2007 national average for a private room in a nursing home is $74,806 a year.[14]
- 44 million Americans give unpaid care to a relative or a friend, and 54 percent contribute to the cost of care.[15]

Life, disability, and long-term care are but a few types of insurance coverage that most of us need. Can you imagine owning a home or a car and not having homeowners or auto insurance? Liability or umbrella coverage is a must these days, given the size of the judgments doled out by juries. Liability coverage takes effect when your personal liability and lawsuit coverage in other policies is exhausted. How about health insurance? My son was a passenger in a car that was involved in an accident in August 2007. His *four-hour* trip to the emergency room cost $17,500. Unlike other countries that offer government-sponsored universal health insurance, the United States considers you personally responsible for your health care needs, as well as those of your family members. The cost of premiums for private health insurance has been skyrocketing at double the rate of inflation.

This chapter will outline the most common types of insurance—life/ health and property/casualty—and focus on the various types of life, disability, liability, homeowners and auto, and long-term-care insurance. It will address the uses of life insurance in wealth management planning; the preferential tax treatment of life insurance policies, and why you should regularly review your life insurance policies and needs.

Insurance—An Overview

Insurance preserves your assets as a policyholder by transferring the risk from you personally or your business to the insurance company in return for a monthly or an annual premium that you would pay. The insurance company pools policyholders' premiums; invests what is not needed for operating expenses or to pay current claims; and reinsures its existing liabilities with other specialized insurance companies to help spread and reduce its risk. Even though the liabilities of insurance companies are enormous, claims are paid on an as-needed basis and are usually spread over time, thus providing the insurance company with the necessary liquidity to meet its financial obligations.

Insurance is a central element to any financial plan. Different types of insurance cover and protect you in different ways against the loss or damage caused by an accident, illness, disability, or death. The insurance industry is divided into two groups: life/health and property/casualty.

In this section, we will describe and review the most common types of insurance:

1. Life insurance—term and permanent
2. Disability insurance
3. Long-term-care insurance
4. Auto and homeowners insurance
5. Liability insurance
6. Health insurance

The insurance industry is regulated by the states. Each state has its own set of rules and statutes. The McCarran-Ferguson Act, passed by Congress in 1945, views the continued state regulation of the insurance industry as being in the public interest. State insurance departments oversee insurer solvency, market conduct, and review and rule on requests for rate increases in coverage, among others. The National Association of Insurance Commissioners develops model rules for the industry, which must usually be approved by the states before they can be implemented.[16]

Life Insurance

Generally, the premium for a life insurance policy is determined by a number of factors, which include the competitiveness of your insurance carrier, your current age and life expectancy, whether you are a male or a female, the state of your residence, your current and past health history, the results of a comprehensive physical exam that is administered by the life insurance company, whether you smoke or not, any riders that you might select for the policy, the amount of death benefit that you select, whether you opt to pay your premium monthly or annually, your credit score, and your financial suitability.[17]

There are two major types of life insurance—term and permanent. Term life is a temporary policy, while permanent life includes traditional whole, universal, and variable universal policies.

1. *Term life.* **Term life insurance** is the simplest form of life insurance. It pays only if death occurs during the term of the policy. Terms can range from one year, which is **renewable annually**, to fixed terms such 5, 10, 15, 20, 25, or 30 years. Some term policies can also be set to a specified age (usually 65). The most commonly purchased term insurance is a 20-year term policy. During the term of the policy, the premium stays the same for most term policies.

With a term policy, coverage expires at the end of the specified term. A **level term** policy pays the same death benefit amount if death occurs at any point during the term of the policy. A **decreasing term** policy provides insurance coverage with fixed premiums for a specified time period, but with a death benefit that drops, usually in one-year increments, over the course of the policy's term. A term life policy has a no-cash-value feature. Some term policies are *convertible* into a permanent type of life insurance without additional evidence of insurability while other term policies come with a "return of premium" feature—the premiums collected or a portion thereof is returned to the client upon the policy's expiration. Most companies will not sell term insurance to an applicant for a term that ends past their eightieth birthday.[18]

A term policy is the least expensive type of life insurance you can purchase. It is most useful for young parents with children who do not have sufficient savings to take care of their family in the event of one of the parents' untimely death. It is also used in buy-sell agreements and when insurance is needed, for personal or business purposes, for a limited period of time. In 2003, about 6.4 million individual term life insurance policies were purchased in the United States. Of these, 97 percent were level term.[19]

Group term is term life insurance offered by employers, fraternal organizations, professional associations, and trade unions. These days, insured adults are more likely to have *only* group life insurance obtained at work. Unfortunately, adults who have only group coverage also carry the smallest amounts of life insurance.[20] Stated differently, more Americans receive their life insurance needs from group policies offered by their employers, and this large group of people carries the smallest amount of life insurance coverage!

2. *Permanent life insurance policies.* There are significant differences between term and permanent life insurance. Here are the most important features of a permanent life insurance policy:

- It provides lifelong protection. It pays a death benefit whether you die the next day or at age 99—a more likely occurrence, given the impressive increases in our life expectancy.
- It has a savings element inside the policy that grows on a tax-deferred basis and may become substantial over time.
- Premiums are generally higher because the policy will continue to be in effect until your ripe old age (unlike the term limits on term policy), when you are most likely to die.
- Annual premiums remain the same and are locked in a permanent policy, while a term policy can go up substantially at the end of its initial term and whenever you chose to renew it.
- It accumulates cash savings. Depending on the type of permanent life policy you select, you may be able to use the cash value inside the

policy to pay premiums, borrow from the insurance company using the cash value in your policy as collateral, or even withdraw cash to help fund retirement.

- Some permanent policies have riders that will allow you to access the death benefit to pay for your long-term-care needs.

In 2003, more permanent policies were issued than term policies. About 7.1 million policies issued were permanent.[21] There are three major types of permanent life policies—traditional whole life, universal life, and variable life, and there are variations within each type:

a. *Traditional whole life*—**Traditional whole life insurance** provides you with permanent protection throughout the life of the policy:

- Both the death benefit and the premium are designed to stay the same throughout the life of the policy, and the policy has a guaranteed cash value.
- The savings element of your policy will grow based on the "dividends" that the insurance company pays you.

b. *Universal life*—In the 1970s and 1980s, life insurance companies introduced two variations on the traditional whole life policies—universal life and variable universal life. A **universal life policy** provides permanent protection with more flexibility than traditional whole life insurance:

- The cash value in the policy earns a money market rate of interest determined by the issuing company, with a guaranteed minimum interest rate.
- You may be able to increase the death benefit, if you pass a medical exam.
- You have the option to increase or decrease your death benefit by paying higher or lower premiums without having to change the policy. You may lower your premium payments, provided there is enough money in your account to cover the costs. This is a useful feature if you are unable to make the full payment because of temporary changes in your economic situation. Coverage stays in effect as long as the policy has enough cash value to cover the monthly expenses and charges.[22]
- Over time, premiums may be increased by the company if mortality costs increase or interest rates are lower than originally anticipated.[23]

c. *Variable universal life*—**Variable universal life insurance** (VUL) provides permanent protection with even more flexibility:

- The policy has a cash value that is invested in variable investment options, which usually include stocks, bonds, and cash. As a result, the value of your policy may grow more quickly but you also have more risk if your investments underperform.

- VUL policies allow you to adjust your premiums and death benefit. Coverage usually stays in effect as long as the cash value in your policy covers the premium and other expenses.

Death benefit guarantees of life insurance policies are based on the claims-paying ability of the issuing company. However, with variable universal life policies, the policy's investment options have value separate from the insurance company's claims-paying ability. Life insurance policies contain fees and expenses such as the cost of insurance, administrative fees, and premiums loads. They have surrender and other charges. Variable universal life insurance policies also have additional charges and fund operating expenses.

Disability Insurance

If you are working and are responsible for some or all of your family's financial security, you may want to consider the purchase of disability insurance. Remember the following:

- One in three workers 20 years or older will likely be disabled for an extended period of time before they retire at age 67.[24]
- 43 percent of all people age 40 will have a long-term disability event (lasting 90 days or more) by age 65.[25]
- Women are more likely to face a disability lasting at least 90 days or more than men.[26]
- Only 58 percent of full-time workers have either short- or long-term disability insurance.[27]
- The primary cause of disability is chronic disease rather than work- or nonwork-related accidents, according to a 2007 study for Life and Health Insurance Foundation for Education.[28]

Disability insurance usually replaces a significant percentage of your lost income, thereby helping you avoid bankruptcy or depleting your savings and other assets to pay for living expenses and the added expenses of medical care. In addition to worker's compensation and/or Social Security disability benefits, many people need protection in the form of either group or individual disability policies.

EMPLOYER GROUP DISABILITY POLICIES Employers cover approximately 40 percent of all workers with some form of company-paid disability insurance.[29] This is required in most states. Disability insurance is categorized as either short or long-term. **Short-term plans** provide an income to employees who cannot perform their regular duties due to illness or injury. Benefits usually last up to 26 weeks but may go up to two years and have a waiting period of 0 to 14 days.[30] **Long-term plans** provide income benefits after the waiting period such as 26 weeks.

Coverage and terms are not uniform and depend largely on what the company has selected for its employees. Generally, long-term disability replaces up to 60 percent of an employee's income for as long as the person is deemed disabled up to a specified age such as 65, and in some cases extended for life.[31]

INDIVIDUAL DISABILITY POLICIES If your employer does not provide disability insurance or you find it to be inadequate, consider buying your own individual disability insurance. An individual disability income policy is the best way to ensure adequate income in the event of disability. A personal policy is particularly important if you are self-employed, change your job frequently, or want a policy with a more liberal definition of disability.

When you buy your own disability policy, you can expect to replace 50 percent to 80 percent of your income. Insurers will not replace all your income because they want you to have the incentive to go back to work. You should generally try to get a noncancelable policy, which may not be canceled by the insurance company, and a guaranteed renewable, which gives you the right to renew the policy with the same benefits and not have the policy canceled by the company. Elect a policy with benefits for life, or at least, your full retirement age (65–67, depending on your date of birth).

When you pay the premiums yourself, disability benefits are not taxed while benefits from employer-sponsored policies, if paid for by the employer, are subject to income tax.

SOCIAL SECURITY AND OTHER SOURCES OF DISABILITY INCOME The taxes you have paid to the government qualify you to draw on Social Security disability benefits. Realize, however, that Social Security payments tend to be minimal, and have a five-month waiting period. Your disability is expected to last at least 12 months and needs to be so severe that you cannot do any job.

Other sources of disability income replacement may be available through workers compensation (if the injury or illness is job-related), auto insurance (if disability is due to an auto accident), and the Department of Veterans Affairs (if injury was while in military service).

MAJOR DIFFERENCES AMONG DISABILITY POLICIES If you are your family's primary wage earner, you cannot afford to go without disability insurance.

Be mindful, however, of the following major differences among disability policies:[32]

- How does your policy define disability? Some policies pay if you cannot do your work, others if you cannot work at all.
- How long will the policy pay for? It could be up to two years for short-term disability and up to a lifetime or full retirement for long-term disability.
- When does it begin? Some policies have waiting periods of 90 days; others have much longer waiting periods.
- How much of your income will it cover? It all depends on the terms of the employer-sponsored policy or your selection when you purchased your individual policy. Aim to replace at least 60 percent to 80 percent of your salary.
- Does your policy have a cap? Some policies limit payouts to $6,000 or so a month.
- Can the insurance company raise your premium or even cancel your policy, and can you receive higher benefits at a later stage without a medical exam?
- Is your insurance company financially solid, and is it known for good customer service?

Disability is involuntary and devastating. It imposes itself unexpectedly and may wreak havoc on your life and that of your family. With proper planning, you can spare yourself and your family from additional agony and pain. Disability insurance can stave off financial disaster by replacing a majority of the income that you would have received from being gainfully employed and ensuring that at least your basic needs and those of your family are still being met.

Long-Term-Care Insurance

With an aging population and uncertainty about the future of Social Security, long-term-care insurance to cover the high cost of nursing home or at-home health care is the focus of increased concern. This might contradict the good news that we are living healthier, in other words, the need for long-term care is diminishing, and the onset for the need of long-term care is occurring much later in our lives, closer to death (this presumes that future periods of long-term care may be shorter than at present).[33] Nevertheless, if you need long-term care, it can be expensive. Given the increasing costs to the government of providing for the medical care of the elderly, no one is proposing any new benefits. However, Medicaid/Medicare, if they agree to pay for long-term care, will usually cover either nursing home care or in-home care depending on the medical requirements of the patient.

Because of either mental or physical illness, or because of injury, you might find yourself in need of help with eating, bathing, dressing, toileting, continence, or transferring (getting out of a chair or bed). These are the six "activities of daily living," and if you cannot perform two or more of these activities, then you are determined to be in need of long-term care.

Here are the primary reasons why you should consider purchasing long-term-care insurance:

- *Long-term care is expensive.* A four-year or longer stay in a nursing home could cost you between $200,000 to $450,000 in today's dollars and not accounting for future inflation.[34] Long-term-care costs, like most health care costs, are rising faster than the general rate of inflation. In September 2007, Genworth Financial, the largest provider of individual long-term care insurance, announced that it will raise premium for "existing" clients. Genworth, which said previously that it projected premiums would remain static for life, filed in all 50 states for premium increases of 8 percent to 12 percent on most of its policies.[35]

- *You cannot rely on the government to pay for your long-term needs.* Medicare pays very little of the cost of long-term care and Medicaid will pay only for patients who are poor and meet strict eligibility requirements. If you are poor and with little, if any, income, you might not want to buy long-term-care insurance because your state's Medicaid will most likely pay for your long-term-care expenses.[36]

- *Your private health insurance rarely pays any of the cost of long-term care.* Private health insurance companies are mandated to treat an ailment or an injury. Any prolonged hospital stay is usually limited in time and if the need arises for long-term care, private insurance companies pass on the patients to Medicaid, if they are destitute, or long-term-care policies if the patients are lucky enough to have them.

- *Medigap insurance does not cover custodial nursing home costs.* **Medigap** is insurance that can help pay medical expenses not covered by the Medicare system, including long-term hospital care limited to a period of no more than 30 days per event.[37] Medigap policies are expensive and complex.

- *You can protect and preserve your assets from being drained by the cost of long-term care.* It has been suggested that if your net worth is around $1.5 million, not including the value of your home, when you need long-term-care services, then you could forgo purchasing long-term-care insurance and pay for the expenses from your savings.[38] However, you might want to consider the effect this added huge cost will have on your estate and opt to save those assets for your heirs by purchasing the insurance.

- *You can avoid being a burden on your spouse and children.* Unless you are poor (Medicare will most likely pay for your long-term care) or wealthy (you can then afford to pay for your own long-term care), then you need to purchase long-term-care insurance. If your spouse is alive, having long-term-care insurance will preserve whatever assets you might have for him/her and your children will not be burdened with having to pay for your long-term costs.
- *You will have better choices.* If you have long-term-care insurance, you can chose the facility (based on quality or location) where you want to receive your long-term care or elect to have the services provided to you at home.
- *It is tax-deductible.* For qualified long-term-care policies, all or a portion of your premiums may be deductible on your personal federal income tax return.[39]
- *Long-term-care insurance premiums can be deductible as a business expense* subject to limitations. Additionally, businesses can discriminate in offering this benefit among its employees. A business owner can decide which employees can receive this benefit and how much of the premium to pay.[40]

When is the best age to buy long-term-care insurance? It makes the most sense to buy long-term-care insurance before you are 60 and, if possible, even when you are in your forties. The main reasons for this rationale are: The younger you are, the less likely you will be rejected when applying for a policy, presumably because you are healthier. If you apply in your sixties, the chance of rejection is 2 in 10, while if you apply in your seventies, the chance of rejection increases to 4 in 10. The second reason is that the younger you are, the lower will your premium be and the more benefits and features might be available for you.[41]

Considering that only 6 percent of Americans buy long-term-care insurance,[42] and only 11 percent of the workers in 2005 had access to long-term-care insurance,[43] and according to Medicare, about half of all nursing home residents pay for the care with personal savings, the need to plan for or purchase long-term-care insurance is compelling.

Auto and Homeowners Insurance

Auto insurance helps protect you from damage to your automobile and from liability for damage or injury caused by you or someone driving your vehicle. It helps cover expenses that you or someone in your car may incur as a result of an accident with an uninsured motorist.

There are three main components of an automobile insurance:

1. **Liability coverage**—both liability injury and property liability coverage—is mandatory with all policies. The state-required minimum coverage is often too little to provide adequate protection. This insurance helps cover the costs of accidental injuries done to others and to damage to their property. It also covers legal fees in the event you are sued.
2. **Collision coverage** is advisable for a vehicle that has more than minimal value. It covers damages to your vehicle from collision and other types of accidents.
3. **Comprehensive coverage** protects you in events other than collision such a fire, theft, and vandalism.

The cost of auto insurance varies greatly, depending on the company and agent you select, your choice of coverage and deductibles, where you live, the kind and value of your vehicle, and the ages of the drivers in your family. You can usually lower the cost of your insurance if you are a safe driver, a nonsmoker, a student with good grades, commute to work via public transportation, and when you bundle your auto insurance with other types of insurance coverage (such as your home) with the same company.

Homeowners or renters insurance helps protect against loss due to theft, fire, and many other disasters. However, most policies do not cover earthquakes or floods, or protect valuables such as jewelry. You would need to purchase additional insurance to be covered for these. Your homeowners insurance allows you to rebuild and refurnish your home after a catastrophe and also covers the costs of a lawsuit if someone is injured on your property. Full coverage means that the home is insured for at least 80 percent of its value or full replacement cost, which may be different than the market value of the home. The land and foundation will not be covered because they will still be there after a disaster.

You need to review and increase the limit on your homeowners coverage regularly, especially if you have made additions to your house, upgraded it, or if the value of your house appreciated considerably. This does not happen automatically, even though your insurance premium might have increased over time. You need to call your insurance company yourself and request the increase in coverage.

Liability/Umbrella Insurance

Liability or **umbrella insurance** is often the most overlooked type of insurance. Umbrella insurance provides you with additional protection against lawsuits from bodily and personal injury and property damage beyond the amounts covered by your homeowners or auto insurance. It usually takes effect when the personal liability and lawsuit coverage in other policies is exhausted.

An umbrella policy is a must for high-income individuals and those with considerable assets. It is fairly inexpensive, usually costing several hundred dollars a year for a million dollars' worth of coverage. It is a great asset-protection tool. As a general rule, liability coverage should be equal to your net worth.[44]

Health Insurance

There are an estimated 47 million Americans without health insurance.[45] Two out of three Americans depend for their health insurance on their employer-sponsored health insurance programs. The remaining one third are either uninsured or rely on Medicare, the health care system for the elderly, or Medicaid, the health care system for the poor. Many families and individuals purchase health insurance directly from insurance companies. The cost of health insurance is expected to rise by 6.7 percent in 2008 following a rise of about 6 percent for each of the past three years—a figure that remains about two times the rate of inflation. Spending on health care in the United States is expected to reach $4,000 billion in 2015, or 20 percent of GDP[46] (gross domestic product—the sum of the value of all goods and services for the entire country).[47]

Given the spiraling cost of health insurance, there has been a shift from traditional group insurance to managed care programs such as preferred provider organizations (PPOs), health maintenance organizations (HMOs), or the newly introduced concept of health savings accounts (HSAs):

- **Traditional group insurance** are plans that normally provide coverage for both basic medical expenses such as hospital and medical care and major medical expenses such as physician services. You are free to choose your provider, but you are ultimately responsible to pay your bills. Your insurance company will reimburse your covered expenses after deductibles and coinsurance payments have been met.
- **Preferred provider organizations** (PPOs) select a group of doctors and hospitals to provide you with services for a predetermined fee-for-service. You may still pay for deductibles and copayments, but they are generally smaller.
- **Health maintenance organizations** (HMOs) provide comprehensive preventative and medical care, often within one location. You have your own primary care physician who will refer you to specialists if needed. With HMOs, there is usually no paperwork and few out-of-pocket expenses.

- **Health savings accounts** (HSAs) are gaining popularity with self-employed individuals and small business owners.[48] They were introduced in 2003 and allow individuals who have high-deductible health insurance plans to contribute tax-deductible funds into a savings/investment account that can be used for medical expenses. You have to be under age 65; your plan deductible must be at least $1,100 for individuals and $2,200 for families with maximum out-of-pocket expenses of $5,500 for individuals and $11,000 for families. HSAs were intended to encourage people to purchase high-deductible health insurance policies, which would have lower premiums. If you have a generous employer-sponsored health plan or hold a policy with low deductibles, you will not qualify to open a health savings account. If you have an HSA, you must decide how to invest your contributions to this plan—money market account or mutual funds. All funds within HSAs are tax-sheltered, and distributions are tax-free for qualified medical expenses such as drugs and long-term-care expenses.[49]

Hopefully, by now, you have come to appreciate the value of purchasing the appropriate and relevant types of insurance coverage to help you protect yourself, your family, your home, your assets and investments, and your business. Review your insurance policies frequently to assess whether you are unnecessarily overinsured or dangerously uninsured or underinsured. We all need insurance because most of us are unable on our own to recover from catastrophic losses. By purchasing insurance policies, in return for a premium, which is usually a small fraction of any potential catastrophic loss, we shift the onus or risk from ourselves to the insurance company.

Invest in Your Life—Uses of Life Insurance

Property and casualty insurance is designed to "indemnify" you, the insured. This means that it is the obligation of your insurance company to make you whole and restore you to where you were prior to the accident or event that caused your loss. You are not supposed to make a gain from property and casualty insurance. Health insurance is similar to property and casualty insurance because it is intended to treat an injury or an illness and bring you back to health. By contrast, you can use life insurance in many and diverse ways that allows you to make a net gain from having a life insurance policy. In this section, we will discuss the utility and uses of life insurance. Life insurance can protect your family in the future; replace lost income; provide liquidity to your estate; pay for your long-term care; help you transfer wealth to your heirs; maximize the value of your existing assets and gifts; provide for business continuation and transfer upon your death;

reward key employees; provide you with additional retirement income; and help you fulfill your charitable goals. Life insurance is a versatile tool with many uses and tremendous benefits. It is viewed by many experts as the cornerstone of sound financial planning. Life insurance allows you to do eight things:

1. *Provide for your family.* The death benefit or face value of a life insurance policy is the amount that you are insured for minus any loans or withdrawals that you might have taken from your life insurance policy. If your family, particularly your spouse, young children and even your surviving parents depend on your income, life insurance can replace that income in the event you die. Insurance can be especially useful if the government- or employer-sponsored benefits of your surviving spouse or children will be reduced after you die.

   Life insurance proceeds can pay off your debt and the mortgage on your home so that your family can be debt free and live in your home without having to worry about coming up with the monthly mortgage payment. It can also pay for your final expenses such as burial costs, probate and other estate administration costs. You may also have final medical expenses that were not covered by your health insurance.

   After your death, there might be additional direct and hidden expenses that would be lost at death. Your spouse might need to relocate near her family or go back to school to sharpen up her skills and be in a better position to support the family. Life insurance will help replace "hidden income" lost because of your death. Your family might not be eligible to continue receiving the health insurance benefits that your employer had provided. Your death means that you are no longer contributing, nor receiving the matches for a retirement plan. By some estimates, the cost of replacing just your health insurance and retirement contributions could be equivalent to $2,000 per month or more.[50]

2. *Pay taxes and provide liquidity.* Federal estate taxes are due nine months after death. Estate taxes are levied on all your assets within your estate and outside of the allowable exemptions. If you had illiquid assets such as a business, a home, or other real estate, the IRS does not care what your heirs have to do in order to pay the estate taxes on time. Your heirs might be forced to sell those assets in order to pay Uncle Sam. A better option is to have a life insurance policy that is paid to your heirs in cash and is income-tax free to allow them to pay off any debts that you might have had and/or any estate taxes that your estate might owe.

3. *Create an inheritance and an instant estate.* If you were a young physician in your thirties and died unexpectedly, you probably would not have had sufficient time to accumulate wealth to pass on to your heirs.

You were probably still paying off medical school debt, buying a house and beginning to raise a family. Life insurance proceeds can create a substantial inheritance and an instant estate for your loved ones. If you are 35, male, nonsmoker, and in good health, you can purchase a $4.0 million 20-year term life insurance policy for a mere $2,795 a year![51] That is a sizable estate and an inheritance that no other investment or noninvestment vehicle can generate for your loved ones with less than $3,000 a year.

4. *Create a source of savings or supplement your retirement income.* Some permanent life insurance policies with cash value features allow the policy holder to withdraw some of the policy's cash value and take out tax-free loans while still providing a death benefit protection. Some of the cash is used as a source of additional savings, an emergency reserve, a source of funds to pay for your children's college education and, in some cases, as a way to supplement your retirement income. This is how it works:

- You will need to buy a permanent life—not term—policy that accumulates cash.
- As long as the policy is not designated as a Modified Endowment Contract (MEC),[52] you can take tax-free *withdrawals* up to the entire amount of the premiums or cost basis that you have paid into the policy. You can then take tax-free *loans* from the cash value that remains inside the policy.[53]
- The life insurance policy cash value grows on a tax-deferred basis.
- The cash value inside variable universal life policies can be invested in stock and bond funds, which often provide competitive returns.
- The tax-deferral growth, the competitive investment vehicles, and the asset protection features of life insurance policies add up to a prudent way of accumulating additional funds for retirement.
- By attaching a disability rider, premium payments will be continued during periods of disability, thus alleviating the possibility of a policy lapse as a result of nonpayment of premiums.
- Withdrawals from insurance policies are not mandatory and may occur at any time or not at all. This is unlike distributions from qualified retirement plans, which may be subject to an early withdrawal penalty prior to age $59^1/_2$ or mandatory distributions at age $70^1/_2$.

When withdrawing cash or taking out a loan on your policy, remember that these can reduce the policy death benefit and cash surrender value and may even cause the policy to lapse. A lapsed policy can cause the loss of the death benefit and any outstanding loans may cause adverse income tax consequences. You need to consult your wealth advisor and your insurance agent before making any withdrawals and taking out any loans.

5. *Fund a business transfer, protect from the loss of a key employee, and reward selected executives.* If you are a small business owner, you and your partners have worked very hard at building up the business. The success of the business has depended mostly on your hard work and that of your partners. To ensure the continuity of the business and its future success when one of the owners unexpectedly dies, business partners often agree to a buy-sell agreement[54] whereby the surviving partners buy a deceased owner's share from his or her estate after death. If the transaction is properly structured, the life insurance can be excluded from the insured's estate.[55] Buy-sell agreements may also be structured so that the corporation, and not the shareholders, own insurance on the lives of the shareholders. Upon the death of a shareholder, the proceeds are payable to the corporation to fund the redemption of the shareholder's share. Life insurance on each of the partners provides the liquidity to finance this type of a business transfer; it guarantees a buyer for the deceased owner's share; it sets a fair selling price for the business—agreed upon by all the partners ahead of time—and it ensures that the business ownership stays among the original partners.[56]

Again, if you are a small business owner, the loss of a key employee could be catastrophic. Key employees are difficult to attract and retain. A life insurance policy on the life of the key employee could ease the potential financial strain on the business and ensure its financial viability despite the key employee's loss.

In today's competitive environment, attracting, retaining, and rewarding talented business executives is increasingly difficult. Even though qualified retirement plans have preferential tax treatment, employers must include all employees and reward everyone in the same manner regardless of their value to the company. Nonqualified plans allow employers to reward key employees in a discriminatory fashion. An **executive bonus plan** allows the employer to pay a bonus to a key executive by paying the annual premium on a life insurance policy for the executive. The executive will be the owner of the policy and can name his or her own beneficiaries. The executive will own any cash value inside the policy and would be able to access it at retirement via tax-favored withdrawals and loans. Another variation of this plan is more restrictive by creating *golden handcuffs*. With a **restricted bonus endorsement arrangement**, a vesting schedule will be applied to the bonus. The executive's access to the cash inside the life insurance policy is restricted until the executive fully vests or retires, thus providing an incentive for the executive to remain with the employer. If the executive leaves before vesting, the unvested portion of the bonus must be paid back to the employer. And, if the executive stays until full vesting or retirement, whichever comes first, the restricted endorsement is removed and the executive can access the policy value for any purpose, including supplemental retirement income.

6. *Donate to charity and replenish those assets*. If you are charitably inclined, you are most likely donating to charities that support causes dear to your heart on a regular basis. In addition to your cash contributions to the charity, you can designate a charity to receive some or all of your life insurance benefits. By making a charity the beneficiary of your life insurance, you can make a larger contribution (the death benefit) than if you donated the cash equivalent of the policy's premiums, which is usually a fraction of the death benefit.

If you are wealthy, require additional income during your lifetime, and own highly appreciated assets such as stocks or real estate, it makes more sense not to donate cash but, rather, to donate the appreciated assets directly to your favorite charity or even your family foundation.

If you sell an appreciated asset, either to fund some of your living expenses or to donate to charity, you have to take into consideration the capital gain taxes that are due on these assets upon their sale. These taxes may take a significant bite out of your proceeds, and this approach may not be the most advantageous. If your goal is to draw income from a highly appreciated property without diminishing your estate because of taxation, then you should consider setting up a Charitable Remainder Trust (CRT). You donate the appreciated asset irrevocably to the CRT that you set up. The CRT, usually administered by a third party, the trustee, and at its discretion, will sell the donated asset and reinvest the proceeds in a diversified portfolio that can generate income. As a result of your donation, you receive an income tax deduction for the calculated value of your gift to charity. The CRT will provide you with regular income, usually a specified percentage of the value of the trust, for the rest of your life and that of your surviving spouse or for a specified number of years depending on what you have elected in the CRT documents. Upon you and your spouse's death, the assets remaining in the CRT are then transferred to your designated charity which may also be your family foundation.

In order to restore and replenish the value of your estate because of your donation to the CRT, you can purchase a life insurance policy in the amount of the assets donated thus restoring the value of your estate passing to your heirs. Ideally, you can use some of the income from the CRT to fund an irrevocable life insurance trust (ILIT). This ensures that your heirs will receive the entire amount of your estate, and because the life insurance proceeds are paid to the irrevocable life insurance trust, your beneficiaries will receive the proceeds of the life insurance policy income-tax free and estate-tax free. Additionally, because the appreciated donated asset is no longer part of your estate, this should reduce the total estate taxes paid by your heirs.

In short, by following this strategy, you will receive lifetime income; you will get a tax deduction for the donated asset, thus reducing your taxes. Your estate taxes may be reduced because the donated asset is no longer part of your estate; and your heirs will receive, through the proceeds of the irrevocable life insurance trust, the equivalent value of your donated gift, income-tax free and estate-tax free.

7. *Pay for your long-term care.* Some life insurance policies may also help you pay for your long-term care. A number of universal and variable universal life insurance policies are designed with long-term-care riders. These riders are not cost free. However, the cost is usually a fraction of purchasing a stand-alone long-term-care policy. When purchasing the policy, you select the specified long-term-care amount. In many cases, it is either 1 percent or 2 percent of the death benefit value. If your death benefit is $1.0 million, and you have selected as your long-term-care option benefit a 1 percent monthly payout, your benefit would be equivalent to $10,000 a month. Keep in mind, however, that the Health Insurance Portability and Accountability Act (HIPAA) sets and specifies the maximum daily tax-free benefit for long-term care. In 2008, it was $270 a day for nursing home or home care.[57] This amount is indexed to inflation and, in late 2008, the 2009 benefit has not yet been determined.[58] Therefore, your tax-free long-term daily benefit will be the smaller of either the daily amount allowed by HIPAA or the amount specified by your long-term-care policy rider.

The long-term-care benefits are paid out monthly income tax-free after you have been certified by a physician that you need long-term care services.[59] These benefits can be used for home health care, as-sisted living, or a nursing home. If you needed to use the long-term-care-rider, the death benefit is reduced by the amount used up by long-term-care needs. Your million-dollar policy will be reduced by $250,000 if that is the amount paid out to pay for long-term care. But, if you never needed long-term care, your beneficiaries will still receive the entire death benefit, income-tax free.

This provision may not cover all the costs incurred with long-term care, especially if your policy death benefit is small or if you have had a prolonged need for long-term care or if you had taken out loans on your policy or withdrew some of its cash value. The long-term-care benefit value can never exceed the death benefit, less any loans or with-drawals, and the rider excludes covering any expenses resulting from an attempted suicide, committing, or attempting to commit a felony, just to name a few exclusions.[60] Since life insurance is regulated by states, the benefits and exclusions are regulated by your state and can differ from state to state.

This innovative inclusion of a long-term-care rider has made life insurances policies even more valuable, not only in meeting the needs of your loved ones after your death, but also in meeting some of your own needs while you are alive.

8. *Maximize assets for heirs.* If you find yourself in the fortunate situation of not needing current income to cover your living expenses from an annuity that you own, the proceeds from your pension, retirement plans, and Social Security, or the income from your accumulated investments, you can utilize those funds, or a portion thereof, to purchase a life insurance policy on your life, or both you and your spouse's lives, and designate family members as beneficiaries. This benefit maximization strategy has multiple advantages and works especially well if you are receiving income from an annuity and or IRAs. Although an annuity is an excellent vehicle for retirement planning and many can provide lifetime income, it is often a poor vehicle for wealth transfer. This is because at death, the annuity is subject to a variety of taxes that eat away at the portion passed on to your heirs. Similarly, an IRA is part of a person's estate at death, and therefore subject to estate taxes. Furthermore, if you inherit an IRA, you would be required to pay income taxes on the distributions you receive from the IRA.

Because annuities and IRAs are poor wealth transfer vehicles, devising a strategy to drain the annuity and the IRA during your lifetime and channeling the funds to pay premium for life insurance can have multiple benefits:

- This strategy potentially increases the wealth transferred to your heirs through the life insurance death benefit, which is usually much larger than the premium paid to fund the life insurance policy.
- If you gift your unneeded income from the annuity and the IRA to an irrevocable life insurance trust (ILIT), your heirs will receive the death benefit of the policy income-tax free and estate-tax free.
- If you utilize your annual gift exclusion amount of $13,000 per person (2009) or any available lifetime unified credit (currently $1.0 million per person), your gift to fund the ILIT is not subject to a current gift tax and the death benefit of the ILIT to your heirs will still be income-tax free and estate-tax free.
- By donating your unneeded income, you are removing the future appreciation of your current income, thus saving on your taxes by removing those funds from your current and future taxable income.

This strategy allows you then to substantially increase or maximize assets left for your heirs, and when utilizing an irrevocable life insurance trust, the death benefit passes to your heirs, income- and estate-tax free.

Life insurance is commonly purchased to provide a death benefit to your beneficiaries. Given its affordability, term life insurance is the most common type of life insurance. Term insurance plays one key role in your wealth management plan—providing a death benefit protection to your beneficiaries for a limited period of time. By comparison, permanent life policies, because of their flexibility, tax-deferred growth, cash withdrawal and loan features, asset protection characteristics, and tax-favored treatment, have emerged as a central tool in wealth management. Permanent life insurance has all of the benefits of term insurance, and the added benefits of creating a source of savings, supplementing your retirement income, funding your children's college education, funding a business transfer, protecting from a loss of a key employee, rewarding selected executives, funding a donation to your charity, and helping you replenish donated funds, paying for your long-term care, and maximizing the assets left to your heirs. Very few, if any other, financial instruments have the versatility of benefits that life insurance can provide.

The Tax-Advantaged Treatment of Life Insurance

Compared to retirement accounts, pensions, and annuities, life insurance policies have been granted unique tax treatment by the Internal Revenue Service. [61] Understanding the tax treatment of life insurance is critical to helping you select the right type of policy and coverage to allow you to meet your needs and take the most advantage of the features available to you. The most important tax-advantaged features of life policies are as follows:

- *Income-tax-free death benefit*—A key tax advantage of all types of life insurance is that the policy's death benefit is generally paid to your beneficiaries free of income taxes.

  However, with life expectancy on the increase, many people with permanent life policies are living to age 100 and beyond. "It is uncertain whether a policy will continue to be treated as life insurance for federal income tax purposes after the insured person's age 100."[62] If the policy is not treated by the IRS as life insurance, death proceeds may be taxable to the recipient.[63]
- *Estate-tax free*—Even though the death benefit generally passes to your heirs, income-tax free, the same death benefit is usually included in your estate for federal estate-tax purposes. However, the death benefit

may be also estate tax-free if ownership of the policy is structured within a properly drafted irrevocable life insurance trust (ILIT). The ILIT becomes the owner of the life insurance policy and is funded by gifts that you make to the trust.

- *Tax-deferred accumulation*—The cash value within permanent life insurance policies grows and accumulates on a tax-deferred basis. You do not pay taxes on gains (nor can you recognize potential losses). This is why life insurance is an attractive wealth accumulation and tax reduction vehicle.

- *Cash accessed tax free*—With a cash value life insurance policy, you can take *tax-free loans* against the cash value. You can also take *tax-free withdrawals* but only to the extent of total premiums paid.[64] The policy cost basis may be withdrawn before any gain is recognized. Withdrawals beyond your policy cost basis will be taxed at ordinary income rates unless they are taken out as loans from the cash value of your permanent policy. If the policy lapses or is surrendered, any outstanding indebtedness will become taxable.[65]

  As long as your policy is not designated as a Modified Endowment Contract (MEC), policy withdrawals are income-tax free up to the amount of the total premiums paid or your cost basis. Once you have withdrawn your entire cost basis, you may still have tax-advantaged access to your cash value as long as you do so in the form of loans from your policy and, as long as your policy is not designated as a Modified Endowment Contract. The policy is designated as MEC if you exceed federal guidelines for the amount of premium paid into a permanent life insurance policy.

  Serious penalties apply to withdrawals and loans from a policy that is designated as a Modified Endowment Contract. Loans and withdrawals are taxed at ordinary income rates, and a 10 percent penalty is levied on distributions (withdrawals and loans) taken prior to age $59^1/_2$. Additionally, withdrawals and loans from an MEC are taken from any gain first, before the tax-free use of the cost basis.[66]

- *No age-related penalties when using loans and withdrawals*—As long as the permanent life policies are designated as non-MEC, you can withdraw some or all of your cost basis and take out tax-free loans regardless of your age. This is unlike withdrawals taken from retirement plans, pension and annuities.

  Although retirement plans, pensions and annuities are excellent vehicles for retirement planning, they are generally poor vehicles for wealth transfer. This is because at death, retirement plans, pensions and annuities are subject to double taxation—income taxes and estate taxes. This double taxation could diminish the value of these retirement assets by up to 70 or 80 percent.[67] By the time your heirs or beneficiaries pay federal and state income taxes in addition to estate taxes on these inherited assets, they might collect a mere 30 cents on the dollar!

If you do not need the income from your retirement plans, pensions and annuities,[68] consider depleting those resources at a faster rate than other assets that you might have. By taking current income or distributions from these assets and gifting the after-tax amount to an irrevocable life insurance trust (ILIT), you can increase the wealth transferred to your heirs by leveraging the premiums paid for a much larger death benefit payout. More importantly, a properly structured ILIT will ensure that the proceeds are received by your beneficiaries, income-tax and estate-tax free. If you compare the value of the assets inherited by your heirs utilizing this maximization strategy to the value of the assets had they directly inherited your retirement plans, pensions and annuities, the difference in value of inherited assets could be staggering. That is largely due to the difference between the government's tax treatment of inherited retirement plans, pensions, and annuities compared to the tax-advantaged treatment of a life insurance's death benefit (income-tax free), particularly if it is inside an irrevocable life insurance trust (estate-tax free as well).

How Much Life Insurance Do You Need?

The amount of life insurance you should purchase depends on your goals and needs and can range from nothing to as much as 20 times your current income. The average industry recommendation is to have enough life insurance to replace income for 7 to 10 years.[69]

- If you have no dependents and have enough money to pay your final expenses, then you do not need to buy any life insurance.
- If you want to create an inheritance for someone you care about or leave a sizable gift to a charity, buy enough insurance to achieve those goals.
- If you own a family business and you expect estate taxes to be owed, buy life insurance to provide your heirs with liquidity to pay those estate taxes without having to sell the business.
- If you are wealthy and have an estate larger than the excludable amounts at death ($3.5 million per person in 2009), buy life insurance to pay for the estate taxes and equalize the inheritance among your heirs.
- If you have dependents, life insurance is a must, and how much to buy can be complicated. However, it is best to err on the side of caution and buy more rather than less life insurance based on what you think your dependents might need.

Here are five factors that you should consider when deciding how much life insurance to buy:

1. How much income are you generating, and how much life insurance is needed to replace that income until your children are adults and your spouse is at the age when he or she can receive Social Security and other benefits?
2. Add to the income other new expenses that will be incurred by your family after death because you are no longer there to take care of some of those responsibilities, such as preparing your taxes, mowing the lawn, cleaning the pool, and so on.
3. Add the cost of sending your children to college. If you were alive and working, your salary would have offset some of those costs. Now your surviving spouse and dependents have to rely on themselves and what you leave them.
4. Replace "hidden income" that would be lost at death. Your employer subsidized your health insurance plan, contributed to your 401(k), funded a pension plan, and possibly gave you stock options in the company. All these benefits will cease upon your death. According to some estimates, the cost of just replacing your health insurance and retirement contributions could be equivalent to $2,000 per month or more.[70] Multiply that amount by 10 or 15 years, and we are talking serious money.
5. Pay for expenses that arise because of your death. These include funeral costs, taxes and administrative costs associated with handling your estate and passing property to your heirs. Your surviving spouse might need to relocate or go back to school to help support the family in your absence. Many people also wonder what to do with the existing home mortgage, presumably the family's largest source of debt, and whether to pay it off with the proceeds of life insurance or save the proceeds of the life insurance and continue paying mortgage on a monthly basis.

If you calculate these expenses, they will add up to a sizable amount, especially if you die young and you have young children. Some financial relief is available from the Social Security survivors' benefits. For example, the survivors of a 35-year-old person who was earning $36,000 at death will receive a maximum of $2,400 per month for a spouse and two children under 18. This amount is pegged to inflation, but stops completely when there are no children under 18.[71] This leaves the surviving spouse without income from the age when the children turn 18 until he or she is 62 and can begin receiving Social Security retirement benefits. Your death could leave your spouse without health and disability insurance for an extended period of time.

Some employers may provide survivors' benefits in the form of life insurance or a death benefit if your pension has vested. These benefits are valuable but cannot be counted upon because they disappear if you change employers or happen to die when you are unemployed.

Finally, it is strongly advisable to purchase life insurance on both husband and wife. Most of the discussion here has centered on the primary wage earner. A nonworking spouse should purchase life insurance because his/her death will cause tremendous strain on the functioning of the family. A nonworking spouse shoulders tremendous responsibilities that do not generate income. If the nonworking spouse dies, then all those responsibilities—raising the children, helping them with school and homework, driving them to games, caring for them when they are sick, cooking and cleaning, and supervising them—would have to fall on someone else. The loss of a parent or a spouse is tragic and irreplaceable but, realistically, the proceeds of life insurance could help in paying for many of the added expenses of losing one of the parents.

You should also consider purchasing life insurance on your children.[72] Clearly, the child is not generating income, and life insurance, in this case, is not intended to replace lost income. It could pay for final expenses such as a funeral, burial and related expenses. These expenses could cause a financial hardship on some families. Another reason for buying life insurance on a child it to guard against the possibility that, when the child is older, he/she might not be able to buy life insurance because of an illness or an accident. This way, your child is guaranteed to have life insurance. A permanent cash-value life insurance could be a valuable gift for your child. You can transfer ownership of the policy to the child when he or she turns 21 and provide them with a lifetime gift, particularly if you opt to continue paying the premium on your child's policy.

Here are six helpful hints when considering how much life insurance you should buy for yourself, your spouse, or your child:

1. There is no universal formula that exists to guide you in determining how much you should buy in life insurance. Each situation and family is unique.
2. It is better to overinsure than underinsure.
3. It is best to buy life insurance when you are young and healthy.
4. Spend your life insurance budget wisely and prioritize your goals. Buy life and disability insurance on the wage earner first, then the spouse, and then consider buying insurance on your children's lives.
5. Even if you already have life insurance coverage, evaluate regularly if you are properly covered. Your needs change over time based on developments in your financial, business, and personal life.

6. Seek advice. Sit down with your wealth advisor and/or your insurance agent and evaluate your goals, needs, and concerns. Come up with a plan and a level and type of coverage that will meet your needs now and in the foreseeable future.

Six Reasons Why You Should Review Your Life Insurance Policies Regularly

In 1990, a healthy 40-year-old male would have paid around $1,400 a year for $500,000 in insurance for a 20-year term period. That same policy today costs 40 percent less, or about $1,000 a year.[73] The Insurance Information Institute is predicting that in 2007, life insurance premiums will fall another 4 percent, their lowest ever in real terms.[74] If falling rates are not a good reason why you should review your existing life insurance policies, especially if they are 5 years or older, then here are six other reasons why you should:

1. *Get more coverage for the same premium.* Insuring life is becoming less expensive because we are living longer, the key determinant in the cost of life insurance. Improved technology has allowed insurance companies to become more efficient at collecting information and better assessing potential life insurance candidates. For the same amount of premium that you were paying for a policy that you took out 10 or more years ago, you are likely to receive today substantially more life insurance coverage, especially if your health situation has not changed much over that period of time. It has been estimated that 74 percent to 87 percent of trust-owned life insurance could be restructured to provide either a 40 percent increase in death benefits or a 40 percent reduction in premium.[75]

2. *Meet your changing needs.* Your life and that of your family are constantly changing, and each change can affect your financial situation and needs. The effectiveness of your life insurance coverage can be altered without your realization. For example, a wedding, a birth, the purchase of a new home, an inheritance, a new job or a promotion, and an increase or decrease in debt levels are all factors that affect your life insurance needs. In 2007, 56 percent of married parents believed that their current life insurance coverage was inadequate![76]

3. *Take advantage of new product offerings.* If your existing life insurance policy does not offer a long-term-care rider, a fairly new feature in life insurance policies, a review of your existing policies could help you take advantage of new product offerings that could help you meet, for example, your need for long-term-care insurance.

4. *Evaluate the ownership structure of your policy.* Will the current own-ership structure of your life policies result in the lowest tax liability, or is there an alternate solution that could save your beneficiaries money in the long term? If your existing life policies are placed in a prop-erly designed ILIT, the proceeds of your life policy could pass to your beneficiaries, income-tax free and estate-tax free. Often, life insurance proceeds are the largest portion of people's estates. Why not shield those proceeds, with minimal expense, from the significant bite of es-tate taxes?

5. *Monitor your investment returns.* Variable universal life policies allow you to invest the cash value of your policy in investment vehicles, usually mutual funds. When creating your initial life insurance policy illustration, you or your agent were asked to make assumptions with regard to the projected returns on your investments inside the policy. Most illustrations these days are run with an 8 percent assumed rate of return. If your funds underperformed, then your policy cash value might be lower than what you had projected initially. In this case, you might need to either change your investment allocation or add more premiums to the policy to ensure that the cash value grows at a rate that would sustain the policy over time. You need to regularly monitor the performance of the underlying investments inside your variable policy.

6. *Review your beneficiaries.* This is one of the most serious and frequently overlooked mistakes. With an extremely high divorce rate, often divorc-ing couples forget or are unaware that they need to update the named beneficiaries on their life insurance policies. Neither a divorce decree nor a will can change the beneficiary of a life policy. Life policies are passed on to heirs by contract, and the only way you can change the named beneficiaries is through the proper change of beneficiary des-ignation form. On other occasions, you might change the beneficiary because the existing beneficiary, an older son, might no longer need the proceeds of the life policy in the event of your death, while the younger children will still need to pay for schooling, living expenses, and other needs.

Effective policy reviews on a regular basis can help you make sure that your goals for purchasing the life policies are met, despite your constantly changing circumstances; that you are not overpaying for the policies that you own; that your investment vehicles within the variable policies are meeting or exceeding your projected goals; that you are taking advantage of lower premiums and better features; that the policy owner structure allows your beneficiaries to pay the least amount of taxes; and, most importantly, that the recipients of your death benefit are your intended beneficiaries.

Concluding Remarks

In the past, children worked alongside their parents to till their farmland or participate in a family business. The family unit pulled together to help each other. If someone fell ill, the family took care of that individual and his/her work was taken over by another member of the family. Parents relied on their children to take care of their health and living needs in their old age. Modern age has significantly changed society's fabric and its legal and financial structures. We are now living in the age of individualism. As a result, we are less reliant on the family unit and more reliant on our own means. In the face of a more challenging world, even the most resourceful, self-reliant, and wealthy among us have insufficient means to meet life's catastrophic challenges.

In the absence of our old-style cohesive family unit, you need a safety net to help you wade through challenging and difficult times. You need some sort of insurance to give you peace of mind that in the event you die, you fall ill, you become disabled, or you get into an accident, you have the means to take care of your loved ones and to help offset the added cost of these unexpected and unpleasant developments.

Insurance has become a must. It is no longer a choice or a luxury expense item. The use of insurance has expanded significantly beyond life, health, property, and disability coverage. Insurance is now an estate planning tool that can help provide for your loved ones after your death. Life insurance proceeds are income-tax free and, if properly structured, can pass to your heirs estate-tax free. Insurance is used in business for buy-sell agreements or to protect against liability and work-related lawsuits.

The message of this chapter is straightforward:

- You need insurance to protect yourself, your family, and your business.
- You need different types of insurance—health, life, disability, accidental, property, and liability, just to name the most common types.
- You need different layers of insurance—for example, you need to buy liability insurance to add more protection to your auto and property insurance.
- The uses of insurance have expanded tremendously—it is used, for example, to fund a buy-sell agreement among business partners to ensure the viability and the continuity of a business. It is used to reward key employees and as an additional source of retirement income.

- Insurance has become a powerful estate and wealth management tool that could provide your loved ones with an instant inheritance and possibly reduce your estate taxes.
- No matter what your personal resources might be, it is usually more cost effective to have insurance than to have none or be underinsured.

In the event you will ever need to use your insurance and, if you are like most of us, you will, you have already discovered that the cost of some insurance premiums, even though they are increasing at a more rapid rate than inflation, pales compared to the cost of one hospital visit, a disability incident, needing long-term care, the damage caused by a car accident, or a fire that ravages even a small portion of your home. Consider the peace of mind of knowing that whenever you die, your family will have the financial means to survive because of the death benefit paid by your life insurance. Add to all this, the slew of other benefits and uses of life insurance, and you then come to the unmistakable conclusion that most of us can no longer function without proper insurance coverage and that the premiums are a necessary evil, or an investment, that allow us to collect on all these benefits. Insurance coverage, with all its types, has become a must, and is critical to your overall financial security. It is a vital component in your comprehensive wealth management plan.

CHAPTER 7

How to Plan Your Gifting and Maximize Its Value

You have worked hard, earned every bit of what you own, and along the way you paid taxes on both your income and capital gains. Now, you want to gift some of your hard-earned money or accumulated wealth to your children, loved ones, and your favorite charities. It is your right to give away to whomever you want whatever is yours, right? Yes, but be careful! The process is not as simple as it appears. You have to be smart about your gifting habits and strategy. The reason is simple—Uncle Sam wants his cut when money or gifts exchange hands, especially if your gifts exceed certain amounts. The IRS contends, however, that "most gifts are not subject to the gift tax and most estates are not subject to the estate tax. (Only 2 percent of all estates are subject to the estate tax.)"[1]

Gift and estate taxes are an integral part of our legal tax code, and there are government rules and regulations that dictate how much you can give away without incurring government-imposed gift taxes. It might seem unjust to you to pay yet another tax on funds or assets that have already been taxed, and you are not alone. Many Americans and government officials agree with you. That is why the estate tax, for example, is called the **death tax.**

Estate tax laws were enacted in 1797 and were known as the Federal Stamps for Wills and Estates. In 1862, during the Civil War and, in 1898, during the Spanish-American War, they were reintroduced. The laws were all repealed within a few years. The current estate tax law was enacted in 1916 and has seen frequent modifications over the years; the most recent was in 2001.[2]

Your prudent and most productive course of action is to take advantage of the tools that are legally available to you to maximize your gifts to your loved ones, during your lifetime and at death, to the utmost extent permissible by law.

You need to understand these gift and estate taxes and when they do or do not apply, especially since the passage of the Economic Growth and Tax Relief Act of 2001 signed by President George W. Bush on June 7, 2001. This law contains several changes, some of which are retroactive. The law and the changes are complicated and uncertain, making estate planning all the more difficult.[3] If you are a resident of Connecticut, Louisiana, North Carolina, Tennessee, or Puerto Rico, you may owe gift taxes to your state as well.[4] The three types of state death taxes are estate tax, inheritance tax, and credit tax, also known as a sponge or pickup tax. The estate and inheritance taxes are known as basic taxes, and some states impose one of the two. All states impose the credit estate tax, either alone or in addition to a basic tax.[5]

As a result, gifting is not necessarily a straightforward exercise. A number of factors, however, can help you maximize your gifts to your loved ones or to your favorite charities:

- Be aware of the allowable limits—the annual, lifetime, and at death limits. These have changed over time and continue to change.
- The timing of your gift is important. Gifting limits during your lifetime and at death are different and change.
- The person or entities to whom you gift determine the amount of your gift that is not subject to a gift tax. Gifting limits to your spouse, loved ones, political organizations, and charity are different.
- The frequency and consistency of your gifting is critical. You are allowed to gift a certain amount of money during a calendar year without that gift being subject to a gift tax. However, if you do not gift each year what is called the **annual exclusion amount,** you lose the privilege for that year.
- Take advantage of opportunities to maximize your gifts. You can make outright gifts of cash or, instead, use the cash to buy a life insurance policy in an irrevocable life insurance trust that pays death benefit amounts that are many times the value of the cash gift income- and estate-tax free.
- Plan your gifting strategy in advance, especially if you are married. Set up a "credit-shelter" trust so your heirs can benefit from your and your spouse's estate-tax exemptions, rather than just one.
- Never ever give away what you might one day need. It is a virtue to be generous, and it is smart to want to reduce your gift taxes. However, it is detrimental and unwise to give away funds that you might need to sustain you in your retirement, or pay for your long-term care and final expenses. In this case, it is best to keep your money and have your heirs worry about paying the required estate taxes.

This chapter will help you wade through the maze of gifting by identifying and analyzing the following:

- Your primary gift recipients—your spouse, loved ones, and charities, and how gifting to each is treated by the tax codes
- Gifting during your lifetime
- Estate gifting
- Six ways to maximize your gifts[6]

Your Primary Gift Recipients

Your primary gift recipients are usually your spouse, your children and loved ones (including, at times, your pet), political organizations,[7] and your favorite charities, including support for the arts, education, and alumni and fraternal associations. The tax treatment of gifting to each recipient is different, and it depends on the following factors:

- Your relationship to the gift recipient
- The size of your gift
- The nature of your gift (cash or life insurance, for example)
- The timing of your gift
- The legal vehicle used to pass on the gift—for example, a family limited partnership

Gifting to Your Spouse

The unlimited gift tax marital deduction enables you to transfer an unlimited amount of assets—up to the entire value of your estate—to a surviving spouse, free of federal and estate taxes. During your lifetime, each spouse can gift to the other, at any time, any amount without any of that gift being subject to any type of gift tax.

Even though this appears to be the most straightforward and least complicated gift that you can make, at least two situations may arise that you have to be vigilant about:

1. Transfers to spouses who are not U.S. citizens are not protected by the gift tax marital deduction.
2. Assets transferred to your spouse, using the unlimited marital deduction, are included in the surviving spouse's taxable estate when he/she dies unless you set up a "credit-shelter" or "bypass" trust.

CITIZENSHIP   *If your spouse is not a U.S. citizen, he/she will not qualify for the unlimited marital deduction.* The rationale for such a rule is to ensure that the property for which the marital deduction is allowed will later be subject to federal estate tax in the surviving spouse's estate. In other words, the IRS wants an assurance that some time in the future, after the death of the surviving noncitizen spouse, those assets will be subject to estate taxes. When the IRS is convinced that the assets will be subject to federal tax in the surviving spouse's estate, "the IRS permits an exception to the above rule."[8]

In the meantime, any gifts to a noncitizen spouse in excess of $128,000 per year for 2008 would have been subject to federal estate taxes. The tax marital gift deduction for noncitizen spouses is indexed for inflation[9] and, therefore, at the time of writing this book, the new figure for 2009 had not been released. This gift can be in addition to the annual exclusion amount of $12,000 for 2008 and which is likely to go up to $13,000 in 2009 since it is also indexed to inflation. Both gifts can be made to a noncitizen spouse without triggering a gift tax.[10] Transfers at death of a U.S. citizen to a noncitizen spouse will be subject to federal estate taxes unless the assets pass through a Qualified Domestic Trust (QDOT) for your spouse. The QDOT is not a separate type of marital trust; rather, it is a marital deduction trust that has additional requirements because the surviving spouse is not a U.S. citizen.[11]

If the assets in the QDOT exceed $3.5 million (in 2009), the U.S. trustee must be a bank, or the individual U.S. trustee must furnish a bond for 65 percent of the value of the QDOT assets at the U.S. citizen's death or must furnish an irrevocable letter of credit to the U.S. government for 65 percent of the value. Up to $600,000 of the value of the personal residence (in the QDOT) may be excluded in determining whether the $3.5 million threshold has been reached.[12]

The QDOT must also satisfy the rules of a lifetime qualified terminable interest property (QTIP) trust—a trust that receives assets qualifying for the marital deduction and which provides benefits for the surviving spouse. Under the QTIP, the noncitizen spouse is entitled for life to all or a specific portion of the income from the entire trust, and the income payable to the spouse must be payable at least annually.[13]

If this all seems confusing, it is. If either you or your spouse is a noncitizen, seek the proper legal and tax advice. Otherwise, the surviving noncitizen spouse could face potential future hardships or could end up paying substantial estate taxes.

TAX ISSUES   *Using the unlimited marital deduction may be a tax trap.* If you leave all your assets to your spouse, it could cost you unnecessary taxes, especially if your combined estate is worth more than $7.0 million in 2009.

Although estate taxes will not be due when you die, all the remaining assets will be part of your spouse's taxable estate when he or she dies. So, at your spouse's death, your children will inherit the entire estate of $7.0 million[14] and get the benefit of only your spouse's $3.5 million estate-tax exemption. However, if you had put $3.5 million into a **credit-shelter** or **bypass trust,** your spouse could still have access to the principal or income of your bypass trust. And, upon your spouse's death, your heirs will inherit the $3.5 million in the bypass trust, along with $3.5 million of your spouse's estate, free of federal estate taxes.

To put it numerically, if you had a combined estate of $3.5 million and you died without having set up a bypass trust and, if your spouse dies in 2009, your heirs would inherit your spouse's $3.5 million exclusion amount, estate-tax free. The remaining $3.5 million that you left your wife would be subject to a 45 percent estate tax amounting to $1,575,000 in estate taxes.[15] In short, if you did not set up a bypass trust, your heirs, upon your spouse's death, would receive $5.425 million, while if you had set up a bypass trust, your heirs would receive the entire $7.0 million. Planning ahead could save your loved ones from paying unnecessarily substantial amounts in estate taxes.

Gifting to Your Loved Ones

Except for gifts to your spouse, political organizations and charity, the tax code does not distinguish between gifts given to anyone else on the basis of whether they are related to you. Your gift to your children, mother, siblings, or neighbors are treated by tax codes in the same manner in that they are subject to the same limits and exclusions. In this case, the identity of the individual receiving the gift does not matter for gift tax purposes.[16]

A gift must be complete and irrevocable for gift tax purposes. Gifts made to minors through (in most states) a Uniform Transfers to Minors Act (UTMA), or (in others), the Uniform Gifts to Minors Act (UGMA), are treated by the IRS as complete and irrevocable gifts, even though they are actually placed with a custodian. The custodian—a parent or any other adult—holds the funds in the minor's name, and these funds can only be used for the sole benefit of the child. When the child turns 18 or 21, depending on the state where he/she resides, then the UTMAs and the UGMAs are transferred to the child's (now adult) sole name.

If you are a parent with a disabled child, be careful how much you gift to your child. Because the disability of a child usually lasts a lifetime, you need to preserve the public assistance benefits available to your child. The Medicaid program, which pays medical expenses for the poor, imposes limits on the amount of assets that a recipient can own or can earn each year that welfare benefits are received. If your disabled child inherits assets from you, even inadvertently, or is gifted assets by you, he or she may lose current government benefits. In this situation, you are faced with a dilemma—either disinherit your child with a disability to preserve the significant government benefits or use a special needs trust.

Special needs trusts are generally established by the parents or relatives of a disabled child. The trustee has absolute discretion over how to spend the trust funds for the benefit of the disabled child. In this case, government benefits should be used to meet basic needs such as food, clothing, and shelter. The funds from the special needs trust should be used for supplementary needs such as utilities, medical care, special equipment, education, job training, or entertainment.[17]

Individuals can set up trusts to benefit even their pets. As of 2007, 39 states and the District of Columbia had enacted laws recognizing the so-called pet trusts. When she died in August 2007, Leona Helmsley left to her dog $12 million in a trust so it could live out its life in luxury. However, Helmsley, a hotel and real estate magnate, did leave the bulk of her multibillion estate to charity.[18]

Gifting to Charities

Americans are extremely generous. In 2006, U.S. charitable giving set a new record and reached an estimated $295.02 billion—a 4.2 percent increase over 2005.[19] About 65 percent of households with income less than $100,000 gave to charity. That is more than the percentage of people who vote or read the Sunday newspaper. Individuals, as opposed to corporations or foundations, are always the largest single source of donations to nonprofit organizations. Individuals contributed 75.6 percent of all giving in 2006, charitable bequests represented 7.8 percent, foundations gave 12.4 percent, while corporations and corporate foundations donated a mere 4.2 percent of total giving.[20]

Americans give to charities and nonprofits for manifold reasons. Here are the seven most common:

1. They give because they are asked. With a large number of worthy causes domestically and internationally, donors respond to requests of assistance primarily because someone asks them.
2. They give out of conviction in the cause or issue.
3. They give to take advantage of the tax deduction generated by their gifts. Contrary to widely held views, however, giving to receive a tax deduction is not the primary reason why people give.
4. Gifting puts current assets and their future appreciation out of the donor's estate, thus reducing future estate taxes.

5. Gifts of appreciated assets to a charitable remainder trust escape capital gains taxes, generate a tax deduction, and provide lifetime income to the donor. Upon the donor's death, assets go to the charity.
6. There are no probate expenses for gifted assets.
7. Large donors often gift to leave a legacy behind them.

The Internal Revenue Code (IRC) allows *unlimited gifting*—in other words, gifts that are not subject to gift or estate taxes—to the following:

- Federal or state governments or their subdivisions to be used exclusively for public purposes
- Nonprofit organizations, trusts, or foundations "operated exclusively for religious, charitable, scientific, literary, or education purposes, which do not attempt to influence and are not substantially engaged in carrying on propaganda or influencing legislation"[21]
- Fraternal or veterans organizations

Additionally, your outright donations to the charities or entities listed here yield a gift-tax deduction (if made during your life) or an estate-tax deduction (if made after your death). The IRC encourages donations to charity and has proven flexible in that regard. For example, your gift in trust to a charity can result in income-tax savings even though you retain certain financial benefits from the assets donated for a substantial period of time after you donate. This is the case when you donate to a **Charitable Remainder Trust (CRT)**. When you set up the CRT and fund it, you get an income-tax deduction for the present value of the gift that ultimately goes to charity. You will continue to receive income from the assets placed in the trust. Upon your death, the charity receives the balance of the assets in the trust.

A **Charitable Lead Trust (CLT)** is the opposite of a Charitable Remainder Trust. With a CLT, the charity receives the income from the trust and delivers to your heirs (your spouse, children, or someone else), the assets donated to the CLT when the trust's terms ends.[22] During the term of the CLT, you may get a current income tax deduction for the value of the charity's income from the trust assets.

Gifting During Your Lifetime

The federal government has a unified tax system that imposes taxes on asset transfers that occur during your lifetime and after your death. Some states also impose either estate or inheritance taxes on asset transfers. Gift taxes are imposed on transfers made during your lifetime, and estate taxes are imposed on transfers made at the time of death.

You can gift either during your lifetime or at death. The limits on gifts during your lifetime are different from the limits on gifts made upon your death. The limits have changed over time and are expected to change in the future.

The Economic Growth and Tax Relief Reconciliation Act (EGTRRA) of 2001 controls the current federal gift tax law. Major highlights of EGTRRA include the following:

- It set the lifetime gift tax exclusion at $1.0 million from 2002 to 2010.
- The highest gift tax rate on amounts above this $1.0 million limit is reduced from 50 percent in 2002 to 35 percent in 2010.
- It increased the estate tax exemption (at death) from $675,000 in 2001 to an unlimited amount in 2010.
- It decreased the highest estate tax rate from 55 percent in 2001 to zero in 2010.
- It included a sunset provision that stated that unless additional legislation is enacted, the act would terminate on January 1, 2011, and the exemption amounts and estate tax rates would revert to laws in place in 2001. (The estate tax exemption would be reduced to $1.0 million and the highest estate tax rate would increase to 55 percent, while the lifetime gift tax exemption would be $1.0 million and the highest gift tax rate would increase to 55 percent.) The sunset provision can be eliminated if Congress votes 60 percent in favor of terminating it.[23]

During your lifetime, you can use three types of gifting exclusions, up to certain limits, before your gift is subject to a gift tax.

1. *Annual exclusion gift.* Every person is allowed to make annual gifts of up to $13,000 (2009) per person each year without having to pay gift taxes.[24] You can make as many annual exclusion gifts to as many people as you desire in any given year, free of gift taxes. A married couple filing jointly can give a total of $26,000 per person per year. So, if you have four children, you can give them annually, between you and your spouse, a total of $104,000 a year—a significant tax-free transfer of wealth over time, particularly if you gift annually or on a regular basis. Keep in mind that if you do not take advantage of the annual gift exclusion, you lose that privilege for that year. In other words, the annual exclusion is not cumulative. It cannot be carried over from one year to the next. To take full advantage of the annual exclusion gift, you need to, although you do not have to, make those gifts every single year.

Over a period of time, a planned giving program using annual exclusion gifts can remove a significant amount of property from your gross estate without incurring any transfer tax or using up any of your lifetime gift tax exemption. Additionally, any future appreciation and income generated by the transferred assets is also removed from your gross estate, further reducing your future estate tax liability.

Another benefit of annual exclusion gifting is the avoidance of the gross-up rule. Under this rule, gift taxes paid by you on transfers within three years of death are included in your estate. However, because annual exclusion gifts are not subject to federal gift tax, you avoid the gross-up rule. This will help reduce the estate taxes that would be payable on gift taxes actually paid.[25]

2. *Lifetime gift tax exemption.* The Economic Growth and Tax Relief Reconciliation Act (EGTRRA) of 2001 set the lifetime gift tax exemption at $1.0 million between 2002 and 2010—this is the amount that you can transfer during your lifetime that is not subject to a federal gift tax. Unlike the estate tax and the generation skipping tax, the gift tax will not be repealed and will remain in place after 2009. The gift tax was retained to deter income tax avoidance schemes. Under the Act, however, the maximum gift tax above the allowable lifetime exemption is scheduled to decline from 50 percent in 2002 to 35 percent in 2010 and back to 55 percent in 2011.

This $1.0 million gift tax exemption amount is in addition to the annual exclusion amount of $13,000 per year (in 2009) that you can give to as many people as you wish. Your lifetime gifting can be made on a sporadic and nonconsistent basis. You do not have to give an equal amount over a period of time, nor do you need to make any gifts at set periods of time. Federal gift tax law requires that the value of all taxable property given each year be accumulated into one total before computing each year's gift tax. For example, if you give a $50,000 gift to your child in 2009, then the amount subject to a gift tax would be $37,000—the $50,000 minus the $13,000 annual exclusion gift. The excess gift of $37,000 would be credited to the $1.0 million lifetime gift exclusion and would reduce the available lifetime gift tax exemption by $37,000. Taxable lifetime gifts from prior years—since 1976, when the estate and gift taxes were unified[26]—must be added to current gifts to determine when the lifetime exemption amount has been exceeded.

3. *Unlimited tuition and medical expenses.* You can give, free of any gift tax, an unlimited amount to pay for someone else's qualified medical expenses and/or tuition (not books, supplies, or other expenses). Tuition payments must be made *directly* to the educational institution to qualify for this exclusion, while qualified medical expenses must be paid directly to the health care provider, and not to the beneficiary.[27]

This exclusion is especially valuable to wealthy grandparents, because their payments of a grandchild's tuition and medical expenses are: (1) unlimited in amount; (2) free of gift tax; and (3) free of the generation-skipping transfer tax (GST).[28] Additionally, these gifts remove large amounts of funds from their estates and give the grandparents control over the use of the gifts by making the payments directly to the educational institution and medical provider. The unlimited exclusion of the tuition and medical expenses is also in addition to the annual exclusion gift that the grandparents may give to their grandchildren.

Estate Gifting

Gifts at the time of death, or **bequests,** as they are known, may be subject to estate taxes if they exceed certain exempt amounts. The federal tax is an excise tax on the right to transfer property at death. The gross estate includes the fair market value of all assets owned by the decedent as of the date of death, including life insurance policies. Under the Economic Growth and Tax Relief Reconciliation Act (EGTRRA) of 2001, the tax applies only to taxable estates that exceed $3.5 million in 2009. The estate tax is completely repealed in 2010 and then reverts to the much lower limit of $1.0 million, unless Congress acts before that time to continue its repeal or to alter the taxable limits.

Generally, the value of gifts (other than gifts of life insurance) made by a person who dies within three years of death is not included in the gross estate. However, if these gifts exceed the annual gift tax exclusion, they may be added to the taxable estate as adjusted taxable gifts. Gifts of life insurance policies are included if made within three years of death.[29] Other transfers or gifts made during one's lifetime that may be brought back into the decedent's estate include: (1) transfer of an asset from which the donor retains an income for his or her lifetime; (2) transfer of an asset where the donor retains the right to alter or terminate the transfer; and (3) assets placed in joint tenancy with another person.[30]

It is important to note that the $3.5 million (in 2009) estate tax exemption amount is inclusive of the $1.0 million lifetime gift tax exemption. In other words, of the $3.5 million amount, up to $1.0 million may be transferred over a person's lifetime without incurring taxes. Overall transfers that exceed $3.5 million are subject to an estate tax rate of 45 percent (in 2009).[31]

For asset transfers either during life or at death to persons in a generation more than one generation below that of the transferor, to grandchildren for example, there is a **generation-skipping transfer (GST) tax** on transfers that exceed $3.5 million in 2009. In 2010, it is slated to be repealed, unless Congress takes action before that time. The GST is imposed in addition to, not instead of, federal gift or federal estate tax. You need to be aware that if you make cumulative generation-skipping transfers in excess of the GST exemption of $3.5 million in 2009, a flat tax equal to the highest estate tax bracket in effect in the year you make the transfer is imposed on every transfer you make after your exemption has been exhausted.[32]

Six Ways to Maximize Your Gifts

If gifting is planned carefully, there are tools and techniques that you could employ that would significantly increase the value of your gift over time, decrease your income and estate taxes, and provide liquidity to your estate. Some of the most common gifting maximization strategies include purchasing life insurance policies with cash that would have been gifted outright, leveraging the annual and lifetime exclusions with discounts, and gradually transferring a closely held family business:

1. *Gift life insurance.* One very effective way to use annual exclusion gifts or even lifetime gifts is to purchase a life insurance policy inside an Irrevocable Life Insurance Trust (ILIT). If you and your wife use your annual gift tax exclusion of $13,000 each (in 2009) for a total of $26,000 per year to purchase a life insurance policy, on either one of you, inside an ILIT, then, upon your death, the death benefit is paid to the beneficiaries income-tax and estate-tax free.

   In 2002, a couple, both 70, utilized their lifetime gift tax exclusion of $1.0 million each to purchase a second-to-die life insurance policy.[33] The premium was paid over a five-year period to help better manage their cash flow. They were able to purchase a policy with a $9.4 million death benefit payable upon the second spouse's death. Because the policy was inside an ILIT, their heirs will receive the $9.4 million death benefit income-tax and estate-tax free. By employing this strategy, the couple was able to:
   - Reduce their estate by $2.0 million, thus saving on potential future estate taxes.
   - Increase the value of their gift from $2.0 million to $9.4 million. Because their $2.0 million gift represented their lifetime allowable gift tax exclusion, and because they purchased the life insurance inside an Irrevocable Life Insurance Trust, the death proceeds will be paid to their beneficiaries, income-tax and estate-tax free.
   - Protect their gifted assets from creditors, avoid probate in the future for the gifted assets, and protect the family's privacy.

     In this case, the disparity between the annual cash gift and the future gift is substantial and, in many cases, it makes economic sense, especially if the gifted cash is not needed by the recipients to pay for daily living expenses.

2. *Utilize discounts.* The valuation of assets can play an important role in planning for the disposition of assets during life and at death. Certain techniques can be used to decrease the value of an asset prior to giving it away in order to reduce any gift or estate tax liability. Such techniques use fractional interest discounts, minority interest discounts, lack of marketability discounts, and discounts on capital gains as a way of reducing the value of an asset.[34] If you structure a gift so that valuation discounts apply to the transfer, you will then be able to leverage the amount of property transferred, using either your annual gift or lifetime gift exclusion.

   For example, if an appraiser determines that a 50 percent discount is applicable to the transfer of limited partnership interests, then a gift of $13,000 of limited partnership interests represents $26,000 of underlying value.

3. *Shift income and growth.* Annual and lifetime exclusion gifting can help reduce your family's overall income tax liability. You can achieve this by gifting not cash, but income-producing assets, to family members in lower tax brackets or by gifting appreciating assets, such as stocks, to a family member who may be subject to a lower capital gains tax rate or who can offset the gains with losses when they sell the appreciated asset.

   If you are married and file your taxes jointly, instead of giving your two children cash in the amount of the annual exclusion ($13,000 each in 2009), you gift to each of them mutual fund shares worth $26,000 ($13,000 from you and $13,000 from your spouse) every year for five years, the total value of your gift to them will be $$130,000. If these shares doubled in value by the time you and your spouse died, your children would have avoided gift and estate taxes on $260,000—the gift's original value plus the growth. Assuming a federal estate tax rate of 45 percent in 2009 above your lifetime exemption, your tax-efficient gifting saved your estate $117,000 in estate taxes.

4. *Gift to vehicles that grow tax free.* If you use your annual or lifetime exclusions to gift to a 529 higher educational plan, the assets in the plan will grow tax-deferred and can be withdrawn completely tax free so long as they are used for higher educational purposes. Additionally, if you have a child or a grandchild who is working and earning reportable income, you can offer to fund their Roth IRA for them up to the maximum allowable by law ($5,000 in 2008). This $5,000 amount will be indexed for inflation thereafter. The IRS may adjust it annually for inflation. However, any adjustments will be in $500 increments. Roth IRAs will grow and can be withdrawn completely free of tax, provided they

are used upon retirement or for expenses prior to retirement allowable by the IRS, such as the down payment on a first residence or to cover eligible medical or educational expenses.

5. *Save on state gift tax.* Annual exclusion and lifetime gifts can reduce your overall *state* tax liability. Most states impose some kind of death tax—estate, inheritance, legacy, or succession tax—after a donor's death. However, not all state impose a gift tax, and those states that impose a gift tax do so at lower tax rates than the death tax rates. Therefore, making gifts, especially the annual exclusion gift, over time can result in considerable state transfer tax savings.[35]

6. *Be selective in what you gift and when you gift it.* In planning your gifting, you should be mindful that property transferred by *gift* retains your cost basis, while property transferred *upon your death* gets a step-up in cost basis as of its fair market value on the day of your death. In determining which assets to gift during your lifetime and which to give upon your death, you should consider the amount of appreciation in the gifted asset and the likelihood that this asset might or might not be sold in the near future.[36] For example, you should consider gifting during your lifetime assets that have not appreciated much since you purchased them, because your cost basis will become the cost basis of the recipient. If these assets have tremendous growth potential, then you are also shifting the growth to the recipient who might be in a lower tax bracket. Conversely, consider gifting in your will or trust an asset that has appreciated considerably because, upon your death, this asset gets a new stepped-up cost basis—the fair market value on the day of your death. And, as long as the asset is within the applicable estate exclusion of $3.5 million (in 2009), there would be no federal estate tax on the property.

Any applicable combination of these gift maximization strategies will allow you to take the most advantage of your gifting. Put some thought in your gifting process and consult your legal or tax advisors to help you make a better-informed decision.

Concluding Remarks

Gifting is an expression of love and affection. By gifting, you are giving away something of value to someone you care about. Your loved ones get to use and enjoy their gift. Gifting, however, can serve other purposes. Gifts can give children the opportunity to participate in the management of a family business, help finance a college education, or pay medical bills.

Gifting should be an integral part of your overall wealth management plan. Gifts are an important estate planning tool for those with taxable estates. For a well-designed and properly executed gifting plan, you should do the following:

- Seek proper legal and tax advice. Tax laws, exemptions, and rates are constantly changing. You need to keep abreast of these changes.
- Be disciplined in gifting. Gift regularly to take advantage of the annual gift exclusion. This could significantly reduce your taxable estate over time.
- Reduce your estate taxes by gifting during your lifetime, and shifting income and asset growth to recipients in lower tax brackets.
- Maximize the value of your gift. By leveraging cash that you would have gifted outright to buy a life insurance policy, you could significantly increase the value of your gift and, if purchased inside an irrevocable life insurance trust, your gift would pass to your heirs income-tax and estate-tax free.
- Set up a bypass trust, if you are married, to take advantage of your individual $3.5 million estate tax exemption (in 2009). Otherwise, your estate could end up paying estate taxes on at least $2 million of the $9 million in your combined estate. In 2009, the estate tax exemption is $3.5 million per person. If a husband and a wife die during 2009, they can leave up to $7.0 million to their heirs estate tax free. Anything above the combined $7.0 million maximum estate tax exemption for a couple is subject to the 45 percent estate tax.
- Do not underestimate your net worth. Your estate could end up paying estate taxes if you miscalculate the value of your estate when it exceeds the allowable lifetime exclusion.
- Review your will, trust, and estate plan periodically, especially if the value of your assets, the make-up of your family, your wishes for sharing assets, and the tax laws change, or even if you move from one state to another.
- Provide your estate with liquidity if you expect your estate to be taxed.
- Consider charitable bequests to reduce your taxable estate, to help a cause dear to your heart, and to leave a legacy behind.
- Stipulate that cash gifts made to your children be kept in a separate account solely in your child's name. Typically, those accounts will not be included in divorce settlements, so the funds will stay with your child.
- File the 709 Federal Gift Tax return every year you make a gift to someone other than your spouse, a political organization or a charity, that exceeds the annual exclusion limit. You will not owe gift

taxes, but the excess amount will be counted toward your lifetime gift tax exclusion.

- Beware that gifts of life insurance and gift taxes paid within three years of death will be included in your gross estate.
- Establish a special needs trust for your disabled child. Otherwise, your disabled child might lose his or her government benefits.
- Realize that the unlimited marital exemption does not apply to a noncitizen spouse. Be mindful of the limited annual gift and estate tax exemptions. With millions of noncitizen immigrants in this country, this is a commonly overlooked issue.

This list is neither comprehensive, nor does it address unique circumstances that might affect you. It highlights a few of the most common elements that need to be carefully looked at in a comprehensive and well-planned gifting strategy.

CHAPTER 8

Asset Protection Strategies

If you are like the majority of Americans, you tend to focus your energies on working hard to meet your daily needs, pay for health care, buy a house, educate your children, help your parents, save for retirement, and plan for the occasional vacation. You pay little if any attention to protecting those assets that you have worked so hard to accumulate. Unfortunately, your financial security can be easily derailed and threatened, often for frivolous reasons, by an unexpected lawsuit.[1]

For many people, it is no longer a matter of "if" you will ever be sued but "when." One million lawyers file 19 million lawsuits each year. Of the 100 million adults in this country, 30 million are people with some valuable assets that someone would love to go after.[2] It is no longer only the wealthy get sued. If you are a person with moderate means, you have a home with equity, savings, liability insurance, or retirement accounts, you could be at risk. You are especially vulnerable if you are a business owner or a professional such as a physician, dentist, lawyer, accountant, real estate agent, or even an architect. You are vulnerable to claims from customers, patients, suppliers, employees, or tenants.

Lawsuits can be expensive and are generally time consuming. It can cost you tens of thousands of dollars to defend yourself. Whether you are able to ward off a lawsuit or not, come out a winner or loser, you generally end up paying the cost of your own defense. Sometimes, defendants end up settling a lawsuit, even though they are innocent, because it is generally less costly to settle a lawsuit than to spend the time, money, and mental agony in defending oneself.

We live in a society where you are a prey and a hostage to potential lawsuits. You need to take matters into your own hands. Your best defense is to educate yourself on the risks that you face, work with advisors that will help you implement asset protection strategies but do so in a planned manner ahead of any potential threat. Advance planning is critical to your offensive strategy.

This chapter will define and address the need for asset protection, discuss the basis of asset protection strategies, dispel some of the common myths, outline and evaluate the most commonly utilized asset protection strategies and vehicles, and conclude with a summary of things to do and not do.

Who Needs Asset Protection, and Why

Just about anyone is liable to get sued. However, the "reality of our legal system is that people are named as defendants in lawsuits not because of their degree of fault but because of their ability to pay."[3] As a result, three categories of people are the ones most likely to get sued—the "deep pocket defendant," the one engaged in any business activity, and the one with a professional practice.

If you are wronged or suffered a loss because of someone else's action or negligence, you should be expected to fairly compensate the victim. However, our legal system has been skewed by the excessive number of lawsuits, especially the frivolous claims, the continually expanding theories of liability, and the exorbitant damage and punitive damage awards that have now become the norm.[4]

A lawyer will most likely not sue someone who is unable to pay because that person had no assets or was not covered by an insurance policy. Frequently, a lawyer will accept or decline a case based not only on the legal merits of the case but the financial ones, specifically the ability to locate someone that could, even remotely, be tied to the case and that could be held liable. If two people are involved in a car accident and the person at fault has no insurance or significant assets, the lawyer would want to determine if the alleged culprit was on an errand for his employer, whether he had alcohol in his system and which restaurant served it to him, whether he had traces of medication, which physician prescribed it and which pharmacist filled it out, whether the accident took place in front of a homeowner whose bushes might have covered a street sign, on a crossing where the city should have had a stop instead of a yield sign, and whether the car had structural defects that could be traced back to the manufacturer and that could have contributed to injuries of the victim. In these cases, most lawyers get paid on a contingency basis, generally 30 to 40 percent of the award. Litigation is time consuming and can be expensive. A lawyer would not want to take on a case that would tie him down with little hope of getting paid. Hence, this explains the lawyer's pursuit to locate the "deep pocket defendant."[5] If you have personal assets, a business, or insurance, you have deep pockets and you are more likely to get sued.

Physicians, rental property owners, officers and directors of companies, and real estate developers are among the businesses and professionals that are high on the list of lawsuit targets. According to one estimate, the odds are 1 in 4 that if you are a physician, you will be sued this year. Therefore, it is virtually certain you will face a lawsuit within four years. Also, if you are a physician under 40, expect to be the subject of a lawsuit four times in your career.[6] It has been estimated that between 70 and 80 percent of all obstetricians have been sued, while other medical specialties, including neurosurgeons, are equally high.[7] As a result, many physicians have tended to narrow the scope of their practice to reduce the likelihood of getting sued.

If you are a rental property owner, you are a prime target for a lawsuit. Even if you comply with all the building codes and safety requirements, you might be sued for a fire that breaks out in one of your rental units or if someone is shot in the alley behind your building, presumably because you could have taken additional unspecified measures to retard the spread of a fire or provide better lighting for security purposes for the alley behind your building. Having insurance on the property does not guarantee that you are free from personal liability. Insurance policies have a laundry list of exclusions and, if the insurance does not cover all the judgment against you, then your personal savings, your home, and other assets will have to be used to satisfy the judgment. "Any real estate—whether or not you have any equity in the property—represents an enormous source of liability to you and poses a danger to all other assets that you have accumulated."[8]

Real estate developers and construction companies represent another group with potentially significant personal liability. Even after you develop and sell property, latent or unseen construction defects may be uninsurable or may surface after a policy has expired. In California, for example, a builder remains legally responsible for latent defects for up to 10 years after the completion of the building. Geologists, architects, and engineers, among others, can be held liable because the lawsuits can target almost everyone involved in the construction.[9] Even purchasers and repurchasers of properties sold and resold are potentially liable for many years to come.

Because of the required disclosures pertaining to publicly traded companies, ample information is available on the executives, officers and directors of those companies. Sharp declines in the price of a stock could trigger an innovative lawyer to organize a class action lawsuit on behalf of current or former shareholders for presumably failing to disclose certain material information. Whether the defendants chose to fight the lawsuit or settle it, the cost of litigation, the drain on time and resources could be substantial.[10]

The scope of those who might be the subject of lawsuits is unlimited—just about anyone with assets (personal, business or covered by insurance), whether directly or indirectly-related to an alleged grievance or incident. Protecting assets is critical for people of wealth who face liability threats from many sources—what they own, their occupation, their business or investment activities, philanthropic involvement or hobbies. Rising malpractice insurance rates are believed to be a key reason why some doctors have dropped coverage altogether and have opted instead to use alternative asset protection tools. A 2005 survey conducted by Prince and Associates of affluent investors (with investable assets of $0.5 to $5 million) found that 47.3 percent of respondents were concerned about being sued, while a mere 12.9 percent of these affluent investors had a formal asset protection plan.[11]

The Fundamental Elements of an Asset Protection Plan

There is no one strategy or structure that should be employed to protect your assets, whether personal or business, Your best plan, working with expert tax and legal advisors, is to use a combination of multiple strategies and structures. Asset protection is a complex field that entails awareness, timing, deterrence, repositioning of assets, the use of federal and state laws, international jurisdictions, and the structuring and creation of mechanisms intended to put significant barriers between your assets and potential creditors. Asset protection "*is* about arranging assets in such a way that they are less vulnerable to claims of *future* creditors."[12]

There are 12 fundamental elements of asset protection plans:

1. Awareness
2. Deterrence
3. Timing
4. Gifting
5. Asset titling
6. Use of existing federal and state laws
7. Use of insurance
8. Converting nonexempt assets to exempt assets
9. Use of trusts
10. Use of business structures
11. Use of nonqualified assets first
12. Seeking expert advice

The complexity of the issue of asset protection should not be underestimated. This chapter seeks to cover some of the basic concepts and strategies in a general way and should not be considered or relied upon as legal advice. It is intended to raise your awareness and educate you in a general way.

Awareness

You need to be aware that asset protection is a critical aspect of your overall wealth management plan. Living in a highly litigious society as we do, we need to take action, sometimes simple and other times complicated, in order to protect those assets. If you are a professional, particularly if you are a physician or a lawyer, you are the frequent target of lawsuits because of the nature of your profession, but also because you are perceived as someone with deep pockets. If you are even moderately wealthy, you need to devise an asset protection plan also, because you are perceived as someone, if sued, who would be either insured or have the assets to pay for a judgment against you.

Deterrence

You are more likely to succeed in discouraging lawsuits against you by holding your assets in a protected manner, without disclosing to the public what you own and how much you have and by holding as many assets as possible in the exempted category. The exempted category includes those vehicles such as retirement plans, insurance policies, your home, and annuities that are provided different levels of protection by federal and state laws. Being aware of the dangers and damage of lawsuits, frivolous or not, and taking preemptive action to protect your assets is your first line of defense.

Asset protection entails comprehensive planning, which will be outlined in this chapter, but also includes avoiding certain situations. The Asset Protection Law Center advises that you "should never enter into a [general] business partnership with anyone."[13] As a co-general partner, you are responsible for all partnership debts and any negligent acts of your partners, even though these potential liabilities that are not your fault.

The Asset Protection Law Center also advises that even though much protection can be accomplished with the set-up of a corporation, much of this protection will be lost if you give a personal guarantee of a corporate obligation.[14] If you sign a personal guarantee, "you are placing all of your assets at the mercy of a particular business deal and you are undertaking a risk with odds much worse than those offered in most gambling casinos."[15]

Timing

An important asset protection tool entails transferring assets to your spouse, child, or a trust for the benefit of these individuals to protect those assets from creditors' claims. However, the timing of the transfers is crucial. The Uniform Fraudulent Conveyances Act, which most states have adopted, states that "if a transfer is made with actual intent to hinder, delay, or defraud any creditor of the debtor, it is fraudulent as to a creditor whose claim arose before or after the transfer date."[16] Also, if the transfer renders you unable to meet your expected debts or obligations or is for less than fair value, it is deemed fraudulent, irrespective of your intent. Like purchasing homeowners insurance, the time to implement asset protection strategies is when there is no threat and it is initiated on a preemptive basis and, ideally, as an integral part of your estate planning and asset protection process. The time to plan and implement your asset protection strategies is well before the emergence of any threats. Simply put, "think of asset protection planning as a vaccine, not a cure."[17]

Gifting

Gifting is the easiest basic strategy to protect your assets. You cannot be sued for what is no longer yours. Gifting can be made to a spouse, children, family members, friends, and charities. Currently, you may gift on an annual basis, up to $13,000 (2009), to an unlimited number of recipients without those funds being subject to a gift tax. In addition, you may gift during your lifetime a total of $1 million, the gift tax exclusion, without being liable for a gift tax. These limits are doubled for a husband and a wife. There is no limit to the amount of a gift that you can provide to someone else for medical and educational reasons, provided those expenses are paid directly to the health provider and the educational institution. Gifts made to a spouse are eligible for an unlimited marital tax deduction and have no gift tax consequence.

The downside of giving away your money is that you lose control and enjoyment of those assets. If you ever exhaust your remaining funds and need those funds in the future, they are no longer yours and you most likely will not have access to them. If you transfer your assets to your spouse's sole name and then there is a divorce, you are out of luck. When giving to your children, be aware that those assets could pass on to your child's ex-spouse in the event of a divorce or, if your adult child is sued, then those assets could be subject to his creditor's claims. But keep in mind that there are ways to avoid even these results by making gifts through a trust.

Gifting assets is an important asset protection strategy. It allows you to help others, reduce the size of your estate, and protect those assets from future creditors. Effective gifts are irrevocable. If you retain too much use or control of the gifted asset, then it is an uncompleted gift, and those assets could be subject to your creditors' claims.

Use of Existing Federal and State Laws

Federal and state laws protect different types of assets from creditors. In general, federal law shields certain retirement plans under its ERISA (Employee

Retirement Income Security Act) rules. Therefore, consider maximizing your contribution to your qualified retirement plans. They enjoy optimum creditor protection under federal law. In addition, state laws shield certain assets from creditors known as *exempt assets,* as they are exempt from seizure in a lawsuit or in bankruptcy. The most common exempt assets are a home, individual retirement accounts, life insurance, and annuities. These assets may be wholly shielded or shielded up to a specified dollar limit. These limits will vary from state to state. In most states, federal bankruptcy laws will look to the state exemption limits for bankruptcy purposes.

In those states that do not look to the state exemption limits, federal law definitions will apply. In these states, the Bankruptcy Abuse Prevention and Consumer Protection Act of 2005 explicitly extended bankruptcy protection to retirement savings held in IRAs. Prior to a U.S. Supreme Court decision in April 2005, retirement assets enjoyed varying levels of creditor protection. Creditor protection for IRAs was covered by state law. The Supreme Court in 2005 added IRAs to the list of federally protected retirement assets. Even though the new bankruptcy act capped the IRA exemption at $1 million, there is no exemption limit on amounts rolled over to IRAs from other qualified plans, including 401(k)s, potentially lifting the limits on the size of a combined IRA and those funds rolled over into the IRA.[18] Funds held in SEP IRAs and SIMPLE IRAs also gained unlimited protection from creditors under the legislation and are not counted toward the $1 million IRA limit.[19]

As already noted, assets that enjoy creditor protection under state law include the primary residence, or what is known as the **homestead exemption**.[20] Some jurisdictions, such as Florida and Texas, provide unlimited homestead exemption, while others, such as Delaware, Washington, D.C., New Jersey, and Pennsylvania provide no specific homestead exemption.[21] Wages, personal property, annuities, and insurance (life, disability, illness, or unemployment benefits) are also considered exempted assets in varying amounts from state to state.

Asset Titling

The way you title your assets could determine the level of asset protection those assets may enjoy from creditors. The titling of assets is a function controlled by state laws. If you are highly exposed to potential liability because of your profession, the nature of your business, your holdings, and your public exposure, some of the options that you have to protect your assets include the following:

- *Partitioning the community assets into separate properties and then titling them separately between you and your spouse.* You solely own the cars, and she solely owns the home equity. Once assets are segregated, "follow proper procedures to avoid commingling of assets," advises Ann Couch, a prominent Arizona CPA.[22] Separate assets are no longer shielded if commingled.

■ *Giving up your share for the benefit of your spouse through a title change.* This works even if you live in a community property state. One spouse owns solely the house, the vacation home, the cars, and so on. The primary danger of transferring assets to your spouse is in the event of a divorce, at least for the nonowner spouse! Accordingly, this type of planning presumes an ironclad marriage.

■ *Titling your assets as "tenancy by the entirety."* Under some circumstances, assets can be protected without having to give up all ownership interest. **Tenancy by the entirety** is an example. It is a form of ownership, recognized in some states, and is permitted only between a husband and a wife. It has survivorship rights that generally cannot be terminated without the consent of both parties. If either one of you is sued, this type of ownership protects your property from your separate creditors. However, tenancy by the entirety does not protect you in the event both of you are sued. Further, tenancy by the entirety is not automatic. You have to file to have your home or other assets titled this way. Moreover, with respect to assets held as tenant by the entirety *other than real estate,* the courts are divided as to whether a creditor of one spouse could seize all or portion of the asset to satisfy a creditor's claim.[23]

■ *Using "tenants in common."* This is form of property ownership in which two or more persons own an undivided interest. Interests need not be equal for **tenants in common,** and, upon death, each tenant's property interest passes to their estate not to the other tenants. Because the portion of the asset owned is not specifically identified and a creditor would have to petition the court to have the asset partitioned, it offers limited asset protection.[24]

■ *Avoiding "joint tenants with rights of survivorship (JTWROS)."* This type of ownership should not be confused with tenancy by the entirety. JTWROS is also a form of property ownership in which two or more individuals hold an undivided interest in property and upon the death of one, full title of the property passes to the survivor by operation of the law. The crucial difference is that tenancy by entirety cannot be terminated without the consent of both parties, and it is a form of joint ownership allowed only between a husband and a wife. Although JTWROS is a convenient and frequently used form of ownership, it is risky because it exposes the jointly owned asset to the creditors of both sides. Many lawyers advise parents to never title assets as **joint tenants with rights of survivorship** with their children.[25] If your child is involved in an auto accident and the child is sued, creditors can seek your jointly held JTWROS property to satisfy the judgment.

Use of Insurance

When you think of asset protection, it is not uncommon to immediately think of insurance. You buy a home insurance policy to protect your house against loss in the event of fire, flood, or hurricane.[26] You buy auto insurance to minimize your losses in the event of an auto accident. Usually, your car, the damage to other vehicles or properties, the medical care of those injured, and a death benefit if there is a fatality are all covered. Your coverage is determined by many factors, most importantly, the terms of your auto policy, whether you are at fault or not, and the monetary limits that you have purchased. Excess liability insurance, often called the umbrella policy, provides additional liability coverage beyond that of the home and auto insurance.

If you are a professional, you should purchase professional liability insurance. Depending on your occupation, you may have medical or legal practice insurance. If you own a business, you should have premises liability insurance and, if your business makes a product (toy, auto, or parts), then you should have product liability insurance. It will protect you from claims when a product you sell malfunctions and causes bodily injury and damages.

Purchasing property and casualty insurance is one of the most basic tools of protecting your assets. The most common types of property and casualty insurance are automobile, homeowners and renters, umbrella liability, professional liability, medical malpractice, general liability, flood, earthquake, premises liability, errors and omissions, products liability. Property and casualty insurance is designed to "indemnify," "make whole," restore, and put you back in the same financial position that you were before the loss (minus any deductibles or copayments). Property and casualty insurance also covers your legal bills, which is important, because these may be significant if you are sued.[27]

By comparison, the other major category of insurance protection is life and health. This category includes all life and health insurance as well as long-term-care and disability insurance. Disability insurance provides you with income in the event you are unable to work, while life insurance provides a death benefit to your heirs in the event of your death.[28]

Within the context of an asset protection strategy, one that is intended to help protect you from potential lawsuits and bankruptcies, life insurance and annuities are central. Permanent life insurance policies, those with cash value, are not limited in size. Conceivably, you may have a permanent life insurance policy with hundreds of thousands, if not millions of dollars, in it. The growth in the cash value of these types of policies enjoys income-tax deferral under the law. Withdrawals and policy loans can be taken against the cash account tax free as well. Thus, with permanent life insurance policies, you enjoy a measure of asset protection, tax-deferred growth, and possible tax-free withdrawals.

Unlike the protection accorded to your primary residence, protection of life insurance assets varies between states. Consult your state's exemptions to determine how well you are safeguarded by logging on to www.assetprotectionbook.com/state_resources.htm. In general:

- Some states shield the entire life insurance proceeds from the creditors of the policyholder. Most protect against creditors at the time of death.
- Other states protect a set amount of the proceeds.
- Some states protect the policy proceeds only if the beneficiaries are the policyholder's spouse and dependents.
- Most states exempt term and group life insurance policies.
- Some states protect a policy's cash surrender value, as well as the policy proceeds. This creates an ideal asset protection strategy.
- No state protects your life insurance from the IRS. If you owe the IRS money, the cash value in your policy, as well as the proceeds can be accessed by the IRS if you owe them money. [29]

If, however, you set up an irrevocable life insurance trust (ILIT), the cash value and the policy proceeds are fully protected from lawsuits and claims.[30] The reason behind this tight protection is the placement of the life insurance policy in an irrevocable trust for the benefit of others. You may not revoke this gift and you completely give up benefit or access to the life insurance policy. This strategy has another tremendous added benefit. The cash value and the proceeds of the life insurance policy, since they no longer belong to you, are taken out of your estate for federal tax purposes, but yet may remain available as a source of payment for the estate taxes payable on other estate assets.

Annuities, whether variable or life annuities, are an ideal tool to safeguard wealth, especially in those states that protect annuities from creditor claims. As of May 2007, only two states—Arkansas and New Hampshire along with the U.S. Virgin Islands—have not passed legislation providing lawsuit protection to permanent life insurance policies or annuities.[31] Among those states, there are exclusions depending on the state. Some states, for example, do not protect those assets when a person declares bankruptcy or when the insurance assets are pledged as collateral for a loan.

Kenneth Lay, the former chairman of Enron, and his wife purchased a $4 million variable annuity two years before Enron filed for Chapter 11 bankruptcy protection. Starting in 2007, the annuity was slated to provide the couple with an annual income of about $900,000. Texas law, where the Lays lived, provides the maximum degree of protection to investments in variable annuities, leaving them virtually untouchable by creditors. Texas law stipulates that unless fraudulent intent could be proven, that annuity contracts "are fully exempt from creditors and from all demands in any bankruptcy and from execution, attachment, garnishment, or other legal process unless a statutory exemption, such as fraud, is applicable."[32] According to estate planning lawyer, John C. Vryhof, it is possible that Mr. Lay might not have been a creditor to the IRS. State laws that protect either life insurance policies or annuities from lawsuits and creditors are trumped when it comes to funds owed by the IRS.[33]

The protection that insurance provides in general is extremely valuable. The case is made stronger when considering as well the asset protection benefits that life insurance policies and annuities may offer. As much as insurance can provide protection, it is a magnet for litigation because insurance companies are then perceived as deep-pocketed targets.

Converting Nonexempt Assets to Exempt Assets

Exempt assets are those that provide a measure of protection against lawsuits, bankruptcies, or creditor's claims. These include retirement plans, life insurance policies, and annuities. One strategy in helping to increase asset protection is to convert, whenever possible, nonexempt assets to exempt assets. Real estate and business assets can be converted into exempt assets through the use of a debt shield.[34]

In New York, while there is no exemption for real estate holdings, including the vast majority of the equity in your home, state laws provide unlimited exemption for permanent or cash life insurance policies. A New York resident who owns a debt-free million-dollar rental property is able to take a loan on this property for about 80 percent of its value and purchase with the proceeds a permanent life insurance policy. By using this strategy, the New York resident was able to shield $800,000 of an exposed or nonexempt asset by converting it into an exempted asset—the permanent life insurance policy.

Another variation of this strategy is to maintain a home mortgage on your home, especially a line of credit, even if you do not need to tap into it right away or at all. A line of credit will show up on public real estate records, which could discourage someone from suing you. You will have a lien against your property, yet potential litigants will not know how much debt you have incurred.[35]

Use of Trusts

Not too long ago, trusts were used primarily by the wealthiest to maintain privacy, reduce estate taxes, and pass on wealth to succeeding generations. Today, the average family—one with equity in the home, some savings, life insurance policies, and retirement—are using trusts as a critical ingredient in their asset protection and estate plans.

A trust is a written agreement between the person creating the trust, the settlor or grantor, and the trustee. A trust can have one or more trustees, and the main responsibility of a trustee is to administer and carry out the terms of the trust. The trust agreement provides that the person creating the trust, the grantor or settlor, will transfer certain assets to the trustee and the trustee will hold those assets for the benefit of the named beneficiaries.

Trusts are "extremely flexible in form and almost any asset protection and estate planning goal can be accomplished by an attorney who is knowledgeable and experienced in this field."[36] Properly designed trusts are critical planning instruments that can enhance your asset protection strategy, reduce your estate taxes, improve your estate planning, and maintain your privacy. The following is a summary of the most commonly used trusts.

LIMITED TERM TRUST   A **limited term trust** is a trust designed to last for a specified number of years at the end of which the trust assets are returned to the grantor. If you are an individual who is a likely target of being sued, such as a physician or a lawyer, it makes sense to use this trust if the assets in question are not needed for the specified term of the trust, for example, 10 or 20 years. In this situation, you can fund the limited term trust with $1 million, with the provision that the income and principal may be used to pay for the support and education of your children presumably until they complete their education. At the end of that period, the funds in the trust are returned to you, and you may use these assets for retirement or other purposes. This trust arrangement provides asset protection for those funds while you are still practicing medicine and are a target of potential lawsuits.

ESTATE FREEZE TRUST   Investments or assets that are likely to appreciate in value over time, such as real estate, stocks, or ownership in a new business venture, may be moved into an **estate freeze trust**. You and your spouse may gift up to the equivalent of $1 million each to this trust, the lifetime gift tax exclusion, and thus avoid paying gift taxes. If the value of the assets within that trust grows to $7 million by 2009, your beneficiaries will also avoid future estate taxes on the $5 million in appreciation. In this manner, your entire gift of $2 million and its subsequent growth are shielded from any potential claim or lawsuit and the entire value of the assets is thus removed from your estate and is no longer subject to future estate taxes.

PRIVACY TRUST   If one of your concerns is the privacy of your holdings and the avoidance of being a target to lawsuits because you are perceived as a deep-pocketed target, you might consider creating a privacy trust. The privacy trust successfully conceals ownership of your assets—bank accounts, real estate holdings, rental properties, brokerage accounts and interests in other entities. The **privacy trust** acts as an intermediary to remove the connection between you and your assets. "Neither your name, nor Social

Security number, nor any personal identifying information appears in any records"[37] related to your assets. You may include in the privacy trust a corporation, a family limited partnership, or a limited liability company that you might have established for asset protection or estate planning purposes. Thus, the combination of these tools is ideal in providing you with privacy as well as asset protection and estate planning benefits.[38]

IRREVOCABLE LIFE INSURANCE TRUST   An **irrevocable life insurance trust (ILIT)** is one of the commonly utilized strategies for estate planning and asset protection. When you hold existing life insurance policies in an ILIT, the ownership of the policies is transferred to this irrevocable trust, thus providing the cash in the policies and the proceeds to the beneficiaries with asset protection and, at the same time, removing the cash and the proceeds from your estate. Life insurance is commonly used in estate planning to provide adequate living expenses to your family upon your death—cash to meet business liquidity needs and necessary liquidity to pay estate taxes, usually at a fraction of the cost of premiums to purchase the life policy.[39]

QUALIFIED PERSONAL RESIDENCE TRUST   If you are like most Americans, your largest source of savings may be the equity in your home. The most popular strategy to protect your home from lawsuits and claims, especially if you live in a state where only a limited amount of your home equity is protected, is to set up the **qualified personal residence trust (QPRT)** for a term of years.

The QPRT is specifically permitted under the Internal Revenue Code.[40] It allows you to grant your residence to the trust while you or both you and your spouse can be the trustees of the trust. You will then have the full power to buy, sell, or refinance your property. The interest deduction is reported directly on your tax return, and all the advantages of home ownership are preserved. At the end of the term of years, the ownership of the house will transfer to other family members, but if the QPRT is properly drafted, you will continue to live in the home.

Be careful not to place your home in a family limited partnership (FLP) or a limited liability corporation (LLC), because you will then jeopardize the important tax advantages of mortgage interest rate deduction and the ability to avoid up to $500,000 of gain on the sale.

REVOCABLE LIVING TRUST   Although this is probably the most used trust, the **revocable living trust** functions well in helping you avoid probate fees and delays. Trust assets pass directly to designated family members and, in this regard, it is an important basic estate planning tool. However, a revocable living trust offers *no asset protection* to the creator of the trust, since the grantor still maintains control over the assets and can be required to use those assets to creditors and lawsuit judgments.[41] If the grantor's creditors want to seize assets owned by a revocable trust, all they need to do is petition the court to "step into the shoes" of the grantor and revoke the trust themselves. At that point, trust assets will no longer by owned by the trust but by the grantor, or you, personally. The creditors will then be able to seize your assets now that you are the owner.[42] Despite this weakness, the living trust is still commonly used in asset protection strategies if the living trust owns a family limited partnership interest and limited liability membership interests or similar vehicles that provide themselves the asset protection.[43]

SPENDTHRIFT TRUST   You can protect assets from your heirs' creditors by placing them in a **spendthrift trust**. Such a trust is created by inserting a clause that prohibits beneficiaries from selling or assigning their interests, either voluntarily or involuntarily. Also, if you are concerned that your successors will be wasteful and will blow their inheritance, you have a valid concern.

Experts believe that 70 percent of all inheritances are frittered away in the first three years.[44] A spendthrift trust allows the trustee to withhold income and principal otherwise payable to the beneficiary, if the trustee believes that the money would be wasted or might be seized by the beneficiary's creditors. The spendthrift trust or clause protects trust assets from lawsuits, debt problems, divorce, a failing business because the spendthrift trust grants the trustee the authority to withhold payments to a beneficiary who has an outstanding creditor.

Because trusts are governed by state law, the amount of protection depends on the state law regarding the spendthrift provision. As a general rule, "assets in the trust but not income from a trust are protected from the creditors of beneficiaries."[45] However, other than in jurisdictions that have special legislation, a spendthrift trust will not avoid claims from *your* creditors unless you give up any interest in the trust assets.[46]

OFFSHORE ASSET PROTECTION TRUSTS   If your estate is sizable and you are willing to incur significant fees, and are comfortable with setting up your trust in a different state or even another country, you may benefit from the superior asset protection trusts that are offered in a number of jurisdictions. Most states do not provide any protection for "domestic asset protection trusts," and it would be necessary to establish such a trust only in a jurisdiction which has authorizing legislation. In the United States, Delaware, Alaska, and South Dakota are among the most commonly used jurisdictions. As an alternative, **offshore asset protection trusts** "afford protection that can be reasonably ensured."[47] These trusts are attractive for seven reasons:[48]

1. Offshore asset protection trusts are difficult to discover, partly because of the secrecy rules of some of these countries and partly because the information on these trusts are not as readily available as information on domestic U.S. trusts.

2. These offshore countries' are distant from the United States and their very foreignness—location, currency, language, customs, laws, and court systems—is a barrier to attack. A creditor would need to spend the time and money and be willing to go to the extent of tackling a claim in a foreign jurisdiction.

3. You must hire a local attorney who, in most countries and unlike the United States, would not be allowed to work on a contingency basis. In fact, the defendant's legal fees may have to be paid by a losing plaintiff.

4. A forfeitable bond must be posted to cover legal fees for both plaintiff and defendant.

5. The grantor may be a beneficiary, albeit discretionary, and still be protected against creditor attack.

6. If you are interested in establishing a true dynasty trust that spans over unlimited generations into the future, an offshore asset protection trust will allow you to do so.

7. The assets of the trust need not be relocated to the foreign country, and the trust assets are not limited to U.S. government-approved securities.

Other features of these offshore trusts include a higher burden of proof that a transaction was fraudulent; judgments obtained in the United States are not recognized by the foreign country; and there is a shorter statue of limitations, usually up to two years. This means that after that two-year period, no creditors may attach the trust on fraudulent transfer grounds.

These trusts, however, do not avoid U.S. income or estate taxation. They are usually designed as a foreign trust for asset protection and as a domestic trust for tax purposes. Unless you are ultra wealthy and highly exposed to lawsuits, these trusts could be expensive and may not warrant the added expense to set up and maintain. One estimate puts the cost of setting up a foreign trust at $20,000 to $50,000, with an additional $3,000 to $10,000 for annual administrative expenses.[49] Some individuals justify the cost of setting up an offshore asset protection trust as an alternative to liability insurance.

There are an estimated 60 offshore financial centers worldwide, such as in Bermuda, Cayman Islands, and Cook Islands. Each offers different benefits. Therefore, it is not unusual to devise an asset protection strategy that uses multiple jurisdictions.

Given all the attributes of setting up an Offshore Asset Protection Trust, it can be an important component of a complete estate and asset protection plan for the ultra wealthy, sophisticated, and highly targeted individual.

Use of Business Structures

If you are a business owner, the legal entity you select to conduct your business could have serious consequences on the extent to which you are able to shield your personal assets from your business liabilities. Additionally, your legal entity structure could provide you with varying levels of asset protection and estate tax savings.[50]

If you are a **sole proprietor** or a **partner**, you are fully exposed and personally liable for all the obligations of your business. If you are incorporated as **"C" corporation**, you are generally fully protected from business liabilities. However, you are taxed twice on your income—your corporation is taxed on its revenues, and you are then taxed on your income from the corporation. Creditors may still go after your equity stock in the corporation. The use of a corporation does not absolve you from professional liability due to your errors and omissions or those of the employees under your direct supervision.

A **limited liability company (LLC)** and a **family limited partnership (FLP)** are "solid asset protectors because the law gives a very specific and limited remedy to creditors coming after assets in either entity."[51] The structures have differences and similarities. In terms of the differences, only the LLC can be used for a single owner, while a limited partnership must have at least two owners.[52] Additionally, while a general partner in an FLP has personal liability for the acts and debts of the FLP, a managing member of the LLC has no such liability.

The similarities between an LLC and an FLP are noteworthy:[53]

- They are both legal entities governed by state law.
- They each have two levels of ownership—active and passive. The active owners (known as managing members in the case of the LLC and general partners in the case of the FLP) have 100 percent control of the entity and its assets. The passive owners (known as members in the case of the LLC and limited partners in the case of the FLP) have little control of the entity and only limited rights, but they do share in the profits.
- Both enjoy "pass through" taxation, a tremendous advantage over a "C" corporation, which gets taxed twice. Neither the LLC nor the FLP is liable for income taxes. The tax liability for the income and capital gains passes through to the owners (partners or members).
- The cost of setting up either entity by an experienced attorney is fairly inexpensive and straightforward.
- Both provide the limited partner (FLP) and the member (LLC) with protection from creditors.

When a creditor pursues you and your assets, which are owned by the LLC/FLP, the creditor cannot seize the assets in the LLC/FLP. It can, however, go after assets that are in your name. Because members of LLCs and limited members of FLPs do not own assets directly, a creditor must seek a "charging order" from the court to satisfy a judgment. A charging order is "a court order which instructs the FLP/LLC to pay the debtor's share of distributions to his/her creditor until the creditor's judgment is paid in full."[54] The managing member of the LLC and the general partner of the FLP are not obligated to make a distribution to the member or the limited partner. The real deterrence is that a charging order may backfire on creditors. Taxes on FLP/LLC income pass through to the parties who are entitled to the income. Each partner/member is responsible for his/her share of the FLP/LLC income. This income is taxable whether or not the income is actually paid. Because income tax may be due on a distribution owed even though not paid (phantom distribution), the creditor with a charging order can be liable for income taxes on a phantom distribution. A creditor will find it difficult to collect a judgment from an FLP/LLC and would rather settle out of court for much less than the creditor could receive in judgment.

Of the most commonly used business structures—the sole proprietorship, the "C" corporation, the LLC, and the FLP—the last two provide the highest level of asset protection and provide beneficial tax advantages compared to a "C" corporation. The FLP is particularly advantageous, as well as an estate planning vehicle protecting the family assets from divorces and reducing gift and estate taxes on transferred assets.

If you have more than one type of business, you should use different entities for each type of business. The objective is to insulate each separate business from the liabilities that could be generated by the other business. If you own several real estate properties, use different entities to hold each one of them. A lawsuit produced by one rental property will then not endanger your other properties. A restaurant, a business highly likely to produce a liability, should be owned by a limited liability company and not you directly. Any lawsuit against the LLC would not endanger your other personal assets or businesses.

Use of Nonqualified Assets First

If you are retired, use existing cash from your savings and funds from brokerage accounts first before you dip into your retirement funds. Your retirement accounts will grow tax deferred, allowing them to increase at a faster rate because of the tax deferral feature. Also, your retirement and IRA funds, and most of your annuities and cash value life insurance policies, are generally asset protected, depending on the state where you live.[55] Exhaust your "exposed" assets first, and then tap into your asset-protected retirement sources. This is a simple asset protection strategy that requires no paperwork or use of special legal structures.

Seeking Expert Advice

Competent wealth advisors are trained to help you identify potential areas of liability exposures; analyze your current coverage and existing gaps; and create asset protection strategies in partnership with other experts in the areas of legal, tax, and accounting. Your wealth advisor needs to work closely with a team that include lawyers who specialize in asset protection strategies and who are capable of preparing all the documents necessary for asset protection, tax efficiency, and estate planning. Tax advisors and accountants are a critical part of the wealth planning team. They are current on federal and state laws and are aware of what is and is not asset protected. Their job is to prepare your tax documents and help you take advantage of all possible tax breaks.

All of your hard work in the area of asset protection plan will be compromised if your plan is not created in advance of any claim or a threat of litigation. For best results, you must address your asset protection needs before difficulties arise.

Concluding Remarks

Asset protection planning should be an integral part of your overall wealth management plan. Shielding your assets from creditors and lawsuits is a critical step in ensuring that you have those assets when you need them. According to John C. Vryhof, a nationally prominent estate planning attorney, the goal of asset protection planning should be to provide legal structures during your lifetime and upon your death that allow you to do the following:

- Pass property to your designated beneficiaries.
- Avoid claims by any of your creditors.
- Proactively protect your beneficiaries from their future potential creditors.
- Reduce your wealth transfer taxes.
- Avoid other costs and delays.[56]

Here is an abbreviated summary of a well-thought-out asset protection plan:

1. *Be aware* that asset protection is a critical component of your overall wealth management plan.
2. *Deter* potential lawsuits and creditor claims by being proactive and holding as many of your assets in protected legal vehicles.
3. *Plan* your asset protection strategies before the emergence of any imminent or potential threat.
4. *Gift* assets that you do not need. There can be no claim against assets that are no longer yours unless, of course, they were

fraudulently conveyed in anticipation of an imminent lawsuit or bankruptcy filing.

5. *Use existing federal and state laws* that shield certain types of assets such as IRAs, retirement plans, equity in your home, cash value life insurance policies and annuities.[57]

6. *Title your assets properly* to take advantage of the protection given to some assets. If you are married, hold your assets in accounts titled "tenancy by the entirety," not "joint with rights of survivorship."

7. *Separate assets* that do not need to be in your name. Asset retitling could be a simple step in protecting your assets.

8. *Use insurance,* as it can preserve your assets and pay to repair damages to your home or vehicle in the case of a fire or an accident. In the event you are sued above and beyond what your home or auto insurance is willing to pay, an umbrella policy could pay for additional judgments against you, thus preserving your assets. Umbrella policies are frequently overlooked, even though it usually costs no more than a few hundred dollars to cover you for a million dollars' worth of coverage.

9. *Convert nonexempt assets to exempt assets* by shifting assets from holdings such as brokerage accounts that can be used to satisfy a judgment against you to holdings that cannot be touched to satisfy a judgment against you, such as annuities and cash-value life insurance policies, depending on the state where you live.

10. *Use trusts* to freeze your estate, hide the ownership of your assets, irrevocably give away some of your assets, and protect your residence. Use offshore asset-protection trusts, despite the added expense and complexity, if your holdings are large and the nature of your business attracts lawsuits.

11. *Use business structures* such as limited liability companies and family limited partnerships to limit and isolate your liabilities.

12. *Use multiple entities* to hold and separate each of your businesses or holdings. Create barriers between you and creditors and among your individual holdings.

13. *Use your exposed or nonprotected assets first.* Leave your protected IRAs and retirement plans to grow tax deferred while enjoying asset protection. Use your retirement funds as needed or required and, preferably, after you have exhausted your nonprotected assets.

14. *Seek expert advice.* You cannot possibly be your own lawyer, tax advisor, accountant, or wealth advisor. These professionals are trained in their field of expertise and can provide invaluable advice and services to help you protect your assets.

We live in a litigious society, whereby if an outcome is not to our liking, our instinct is to sue. The legal system has been clogged with lawsuits and frivolous claims, and judgments have been huge and, mostly, unrealistic. There is not a single asset protection plan that works for everyone, nor is there a foolproof asset protection plan. Your plan is as unique as you are. The nature and complexity of your business, the type of assets that you hold, the state in which you live, your family structure and dynamics, the type and level of insurances that you have purchased, your awareness and diligence, your willingness to listen to the advice of the experts, and how and where you hold your assets are some of the critical factors that will determine the extent to which you are able to protect your assets.

The key, however, is to begin the process well before the emergence of any potential liability and lawsuit against you. All you can hope for is that whatever asset protection plan that you have devised has placed you in a better position than you were before you embarked on implementing your asset protection plan. Here is the bottom line. The system is broken. If you do not take the initiative to protect what you have worked so hard to build, your ability to preserve and grow your future wealth is in serious jeopardy.

CHAPTER 9

Taxes and Tax-Saving Strategies

Y ou often hear, mostly with disdain and quiet resignation, that "two things are certain in life—death and taxes."[1] In 2007, Tax Freedom Day fell on April 30th. That is the day when Americans began to work to support their personal needs, after working for 120 days (up from 112 days in 1982) to pay for government services through taxes. The cost of paying taxes for the average American is currently higher than the cost of paying for food, clothing, and housing combined. According to the Tax Foundation, taxes amounted to 32.7 percent of Americans' income in 2007.[2]

Admittedly, taxes are probably the most unpleasant aspect of personal finance. Nevertheless, every major business and investment decision you contemplate should be taken with an eye on how it will affect your taxes. Keep in mind that a dollar saved on taxes is worth much more than a dollar saved on expenses. Thus, it is important to explore whether a particular business decision, a course of action, or a financial step can help you reduce your tax liability.

Just because you do not like taxes does not mean that you can evade paying them. It is the law, and the consequences of tax evasion are serious. Fortunately, tax laws provide you with tools such as deductions, credits, transfers, and planning and investment vehicles that, if properly utilized, can help you minimize your tax liability. This chapter will cover a brief history of taxation, survey the most common types of taxes, and, from a wealth management perspective, explore the basic tax-saving strategies that can be implemented to help you reduce your tax obligations.

History of Taxation

It is believed that the first known system of taxation existed in Ancient Egypt around 3000 BC to 2800 BC. The pharaoh would conduct a biennial tour of the kingdom, collecting tax revenues from the people. The Bible refers to this tax collection system in Genesis, Chapter 47, verse 24, where it states, "But when the crop comes in, give a fifth of it to Pharaoh." Tax collection in Europe is well documented, especially going back to the seventeenth century. Taxation in Europe was usually calculated as a percentage of production, usually 15 to 20 percent, of final goods.[3]

In modern world history, raising money to finance wars played a critical role in the evolution and permanent introduction of taxation. During the war-filled years of the eighteenth and nineteenth centuries, tax rates in Europe increased significantly as wars became more sophisticated and expensive and as governments adapted, improved and centralized their tax-gathering systems.[4]

In this country, and before the Revolutionary War, the colonial government had a limited need for revenue, while each of the colonies had greater responsibilities and thus needs. These needs were met with different types of taxes. The southern colonies primarily taxed imports and exports, while the New England colonies raised revenue primarily through real estate and excise taxes, as well as taxes based on occupation.[5] In 1765, the English Parliament passed the Stamp Act, the first tax imposed directly on the American colonies, to help pay for its wars against France. The American colonies, which were not represented in the English Parliament, rebelled. Taxes, especially the tea tax, ignited the rallying cry behind the American Revolution that "taxation without representation is tyranny."[6]

In 1789, the federal government was granted the authority to raise taxes. The Constitution endowed Congress with the power to "...lay and collect taxes... and provide for the common Defense and general Welfare of the United States."[7] To pay the debts of the Revolutionary War, Congress levied excise taxes on a number of products such as distilled spirits, tobacco, carriages, and property sold at auctions. During the conflict with France in the 1790s, the federal government imposed the first direct taxes on the owners of houses, land, slaves, and estates. These were considered direct taxes because they were a recurring tax directly paid by the taxpayer to the government based on the value of the item in question. To raise money for yet another war, the War of 1812, Congress imposed additional excise taxes and raised money by issuing Treasury notes. When the Civil War erupted, Congress passed the Revenue Act of 1861 and imposed a tax on personal incomes. The 1862 tax law mandated that taxes be "withheld at the source" by employers. This was done to assure timely collection of taxes and this mechanism is still in force to this day. Between 1868 and 1913, almost 90 percent of the federal revenue was collected from liquor and tobacco revenues. In fact, there was no more need for the income tax and it was abolished in 1872.[8]

The Sixteenth Amendment to the Constitution allowed the federal government to impose tax on individuals' lawful incomes without regard to the population of each state. In 1916, Congress deleted the word "lawful" from the definition of income. Thus, all income became subject to tax, even if it was earned by illegal means. Consequently, many who broke various laws associated with illegal activities and escaped justice for these crimes were later tried on tax evasion charges. The reintroduction of the income tax fundamentally "gave the government the right and the need to know"[9] about all matters of an individual or business economic life. In 1916, Congress recognized the invasiveness of the income tax into the taxpayer's personal affairs and required that information from tax returns be kept confidential.

The entry of the United States into World War I increased the need for revenue, and Congress responded by passing the 1916 Revenue Act. Then after the stock market crash in 1929 and the resulting significant drop in revenue, Congress passed the Tax Act of 1932, which dramatically increased tax rates. The eruption of World War II led to the passage in 1940 of two tax laws that increased individual and corporate taxes. The Korean War then led to the need for additional revenues. In 1953, the Bureau of Internal Revenue was renamed the Internal Revenue Service (IRS) to stress the service aspect of its work. By 1959, the IRS "had become the world's largest accounting, collection, and forms-processing organization."[10]

The Economic Recovery Tax Act of 1981 represented a fundamental shift in the course of federal income tax policy. It featured a 25 percent reduction in individual tax brackets, phased in over three years, and indexed for inflation thereafter. It accelerated the tax depreciation of business outlays for plant and equipment and introduced a 10 percent investment tax credit to stimulate additional capital expenditure. The Tax Reform Act of 1986 brought the top tax rate down from 50 percent to 28 percent, while the corporate tax rated was reduced from 50 percent to 35 percent. In 1990, Congress enacted a significant tax increase, highlighting an increase in the top tax rate to 31 percent. Then, in 1993, Congress enacted a second major tax increase in which the top tax rate was raised to 36 percent, in addition to a 10 percent surcharge. In 1996, an important tax shift occurred on the individual side in the form of the creation of tax vehicles to promote purpose-specific savings such as the Medical Savings Account, the education IRA, 529 College Savings plans, and the Roth IRA. The Taxpayer Relief Act of 1997 made some changes to the tax code and provided a modest tax cut. The centerpiece of this Act, however, was a new benefit to certain families with children through the per-child tax credit.

The Economic Growth and Tax Relief and Reconciliation Act of 2001 lowered marginal tax rates, increased the per-child tax credit but, more importantly, it put the estate, gift, and generation-skipping taxes on course for eventual repeal. This Act has had a fundamental and radical effect on wealth planning, but it remains to be seen whether those changes will become permanent, as they include a sunset provision; it expires in 2011 unless Congress acts prior to that deadline.

In short, federal, state, and local tax systems in the United States have undergone significant changes over the years in response to changing conditions and changes in the role of government. The types of taxes collected, their relative proportions, and the size of the revenues are all different now than they were a few decades ago. Some changes were events-driven, such as wars; others were legislative, giving the power to Congress to levy taxes, while other changes were more gradual, responding to developments in society, the economy, and in the new definition of the roles and responsibilities that government has assumed for itself.

Taxation and Tax Types

A **tax** is a financial charge, a bill, imposed on an individual or a legal entity by a state or its equivalent (such as a revolutionary movement) claiming to have the right to collect taxes. A tax is therefore "not a voluntary payment or donation, but an enforced contribution, exacted pursuant to legislative authority."[11] Wealth transfer taxes, for example, are imposed on the "privilege" of being able to "transfer" property.[12] In modern taxation systems, taxes are levied in money. Tax collection is performed by a government agency such as the Internal Revenue Service (IRS) in the United States. When taxes are not fully paid, civil (such as fines or forfeiture) or criminal (such as imprisonment) penalties may be imposed on the nonpaying individual or entity.

Why Pay Taxes

In the first 182 years of the history of the United States (1789–1970) where financial records were maintained, the United State spent $2.8 trillion altogether. Ironically, $2.8 trillion is also the estimated total government expenses for the 2007 fiscal year alone.[13] Taxes are imposed for a variety of reasons. The main reasons for taxation are:

- Revenue generation
- Redistribution of wealth
- Repricing of assets
- Representation in a political system[14]

The main purpose of taxes is to raise money to pay for economic infrastructure (roads, schools, and hospitals), public works, and the operation of government itself. Governments use taxes to fund welfare, public services, education and health care systems, pensions for the elderly, unemployment benefits, and public transportation. Funds are also used to support internal order and defend from external threats. Taxes also pay for other indirect government functions, such as enforcing the law and maintaining a justice system.

The second reason to pay or raise taxes is redistribution or the transfer of wealth from the rich to the poor in a society. This is an acceptable yet a controversial function in democracies. The third reason to pay taxes is to reprice certain assets. Tobacco, for example, is heavily taxed to discourage smoking. Finally, tax payment is the price you have to pay for the right of representation in the decision-making process. The American Revolution espoused the principle of "no taxation without representation." In democracies, people elect those in charge of establishing the tax system, and the choices made reflect the type of community which the people wish to create. If citizens are to pay taxes, they expect their leaders to be accountable to them.

Tax Rates—Proportional, Progressive, and Regressive

Taxes are most often levied as a percentage of either income or consumption, and that percentage is called the **tax rate**. Governments use different kinds of taxes and different tax rates. This is done to primarily distribute the tax burden among individuals and other taxed entities such as businesses. A **progressive tax rate** describes the way the rate progresses from low to high. It takes a larger percentage of income from high-income groups than from low-income groups. A tax on luxury goods and the absence of taxes on basic necessities may be described as progressive because the tax burden increases on those who can afford high-end consumption and decreases for people who spend mostly on the basic necessities such as food and fuel. Conversely, a **regressive tax rate** goes from high to low and takes a larger percentage of income from low income groups than from high-income groups such as the gas tax. This is because, irrespective of income, people have to drive their cars. The expenditure on gas for a lower-income individual represents a larger portion of their income compared to those with higher incomes. In between is the **proportional tax**. It is an income tax that takes the same percentage of income from everyone regardless of how much or how little an individual earns. The United States does not use this system of taxation, primarily because it is highly debatable as to whether or not it is a fair system.[15]

Despite the government's attempts to distribute the tax burden among various segments of the population fairly and equitably, IRS data for 2005 (updated in October 2007) reveal that the top 1 percent of tax returns paid about the same amount of federal individual income tax as the bottom 95 percent of tax returns. In other words, the tax burden on Americans is top heavy, and those who earn the most ended up in 2005 paying almost 40 percent of all federal income taxes.[16]

Direct versus Indirect Taxes

A direct tax is a tax that cannot be shifted onto others. It is collected directly from the people or organizations on which it is imposed. Income and property taxes are good examples of direct taxes. By comparison, an indirect tax increases the price of a good so that consumers are actually paying the tax by paying more for the products. Fuel, liquor, and cigarette taxes are just a few examples of this type of tax. Indirect taxes are imposed on rights, privileges, and activities. Estate or gift taxes are indirect taxes, because what is taxed is the privilege of transferring property and not the property or the asset itself. The distinction between direct and indirect taxation is subtle but can be important under the law.[17]

Types of Taxes

Governments impose many types of taxes. You pay income taxes when you earn money, consumption taxes when you spend it, property taxes when you own a home or a land, and, in many cases, estate taxes when you die. In the United States, federal, state, and local governments all collect taxes. While the federal government relies primarily on income taxes, state and local governments depend on sales and property taxes as their main sources of income.[18] The number and types of taxes that exist, whether direct or indirect, is extensive. In this section we will only cover the most common types of taxes. These include the income tax, Social Security and payroll tax, property tax, capital gains and dividend tax, the kiddie tax, alternative minimum tax (AMT), property tax, retirement tax, and estate and gift tax.

INDIVIDUAL INCOME TAX An income tax is a tax imposed on the financial income of individuals, corporations, or other legal entities. Individual income taxes often tax the total income of an individual (with some deductions and credits permitted). The U.S. federal individual income tax was enacted in 1913 following the passage of the Sixteenth Amendment. Most states and a small number of local and municipal governments also collect income taxes. Income taxes today provide the largest single source of federal revenues estimated at $1 trillion in 2006.[19] Personal income tax is often collected on a pay-as-you-go basis. Small corrections are made soon after the end of the tax year. You will then pay additional taxes or collect a refund. Compared to other developed countries in the world, U.S. income taxes are some of the lowest. If you are married with two children, you can pay as much as 41.37 percent in income taxes in France, compared to only 11.9 percent in the United States.[20]

CORPORATE INCOME TAX Corporate income taxes often tax net income or the difference between gross receipts, expenses, and additional write-offs.

Like personal income tax, corporate income tax rates generally increase with income. The corporate income tax is one of the most controversial types of taxes. Many economists argue that only real people—such as shareholders who own corporations—can be a tax burden. They also point out that corporate income tax leads to double taxation of corporate income. Income is taxed once it is earned by the corporation, and a second time when it is paid to shareholders in the form of dividends. Corporate income faces a higher tax burden than income earned by individuals or by other types of businesses. This is why legislation was passed in 2003 in attempt to address this perceived unfairness by lowering the tax rate on dividends.[21]

SOCIAL SECURITY AND PAYROLL TAXES As an employer, you must withhold Social Security and Medicare taxes from your employees' wages. You are required to withhold 6.2 percent of an employee's wages for Social Security taxes and match it with another 6.2 percent until the employee reaches the wage base, which is projected to be $106,500 for 2009. The Medicare tax rate is 2.9 percent—half withheld from the employee's wages and the other half matched by the employer. Since there is no wage base for the Medicare tax, both the employer and employee continue to pay Medicare tax irrespective of how much is earned. Payroll taxes are the state and federal taxes that you, an employer, are required to withhold and/or to pay on behalf of your employees. Thus, the total Social Security and Medicare tax comes to 15.3 percent of an employee's salary, up to the annual base of $106,500—not a small percentage, considering all the other taxes that have to be paid as well. Finally, employers are also required to pay state and federal unemployment tax.[22]

PROPERTY TAX A property tax is a tax "on an individual's wealth—the value of all of the person's assets, both financial (such as stocks and bonds) and real (such as houses, cars, and artwork)."[23] A property tax is usually levied on the value of the property by reason of its ownership and, in many cases, it is a recurring tax imposed annually. For a 150-year period beginning in 1695, England imposed a tax on windows! To avoid paying this tax, people would brick up the windows on their buildings.[24] In the United States, there is no federal property tax but state and local governments are the ones who generally impose property taxes on buildings—homes, factories, office buildings—and on land. In 2000, property taxes accounted for a mere 2 percent of state tax revenues and a whopping 72 percent of local tax revenues.[25]

CAPITAL GAINS AND DIVIDEND TAX The capital gains tax is the tax on the profit generated from the sale of an asset, including stocks, bonds, mutual funds, and other capital assets that has appreciated. If you sell those assets at a lower price than what you paid, you can claim a capital loss. The amount of capital gain is calculated by subtracting your cost basis (including the transaction costs to buy and sell your asset) from the sale price. The length of time that you hold your investment determines whether your capital gain is treated as a long- or short-term gain. Since 2003, assets held for longer than 12 months generate a long-term capital gain that is taxed at a much lower rate than short-term capital gain for assets held less than 12 months. For 2007, the capital gains rate was 15 percent if your other income is in the 25 percent or higher tax bracket. It was 5 percent if your other income was in the 10 or 15 percent brackets.[26] The same rates applied to cash dividends from common stocks, nondebt preferred stocks, and qualified mutual funds. Alternatively, short-term capital gains are taxed as ordinary income. From 2008 through 2010, a 0 percent long-term capital gain tax rate potentially applies to taxpayers whose taxable income, which includes long-term capital gains, is less than $65,100 for a married couple filing jointly, and $32,550 for a single filer. After 2010, the rates revert to 10 and 20 percent (up from 15 percent), depending on your income levels.[27]

The IRS allows you to offset your capital gains with capital losses. If your losses exceed your gains, you can offset up to $3,000 of ordinary income in a year. If you have larger capital losses, you can carry over your losses and use them to offset capital gains in future years.[28]

ALTERNATIVE MINIMUM TAX (AMT)   The Alternative Minimum Tax, also known as AMT, is a flat tax of 26 percent on the first $175,000 of AMT income in 2007 and 28 percent on any balance.[29] The AMT is the outgrowth of the minimum tax created in 1969 following congressional testimony regarding 155 taxpayers with income over $200,000 who avoided paying taxes for the 1966 tax year.[30]

AMT was instituted to ensure that wealthy individuals, who could claim many itemized deductions and tax-sheltered transactions, paid at least some minimum amount of federal income tax each year. AMT disallows many exemptions and deductions allowable for regular tax purposes, such as personal exemptions, standard deductions, state and local taxes, and real estate taxes.[31] If you are subject to the AMT, you must calculate your tax liability under both the regular and the AMT method. Your tax liability is based on the higher of the two calculations. The October 2008 bail-out package that was passed by Congress and signed into law by President George W. Bush moved to shield millions of taxpayers from the alternative minimum tax in 2008. The AMT provision would ensure that as many as 25 million Americans do not see a tax increase because of the AMT in 2008.[32]

Tax laws give favored treatment to certain kinds of income and allow special deductions and credits for certain kinds of expenses. The AMT attempts to instill fairness by guaranteeing that all individuals who benefit from these tax advantages pay at least a minimum amount of tax each year. The problem with AMT is that it was not indexed to inflation. As a result, about

23 million unsuspecting middle-class taxpayers were hit with unintended higher taxes. Another 25 million taxpayers would have likely faced higher taxes in 2008 had the law pertaining to AMT was not amended in the October 2008 legislation. For years, Congress was aware of this problem, and it used to pass an annual patch in the law to extend the credits so that unintended taxpayers would not be affected by AMT. By 2007, the number of potential taxpayers who might have been unintentionally subject to AMT grew dramatically to 25 million, making a more permanent fix urgently needed.[33]

ESTATE, INHERITANCE, AND GIFT TAXES An estate tax is a tax on a deceased person's estate, which includes everything that person owned at the time of death such as money, stocks, bonds, real estate, businesses, and proceeds from life insurance policies.[34] An inheritance tax also taxes the deceased person's estate, but only after the estate passes to heirs. Estate and inheritance taxes are collectively called "death taxes."[35] A gift tax is a tax on the transfer of property between living people.

In the United States, the federal government imposes gift and estate taxes, and some states impose inheritance or estate taxes. These taxes are minor sources of revenue because the taxes apply only to very large estates and gifts. In most cases as well, property transferred to a surviving spouse is not subject to taxes. In 2002, less than 2 percent of estates were subject to the estate tax.[36] Estate, inheritance, and gift taxes are controversial. Supporters argue that these taxes are important tools to redistribute wealth in society and to prevent the rise of powerful oligarchies. Opponents respond that if an individual has paid taxes on his/her income while accumulating wealth, why should it be taxed again when the wealth is transferred?

SALES TAX Sales taxes are a form of excise imposed when an item is sold to a consumer. Since people with higher incomes spend a lower portion of their income on sales taxes, a flat sales tax is viewed as regressive. This is why it is common to exempt food, utilities, and even clothing from sales taxes. Since lower-income individuals spend a higher proportion of their income on these basic items, these exemptions would make the tax more progressive.

Some states rely entirely on sales taxes for state revenue, as they do not levy a state income tax. These states tend to have significant amount of tourism, thus allowing the state to benefit from taxing people who would otherwise not pay income taxes. Alaska, Tennessee, Florida, Nevada, South Dakota, Texas, Washington (state), and Wyoming do not impose a state income tax. New Hampshire and Tennessee levy state incomes taxes on dividends and interest income; only Alaska and New Hampshire do not impose a state sales tax.[37]

KIDDIE TAX   The **kiddie tax** refers to the manner in which unearned income is taxed for children. In 2007, the first $850 of unearned income was tax free, the second $850 was taxed at the child's marginal tax rate, and any remaining unearned income was then taxed at the parents' highest marginal tax rate. In May 2007, Congress raised the age limit for application of the kiddie tax to all children under 19 (previously age 18) and to students under age 24 and dependent on their parents, effective in 2008. It was only in 2006 that the kiddie tax age limit was raised from under age 14 to 18. There is an exception, however, to these new age limits. If the earned income of a child over 17 exceeds half her support, the kiddie tax will not apply.[38] Kiddie taxes were imposed because parents used to shift income and assets to their children in the hopes of reducing their household tax liability.

OTHER TAXES   Other existing taxes include import or export tariff (customs duty), value added tax (a tax on a product at sequential points in the production), sin tax (such as taxes on cigarettes and alcohol), excise tax (tax on commodities, facilities, or privileges), toll (a tax or fee charged to travel via a road or a bridge), and pollution tax (levied on a company that produces pollution over a certain level established by the government). There are many other taxes; a comprehensive list and description of these taxes is beyond the scope of this book.

Tax-Saving Strategies

Tax evasion is a $300-billion-a-year problem, according to the Internal Revenue Service (IRS). It is not just about greed. Some people lie because of the thrill of it, or because they think that they are too clever to be caught.[39] More men are likely to lie on their tax returns than women. However, among women, women with college degrees cheat more often than those with less education. On a per capita basis, Nevada and the District of Columbia have the largest number of tax evaders, while the residents of Vermont and South Dakota are the most honest.[40] The IRS estimates that taxpayers voluntarily pay only about 80 percent of the taxes they legally owe, and the greater the individual's tax rate, the greater is the incentive to defraud the government.[41] Please note the difference between tax evasion and tax avoidance. **Tax evasion** is failing to pay taxes that are due and is illegal. **Tax avoidance** occurs when people change their behavior to reduce the amount of taxes they legally owe such as relocating a business to a state with lower taxes. There is nothing illegal about tax avoidance.[42]

There is no question that the vast majority of people do not like to pay taxes, even though many believe that they need to, and are legally bound to do so to help support the political system and services that are provided by the government in return. If the tax bite is distasteful to you, then consider the many tax-saving strategies that exist and that are legal that you, as a tax-payer, can use to lower your tax liability. Of the 132.6 million tax returns filed in 2005 that had a positive adjusted gross income (AGI), 42 million tax returns paid no federal income tax. Using exemptions, deductions, tax credits, and selective investment vehicles and approaches, these taxpayers got back every dollar that the federal government had withheld from their paychecks during 2005, and some even received more money back from the IRS.[43]

This section will provide you with an overview of those money-saving and tax-reducing strategies. As always, please consult your CPA or tax attorney as this information is provided for educational purposes only and is no way intended as tax advice. Many of these tax-saving strategies are covered in various chapters of the book such as the chapters on estate planning, planning for a comfortable retirement, insurance, and gifting. Therefore, some of these strategies will be discussed briefly but should you need more in-depth information and analysis, please refer to other chapters in the book and, most importantly, always consult your CPA or tax attorney before making tax-related decisions.

Maximize Your Tax-Deferred Retirement

If you do not have an existing retirement plan, establish one. If you do, contribute the maximum to it. A major feature of retirement plans is tax deferral whereby money invested in a retirement plan is contributed on a pre-tax basis (thus reducing your tax liability every year you make a contribution) and grows tax deferred (as such it is not subject to annual taxes when realized growth occurs and dividend or interest is generated) until distributions are made at retirement. Over a 30-year period, the value of a tax-deferred account can grow by 75 percent or more as much as a taxable account.[44] Contributions to most retirement plans, with the notable exception of a Roth IRA, will reduce your current-year taxable income, although you still have to pay Social Security and Medicare taxes on the contributions. There are many investment vehicles available to help you save for retirement. These include traditional IRA, Roth IRA, SEP IRA, SIMPLE IRA, Keogh, 403(b) and 401(k). Which one is appropriate for you depends on a number of factors, such as whether you are a sole proprietor, a partner, or an employee, the number of participants in a plan as well as your level of income. While an IRA allows a maximum deduction of $5,000 in 2008 (plus a $1,000 catch-up provision if you are over 50), the new Roth 401(k) allows you to save $15,500 (with $5,000 catch-up contribution if you are over 50), and the SEP allows you to save 25 percent of profits, up to $46,000 (2008). Putting 25 percent of profits into a SEP is like increasing after-tax dollars by 33 percent.[45]

Harvest Tax Loss but Beware of the Wash Sale Rule

Sell investments, usually toward the end of the calendar year, to capture losses on an investment. Capital losses (whether long- or short-term) can offset capital gains (whether long- or short-term) on a dollar-for-dollar basis. For example if your captured gains for a year are $5,000 and your realized losses are $5,000, you then do not owe any capital gains taxes for that year. If your captured losses are $10,000 and your gains are only $5,000, then up to $3,000 of losses each year can reduce, dollar-for-dollar, your ordinary income. If your losses are larger, any excess losses may be carried forward until they are exhausted or until you die. To take a loss in a particular year, your transaction trade date must be no later than December 31st of the calendar year. If you plan to repurchase the same security, do so only after 31 days from your sale date. Otherwise, a **wash sale** occurs and the loss cannot be used for tax purposes. A wash sale occurs when a security is sold for a loss and the same or substantially equal security is repurchased within 30 full days before or after the sale date.

Reduce Alternative Minimum Tax (AMT) Exposure

Investors living in states with high income and property taxes are more likely to be subject to the AMT. If the AMT applies to you and you have large amounts of preference items, you can reduce the AMT by deferring preference items such as delaying the payment of state and local taxes (without making these payments overdue). Deferring local tax payments into non-AMT years can maximize the use of these deductions.[46] Also, taking a sizable long-term capital gain in a year when there is AMT exposure may not be a wise step. You should review your portfolio for tax-exempt bonds subject to AMT. AMT municipal bonds (usually federally tax-exempt) are taxable to holders who are subject to the AMT. You need to review your portfolio with an eye on the impact of investments subject to AMT.

Invest in a Roth IRA

If you qualify for a Roth IRA, take advantage of it. Your contribution is limited to a projected $5,500 in 2009 (plus $1,000 if you are age 50 or over). Since your contribution is in after-tax money, all of your withdrawals—both contributions and earnings—will grow tax-deferred and will be tax free when you retire. If you are single, and your adjusted gross income was below $116,000 in 2008 or married filing a joint return with an adjusted gross income below $169,000 you would have qualified to contribute to a Roth IRA.

Consider Converting a Traditional IRA to a Roth IRA

Currently, you can convert a traditional IRA to a Roth IRA if your income is $100,000 or less. In 2010, this income limitation is eliminated. When you convert a traditional IRA to a Roth, you will pay income tax the year you convert. However, you will gain tax-free distribution in the future. This strategy is ideal if you feel your income tax bracket today is lower than what you think it will be when you retire or if you believe that future tax rates will be higher than they are today.

Gift

Gifting is another way to help minimize your tax obligations. The idea is to give away assets now and, as a result, save on inheritance taxes later. Refer to the chapter on gifting for an extensive discussion on this topic. An important reminder here is that you can make annual gifts of up to a projected $13,000 in 2009. to an unlimited number of people without any federal gift tax consequences. Although you would not receive an income tax deduction for the gift, it will help reduce the size of your taxable estate especially if you (and your spouse) utilize your annual gift tax exclusion privileges on a regular annual basis.

Also, you do not have to gift in cash. A better alternative is to leverage your gift by investing the cash in a way that ultimately increases the value of the donated gift. For example, you can purchase life insurance policies inside an irrevocable life insurance trust. The insurance proceeds would be significantly larger than your cash gift and, upon your death, the proceeds would be exempt both from income and estate taxes. You can use your annual gift tax exclusion to gift interests in a family limited partnership. Or, you may gift appreciated properties or assets and lower your tax liability in the meantime. Another important gifting tool is utilizing your lifetime gift tax credit that allows gifts by each individual of up to $1.0 million during your lifetime, in addition to the annual exclusion. This exclusion is the lifetime total of gifts by one person, the donor, to one or more individuals. You need to keep track of this lifetime gift tax credit by filing a special gift tax return with the IRS every year you use the lifetime credit. It is important to note that it is possible for you to gift $1.0 million a year without tapping into this lifetime credit by utilizing the annual gift exclusion of $13,000 a year in 2009. In this case, you are limited to giving each recipient $13,000, but you can give that amount to 10 or to an unlimited number of people.

Utilize Estate-Planning Strategies

For determining the federal estate taxes, your total assets have to be added up. These could include your qualified retirement plans, your deferred compensation, stock options, annuities, other deferred payout arrangements, your real estate, life insurance, business ownership interests, stocks, bonds, and personal property. Each of these can be subject to federal estate taxes and may also be subject to income and inheritance taxes. Without proper planning, this combination of taxes can drastically reduce what your heirs might receive.

The chapters on estate planning, gifting, and life insurance address many of the issues that could arise and offer ideas to help you reduce your estate tax liabilities. This is a complex area of wealth planning and you should consult your wealth management team early in your life to help you maneuver through these complexities. However, with the proper expert advice, the tools that are available may significantly help you in lowering, if not eliminating, your estate tax liabilities.

In 2007, 1 out of 118 deaths in the United States was expected to leave behind an estate that would have produced the payment of federal estate taxes, compared to 1 out of 54 deaths in 1997. This means that less people are subject to estate taxes today than they were a decade ago. The reason for this decline could be attributed to the more favorable estate and gift tax laws and the higher limits on exemptions. Over the last 10 years, the amount that may be passed estate-tax free onto heirs of a decedent increased from $600,000 to $3.5 million in 2009.[47] Additionally, more wealthy individuals are setting up trusts and better utilizing strategies to help them lower their estate tax liabilities. A U.S. Trust Company- survey of wealthy Americans published in June 2006 indicated that this group's tax-saving strategies included setting up trusts (67 percent), giving money away (55 percent), purchasing life insurance to pay for estate taxes (46 percent), and setting up foundations (18 percent).[48] Finally, because Americans are living longer and health care costs have soared, more Americans expect to leave nothing to their surviving heirs. Sadly, 64 percent of American workers anticipate a total depletion of their life savings during retirement.[49]

Do Not Cash Out an Inherited IRA

If you inherit an IRA, do not cash it out. Instead, keep it and take required minimum distributions over your lifetime. The tax consequences of liquidating an inherited IRA are significant, and you miss the opportunity to get tax-deferred growth on the money. Assume that you inherit a $500,000 IRA at age 50. If you cash it out immediately, you would be taxed at the 35 percent tax rate and net $325,000 after paying income taxes. If, however, you take annual minimum distributions based on an IRS formula, by age 84, the total amount that you would have collected over the years would be $2.7 million, assuming an 8 percent average annual return.[50] Another way to maximize inherited IRAs is to claim an IRD (income in respect of a decedent) deduction. This deduction can be taken against withdrawals when federal taxes have been paid on IRA assets. This deduction can also be used against assets in inherited tax-deferred annuities and 401(k)s.[51]

Save for Your Children's or Grandchildren's Education in 529 College Savings Plans

If you intend to go back to school, or help pay for your children or grand-children's college education, a 529 college savings plan is a great vehicle to invest for that purpose. Unlike a Coverdell education IRA, there is no income limit on who can contribute; you do not have to be a family member to contribute to a 529 plan; you can change the beneficiary at any time (in case your child receives a scholarship or decides not to go to college); there is no age limit as far as the beneficiary is concerned; and the amount of funds that can be contributed to a 529 plan can be as high as $325,000 with some plans. Best of all, any withdrawals used for college costs are not taxable. Very few investment vehicles are available that provide you with these kind of benefits.

If you are wealthy and you are concerned about lowering your estate tax liability, you can gift assets to a 529 plan utilizing your $13,000 annual gift exclusion, or $26,000 if you are a couple. You can gift to multiple beneficiaries in the same year, and if you are really intent on gifting the maximum, 529 plans allow for accelerated gifting. For example, in 2009, you and your spouse can gift $13,000 each, utilizing the annual gift exclusion for a total of $26,000, and you are permitted to fund four additional years for a five-year total of $130,000 per couple. If you have five grandchildren, you can effectively gift to their 529 plans—and not pay any gift tax—a total of $650,000. Keep in mind that no further annual exclusion gifts and/or generation-skipping transfers to the same beneficiaries may be made over the same five-year period, and the transfer must be reported as a series of five equal annual transfers on Form 709 tax return.[52]

529 gifts can reduce your income liability (because you are giving money and its future earning potential away), minimize your estate taxes (in this example, by $650,000), and potentially leave a larger legacy because the funds you contribute will grow tax deferred, allowing your gift to grow faster over time, and then be distributed tax free for qualified college expenses.[53]

Replace Personal Loans with Home Equity-Loan Debt

Interest paid on up to $100,000 of home-equity debt is deductible on your tax return. If you have personal debt such as a car loan, pay off that debt from your home-equity line of credit. Personal interest is not tax deductible, while interest on a home-equity debt is. Remember that mortgage interest is deductible on up to $1,000,000 of original debt incurred to purchase a primary residence.

Transfer Appreciated Long-Term Securities to Older Children

Gifting to a child is a commonly used strategy to manage capital gains taxes. It is especially valuable in 2008–2010 because long-term capital-gains tax rates will be reduced to 0 percent for individuals in the 10 and 15 percent tax brackets. A child would have to be 19 or older, or age 24 and older if he/she is a full-time student. Younger (minor) children will be taxed at the parents' rates, making this technique unavailable and less attractive with younger children.[54] If you are a parent in the 25 percent tax bracket or higher, your long-term capital-gains tax rate will be 15 percent. Your older child is likely to be in the 10 or 15 percent tax rate and would end up paying 0 percent on the sale of the same long-term securities. Thus, by transferring assets, along with their cost basis and holding periods, to your older child, you can potentially eliminate your capital gains taxes. Keep in mind that the portion of your gift of stocks to your child that exceeds the $13,000 in 2009 (or $26,000 if it is a joint gift) annual exclusion limit could be subject to a gift tax if you have used up your lifetime gift tax exclusion.[55]

Shift Investments into Qualified Dividend-Paying Stock

If you want to save on taxes, you can reallocate your portfolio. Qualified dividend income is taxed at the same favorable tax rates that apply to long-term capital gains. Depending on your income, the maximum tax rate on qualified dividend income is 15 percent. However, for 2008–2010, the rate is 0 percent (subject to limitations) if your total taxable income is taxed at the lower brackets of 10 or 15 percent. Therefore, to save on taxes, you may want to shift out of investments that generate income taxed at ordinary rates, such as taxable bonds or synthetic preferreds, into dividend-paying stocks.[56]

Defer Interest Income from One Year to Another

If interest income will put you in a higher tax bracket for the year, consider buying Treasury bills or certificates of deposit (CDs) that mature in the following year and do not have any interest payments in your current year, thus deferring any interest income to the next year.

Postpone the Sale of Stocks to Take Advantage of Long-Term Capital Gains

If you hold stocks for less than 12 months and sell them, your short-term capital gains will be taxed as ordinary income, which could be as high as 35 percent. However, if you hold your stock for more than 12 months, your appreciation will be taxed at the much lower tax rate that applies to long-term capital gains.

Take Advantage of the 0 Percent Capital Tax Rate

Between 2008 and 2010, if you are married and filing jointly and your maximum taxable income is below $65,100 or single and your maximum taxable income is below $32,550, you may qualify for a 0 percent long-term capital gains tax rate. It does not matter when you acquired the asset as long as you hold it in excess of 12 months. The 0 percent rate applies to sales made (trade date) during calendar years 2008, 2009, and 2010. Although you can technically gift appreciated securities to your children and obtain the 0 percent capital gain rate, be careful because your child will be subject to the kiddie tax. Your minor child's income has to be $1,800 or less to qualify. Otherwise, the tax will be the same as the parents' marginal tax rate and neither the child nor the parents will benefit from the 0 percent tax rate. However, if you are near retirement, shifting income between years, or accelerating deductions, may allow you to benefit from the 0 percent capital gains rate on all, or a portion, of your gains.[57]

The Sale of Your Home Provides Tax-Free Capital Gains

Since May 7, 1997, you can exclude up to $250,000 of gain if you sell your home and you are a single taxpayer and up to $500,000 of gain if you are married filing jointly, provided that the home was owned by you and it was your primary residence in at least two of the preceding five years. You do not have to buy another home to qualify for this exclusion. This is not to advocate selling your home just to take advantage of the significant capital gains that can be excluded from your income. The intention here is to make you aware of this important benefit. Another added feature of this benefit is that if you are forced to sell your home in less than two years because of employment relocation, health reasons, or unforeseen circumstances, you can prorate the exclusion amount based on how long you lived in the home.[58] This exclusion may be claimed by taxpayers of any age for an unlimited number of times. However, it may not be claimed more than once in a two-year period.

Senior Citizens Can Benefit from Special Tax Provisions

If you are senior, receive your retirement income in a way that will stretch out your tax liability for as many years as possible. For example, do not take distributions from your IRA or Keogh until age $70\frac{1}{2}$ unless you absolutely need the money to cover basic living expenses. This allows the maximum amount of time for your assets to grow tax deferred. If you withdraw funds from an insurance contract, first take out your original principal that is not subject to taxes, and then receive distributions from the earnings, which are taxable. If you live in a high-tax state, buy bonds issued by the state to sidestep both federal and state taxes. If you are 65 or older, take advantage of the many provisions in the tax code that benefit seniors:

- You must file a return only if you report a gross income of $8,300 or more if you are single, or $14,650 if you are married and filing jointly.
- If you do not itemize, you qualify for a higher standard deduction that could be as much as $1,100.
- You may qualify for a tax credit if you do not receive Social Security or railroad retirement benefits.
- All income you receive from Social Security is tax free if your provisional income is $44,000 or less if you are married and filing jointly.
- If you move into a continuing-care or life-care community, the portion of your monthly fees allocated to health care services is deductible as an itemized expense.[59]

Claim Your Tax Credits

After you determine your income tax liability, you may be able to reduce that liability by claiming one of several available tax credits. Most personal tax credits are allowed to the full extent of your regular tax liability and alternative minimum tax. However, they do not create a refund if they exceed your tax liability, and these credits are mostly geared for lower-income people. Surprisingly, many people do not claim these credits. For example, only 4 percent of tax returns claim the retirement saver's tax credit, according to the Congressional Research Service.[60] The following are the most common nonrefundable credits:[61]

- Child tax credit (for 2009, depending on your adjusted gross income, you generally were able to claim a tax credit of $1,000 for each qualifying child who was under age 17 at the end of 2009.[62] The credit is reduced by $50 for each $1,000 of income above $75,000 for single filers, $110,000 for joint filers—$11,750 is added to the phase-out range for each qualified child).[63]
- Dependent care credit (if you hire someone to care for your children or other dependents while you work, you may qualify for a tax credit for the expenses).
- Adoption credit (a tax credit of up to $12,150 may be available on your 2009 tax return for the qualifying costs of adopting a child under age 18).[64]

- Education credits such as the Hope and lifetime learning credits.
- Retirement savings credit (savers who put money into a 401(k), IRA or other similar plan may qualify for a tax credit).
- Credit for the elderly and disabled.
- Mortgage interest credit.
- Washington, D.C., first-time homebuyer credit.

Refundable credits allow you to receive a refund, even if the credit exceeds your tax liability. Some of the most common refundable tax credits include:[65]

- Additional child tax credit (part or all of the child tax credit may have been refundable as additional credit if your earned income for 2007 exceeded $11,750 or you had three or more children).
- The earned income credit.
- The health coverage credit.
- The long-term unused minimum tax credit (available to those who paid alternative minimum tax in prior years, primarily because of exercising incentive stock options. Starting in 2007 and running through 2012, such individuals may claim a refundable credit usually up to $5,000 annually. Adjusted gross income limitations can disallow high-income taxpayers from claiming this credit).

Other tax credits include the following:[66]

- The residential energy tax credits. The Energy Policy Act of 2005 created a number of limited tax credits for individuals who make energy savings improvements to their homes.
- The alternative motor vehicle credit includes credits for buying hybrid vehicles. However, once a manufacturer sells over 60,000 qualifying hybrids, the credits for all hybrids produced by that manufacturer are reduced by 50 percent for a six-month period and then by 75 percent for the following six-month period. After the end of the second six-month period, the credits simply disappear. Under this arbitrary phase-out rule, Toyota and Lexus hybrids are no longer available, Honda is next in line (estimated to disappear in 2008) followed by Ford and GM hybrids.[67]
- The research and development tax credit. The IRS and many states offer incentives to businesses to invest in research and development. The federal government offers as much as 6.5 percent tax credit for every dollar spent, while many states offer about 5 percent for every dollar spent in new product or process development.[68]

Do Not Overlook Your Tax Deductions

Years ago, former IRS Commissioner Fred Goldberg told *Kiplinger's Personal Finance* magazine that millions of taxpayers overpaid their taxes by overlooking just one of the many tax deductions and credits that they are entitled to claim.[69] Deductions lower your taxable income, and credits lower your taxes. Even though tax credits are more valuable because they reduce your tax bill dollar for dollar, tax deductions can significantly reduce your income that is subject to tax. Examples of tax deductions include the following:[70]

- Home mortgage interest deduction—Home mortgage and home equity line of credit interest are the most common and usually the largest tax-deductible expenses that you can claim. They can significantly reduce your taxable income but are subject to limitations based on the size of your loans.
- State sales taxes—Although all taxpayers can claim this write-off, it is more valuable for those of you who live in states that do not impose an income-state tax. You must then choose between deducting state income taxes or state sales taxes. For most residents of income-state taxes, the income-tax deduction is a better deal. If you bought a vehicle, home building materials, or a boat, you get to add the state sales tax you paid to the amount shown in IRS tables for your state, to the extent the sales tax rate you paid does not exceed the state's general sales tax rate.
- Health savings account—You can take an above-the-line tax deduction for contributions to a qualified health savings account (HSA) plan if you are covered by a high-deductible health insurance plan, and you are not covered by any other health insurance plan.
- $250 educators' expenses—Teachers and their aides can deduct up to $250 they spent in 2007 for books and classroom materials.
- College tuition—You may qualify to deduct up to $4,000 you paid in college tuition in 2007 for yourself, your spouse, or your child. This is a valuable tax break if your income is too high to qualify for the Hope or lifetime learning credit.
- Student loan interest paid by the parents—If you, as a parent, paid back your child's student loan, the IRS views this as though you have given the money to your child, who then pays the debt. So, a child who is not claimed as a dependent can qualify to deduct up to $2,500 of student loan interest paid by the parents.
- Moving expense to take a first job—If you move more than 50 miles to get to your first job, you can deduct the cost of moving yourself and your household goods to your new location, including 20 cents a mile, plus parking fees and tolls for driving your own car.

- Refinancing points—When you buy a house, you get to deduct points paid to get your mortgage as a lump sum. However, if you refinance, you have to refinance the points over the life of the loan. When you sell your house or refinance again, you may get to deduct the remaining portion of the points that was not deducted.
- Contributions to nonprofit organizations—Whether the contribution is to your house of worship, a charity, or your college, donations of cash and property are tax deductible. Out-of-pocket charitable contributions are also tax deductible. For example, if you paid for the stamps for your church's fundraiser, you can deduct that expense as a charitable contribution.
- Alimony—You can claim a tax deduction for the alimony paid to your ex-spouse.
- Early withdrawal penalty—If you incur a penalty for early withdrawal of your certificate of deposit at a financial institution, you can take that penalty as a tax deduction.
- Foreign tax credit—If you live abroad, claiming the foreign tax credit reduces your U.S. taxes by the amount of tax you have paid to foreign governments.

These are but a few of the tax deductions that you might be entitled to claim.[71] Even though your tax advisor is the competent source of advice on these matters, unless you share information with your advisor about your activities throughout the tax year, he or she might not realize that you could claim certain tax deductions.

Special Tax Treatment of Employer Stock Distributions—Net Unrealized Appreciation (NUA)

If you are like most employees, you tend to roll your 401(k) assets into an IRA when you leave your job. Usually, this is a great way to continue deferring taxes until you retire and begin taking distributions. However, if your 401(k) or other employer-sponsored retirement plan includes highly appreciated, publicly-traded stock in the company you work for, you could save thousands of dollars by paying taxes on the stock now rather than later.

Normally, when you take distributions from your IRA, you pay ordinary taxes on those distributions. Company stock rolled into an IRA is treated the same way. For example, if you included your company shares in your IRA rollover, the entire value of your IRA would be taxed at your regular income tax rate when you take withdrawals from your IRA. Depending on your tax bracket, that could be as high as 35 percent.[72] But, if you withdraw your company stock from your 401(k) and, instead of rolling it into an

IRA, transfer it to a taxable brokerage account, you avoid paying ordinary income taxes on the stock's net unrealized appreciation (NUA). The NUA is the difference between the value of the company stock at the time it was purchased inside your 401(k) account and the time of distribution or when transferred out of the 401(k).[73] Pursuing this strategy means that the only part of your company stock that is subject to ordinary income taxes is the value of the stock when it was first purchased inside your 401(k) plan (your cost basis). At the time of the lump sum distribution, there is no tax on the net unrealized appreciation of the employer stock. Because of this NUA tax break, it may be more beneficial for you not to roll over your company stock from the 401(k) into your IRA.

Note that the other assets of your 401(k)—such as mutual funds—do not receive the NUA tax break. Therefore, you would want to roll these plan assets into an IRA and continue deferring taxes on past and future growth. What happens next is that when you sell the employer stock in your new taxable account, the sale proceeds are treated as capital gains or losses, depending on whether the sale price is more or less than the cost basis. If you sell the stock for more, it will be taxed as long-term capital gains on the NUA rather than ordinary income tax rates.

For example, let us assume that you take a lump-sum distribution of your employer's stock in August, and you sell the 1,000 shares in February of the following year. Assume that you bought the stock at a cost basis of $20 a share, the fair market value on the date of distribution in August is $80 per share, and the sale price of the stock in February of the following year is $110 a share. Based on these assumptions, your cost basis will be $20 × 1000 shares, or $20,000. This amount is taxed as ordinary income for the year of distribution. Your net unrealized appreciation will be $80 per share (the value on the date of distribution) minus $20 per share (cost basis) or $60 per share for a total of $60,000. This amount will be recognized as long-term capital gain in the year the stock is sold (no matter what the holding period is). If you hold the stock in your taxable account for less than 12 months, then the difference between your $110 actual sale price minus the $80 per share (the value of the stock at the time of distribution) would be equal to $30 per share, for a total of $30,000—the additional gain in excess of the fair market value on the distribution date. This gain will be taxed as short-term capital gain. If you hold the stock in your taxable account for more than 12 months, then this amount will be taxed as long-term capital gains tax.[74]

There are three additional advantages for this strategy. The employer stock that is taken as a lump sum distribution and deposited in a taxable account is not required to be sold at age $70\frac{1}{2}$ due to IRS minimum distribution requirements. Additionally, upon your death, your heirs will receive a step-up in cost basis of the value of the employer stock for any appreciation from the distribution date.[75] Finally, if you are below retirement age and take a distribution from your 401(k) or IRA, you would normally be hit with a 10 percent early withdrawal penalty. But with the NUA option, the penalty applies to the cost basis only.[76]

Plan Your Employer Stock Option Exercises

To minimize the potential tax impact of stock option exercises, consider a planned multiyear exercise strategy and be aware of the expiration dates on your company stock option awards. You might consider gifts of nonqualified stock options to others, if your employer allows it. This is especially rewarding if the stock price is lower and you are looking to shift potential future appreciation and reduce estate taxes. Also, if you exercise incentive stock options (ISOs) during the year and the stock price decreases from the date of exercise, selling some or all of the stock by year-end can reduce potential alternative minimum tax (AMT) exposure attributable to the stock option exercise.[77]

Contribute Appreciated Securities to Charity

If you contribute appreciated securities to a charity that you have owned for more than a year, you will not be taxed on the unrealized long-term capital gain, and you will receive a charitable deduction for the current market value of the securities contributed. You may deduct charitable contributions of long-term securities up to 30 percent of adjusted gross income, and you may carry forward any contributions in excess of the annual 30 percent limit for up to five years.[78] When possible, do not contribute cash to charity—the tax advantages of contributing long-held appreciated assets outweigh cash contributions. If you donate appreciated real estate or other tangible assets, you will not be required to recapture any depreciation previously taken. If you were to sell that appreciated real estate, previously taken depreciation would have to be recaptured at regular income tax rates. For many years, wealthy individuals have legally avoided paying taxes on appreciated assets and avoided paying taxes on recaptured depreciation taken over the years by donating those assets to charity.[79]

Claim Full Depreciation of Capital Purchases

Depreciation is a write-off of capital purchases over the life of the equipment. Depreciation is usually written off in five or seven years, depending on the item. Section 179, however, allows you to write off $105,000 of capital purchases each year.[80] If you buy a $50,000 machine, take the full amount in expenses, instead of just one-fifth. Clearly, you will not be able to take further deductions in coming years, but at least you will have claimed and locked in the full depreciation of your capital purchases.

Claim the Loss on a Worthless Security

In the days of the technology bubble, many stocks that soared in price for absolutely no fundamental reasons became worthless. To claim a loss on a worthless security, it must be truly worthless. The fact that you cannot sell a worthless security does not automatically prove that the security is worthless. Some brokerage firms, as a service to their clients, would purchase these stocks for a nominal price, to help their clients prove that the security has been sold. If you are unable to sell the security, you can claim the loss only in the year the security becomes worthless; however, you have to prove to the IRS that the security has become worthless. The IRS considers each case individually, based on the evidence presented.[81] Ask your brokerage firm to buy these worthless securities for a fraction of a penny just to complete their sale and to help you document and claim your loss. The financial crisis that began in late 2007 and that decimated venerable financial institutions such Bear Sterns and Lehman Brothers, just to name a couple, have seen the prices of those stocks tumble to the ground like a huge meteorite from outer space. At these levels, these stocks fall in the category of almost worthless stocks. For example, Lehman's stock price on October 9, 2008, was trading at 11 cents from a 52-week high of $67.73.[82] The only consolation for the holders of stocks such as Lehman's is that once sold, the holders would be able to realize huge capital losses that would be carried forward and that could help them offset gains in other investments sometime in the future.

Contribute to a Flexible Spending Account

If your employer permits it, you may contribute pretax money to a flexible spending account that would pay for your medical out-of-pocket expenses. If you elect, for example, to take $5,000 a year, this money is taken from your paycheck on a pretax basis and covers out-of-pocket medical expenses throughout the year. This essentially shelters $5,000 of your income from taxes. However, be careful not to overestimate your out-of-pocket medical expense, because if you do not use these funds during a set period of time, you would then have to forfeit these funds.

Employ Your Minor Children

If you hire your children to work for you and pay them $4,850 each, you can reduce your taxable income by that amount. Your child pays no income taxes because their income is below the single exemption allowance. And, if your children are under 18 and your business is not incorporated, you do not have to pay Social Security or Medicare taxes on their salaries.[83]

Set Up a Home Office

With more workers telecommuting and working out of a home, this practice no longer automatically raises a red flag for the IRS. In 2001, the definition of a home office was revised. In the past, a home office had to be a principal place of business, and there was no other place to do work. The new rules state that if you do significant administrative work regularly and exclusively at a designated space in your home, even though you have an office at your workplace, then your home office is your principal place of business and you can take a home office deduction. If, for example, you use 20 percent of your home's square footage, you can deduct 20 percent of your mortgage interest, property taxes, insurance, repairs, maintenance and depreciation.[84]

Combine Business with Pleasure Travel

If you are traveling on vacation or business, consider including a business portion to your vacation travel, or if you are traveling on business, consider including a pleasure portion. Howard Scott, an author who specializes in tax preparation for small businesses, writes, "If more than half of your time is devoted to business, you may deduct transportation costs (plane, car rental and gas) and any business-related expenses (meals for entertaining clients)."[85]

Increase or Take Advantage of Business Expenses

Expenses that help educate you and grow your business are deductible expenses. For example, a business book that you might have bought, magazine subscriptions that help you communicate with clients, educational courses that improve your management skills, membership fees to associations, and professional organizations that expand your customer base, the use of your home Internet for business, your cell phone if it is primarily used for work, or even your personal grooming expenses because image is important to your business, are all business expenses.[86] The scope of deductible expenses relates largely to your type of business. In 1988, Indiana stripper Cynthia S. Hess became the first person to receive a tax deduction for breast implants![87]

Spend Your Money

You have earned it! It sounds easy, but enjoying your money while you are alive leaves fewer dollars that could be subject to estate taxes when you die.[88]

No matter how well-read and knowledgeable you are about taxes and tax-saving strategies, you should meet regularly with your professional tax advisor. There are constant changes in the tax law, and there are usually changes in your goals and circumstances. Self-reliance in an area that requires specific expertise could be detrimental to your overall well being.

Concluding Remarks

When it comes to dealing with taxes, be smart and proactive. You cannot have an effective wealth management plan while ignoring the consequences of taxes, whether you are dealing with investing, maximizing your income, planning for retirement, gifting during your life or at death, or even managing your debt. The government has provided tax breaks in terms of deductions as well as credits to help ease the burden of taxes and be as fair as it can be in dealing with 300 million citizens. The tax-saving strategies discussed in this chapter are just some of the ways that the government has permitted taxpayers to minimize their tax liability while, at the same time, ensuring a fair and equitable tax system. It is up to you, with the help of your tax, investment, and other advisors, to take full advantage of these tax-saving opportunities. Knowledge and timely action on these and other tax-saving strategies are critical to your ability to succeed in this task.

CHAPTER 10

The Role and Qualities of an Exceptional Wealth Advisor

Your wealth advisor should be much more than just your investment advisor. She is the relationship manager to your overall wealth management plan. She should be able to articulate a variety of wealth management solutions in each of the following areas: investing, wealth building, wealth preservation, wealth transfer, insurance, debt management, asset protection, and charitable planning. She should coordinate your estate planning process and work closely with your wealth management team—the estate planning and tax lawyer, the accountant, the insurance agent, and the trust officer. More importantly, she should understand you and care about your financial goals and personal preferences.

Today, there are 650,000 licensed financial advisors in the United States.[1] They refer to themselves as brokers, financial advisors, financial planners, financial consultants, or wealth advisors. Often, these and other titles are used interchangeably and loosely by individuals in the financial industry. No matter what your advisor calls him or herself or what titles their employer bestows upon them, what really matters are the nature and scope of services they offer (not so much the products), and the qualities and qualifications that these advisors possess.

This proliferation in titles or roles is largely due to the evolution of the financial industry in the United States. In the past, you would call a broker or he would call you to buy or sell a stock, a bond, and other financial instruments. Brokers were intermediaries who, at times, also offered clients advice on their take on stocks and bonds. The stock market crash on October 19, 1987, the infamous Black Monday, saw the decline of the Dow Jones Industrial Average (DJIA) by 22.6 percent in one day—the largest one-day percentage decline in stock market history.[2] Investors and advisors were spooked and began looking for ways to reduce the risk and volatility of their financial investments.

Diversification was viewed as key to lowering risk and volatility. Advisors and investors began relying increasingly on professional money managers, as well as shifting assets to passive investment vehicles to invest their portfolios. There was widespread acceptance and, at times, a "virtual mania" for indexing as a core investment policy.[3] Portfolio managers offered either mutual funds for small investors or separately managed accounts for larger investors. The financial services business was in the process of converting itself from a commission to a fee-based industry.

The Glass-Steagall Act, which mandated the fragmentation of the financial services industry into three uncoordinated pieces—banking, insurance, and investments—contributed to a competing and often counterproductive approach to financial planning. In 1933, in the wake of the 1929 stock market crash, during a nationwide commercial bank failure and the Great Depression, the Glass-Steagall Act was passed by Congress. It separated investment and commercial banking activities. Improper bank activity, namely an overzealous commercial bank involvement in stock market investing, was deemed the main culprit of the financial crash. It was believed that commercial banks took too much risk with depositors' money.[4] The repeal of the Act in 1999 paved the way to the rise of a more coordinated approach to financial planning allowing providers to look at the client's overall needs as opposed to pushing products from competing providers. Large investment firms began bundling their retail products and services into a coordinated, fee-based platform and they began offering formal financial planning. Unfortunately, over the past decade, banks and investment companies developed very aggressive and complex investment structures, facilitated by the availability of cheap credit, in order to boost their returns. They ended up over-leveraging their holdings and utilizing sophisticated and hard-to-understand tools that, once the subprime and liquidity crises erupted, ended up leading to many of these banks and investment banks' demise.

Another evolution in the industry was sparked by the advent and subsequent burst of the Internet and technology bubbles and the market's precipitous decline between 2000 and 2002. The Internet made it dangerously easy for investors to trade on their own accord. Day traders mushroomed, chasing unrealistic returns and attempting to short-circuit the basic principles of proper investing. This suicidal phenomenon led many investors to think that they could do without professional investment advice, and in their minds marked the beginning of the end of the financial advisor.

The ensuing market crash was punishing and brutal. It forced investors and advisors, many of whom were carried as well with the euphoric tide, back to earth. Advisors were reminded again of the basic principles of investing and began directing their attention to wealth management as a way of further diversifying investment risk by providing the clients with comprehensive wealth planning; hence, the emergence of today's wealth advisor. Even a wealth management approach did not shield investors from the latest crisis in the financial markets. However, those investors who adopted and implemented the wealth management principles escaped the worst from the crisis because had they already purchased the necessary life insurance policies to transfer wealth to their heirs and provide liquidity to their estates. They would have been in a much worse position had they not done that because those funds that had been redirected to buying life insurance and annuities, for example, would have unavoidably been subject to the severe downturn in the markets.

This chapter will explore and analyze the evolving role of the new wealth advisor and help guide you in identifying the qualities and characteristics that you should look for in your wealth advisor.

The Role of a Comprehensive Wealth Advisor

Your search for a wealth advisor should begin by asking yourself the following questions:

- Do I have the legal, estate planning, tax, accounting, insurance, or investment expertise to create and implement my own wealth management plan?
- Do I have the interest?
- Do I have the time?
- Am I ultimately better served by seeking the advice of these experts?

Even if you have the interest and the time, no one has the comprehensive expertise to plan and implement his or her own wealth management plan.

The average high-net-worth client in this country utilizes the services of five or more professionals to develop their comprehensive wealth plan.[5] There is the attorney who provides legal advice and drafts legal documents ranging from estate plans to simple wills. The accountant provides tax advice on an ongoing basis and on an as-needed basis, in the development of your overall strategic wealth management plan. The insurance advisor's task is to make certain that you are protected in terms of your overall insurance needs—life, property, health, disability, liability, and long-term care. The trust officer's role is to understand and to help execute your wishes in the ultimate management of your trust. Finally, your wealth advisor devises your investment strategy and assumes the role of quarterback, coordinator, or relationship manager of your overall wealth management plan.

Your multiple experts should be in a position to sit down together or, at least, consult with each other when you initially devise your wealth management plan. They should communicate with one another on an as-needed basis, especially when significant changes in your life occur. Experts might be engrossed in their own world of planning techniques and, frequently, need to hear the perspective of the other experts and discuss the implication of what one expert might recommend, for example, on tax or legal issues. Without a coordinator—your wealth advisor or relationship manager—your plan could be diverted off track by the zealousness or close-mindedness of one of your experts. Ultimately, the goal is to do what is best for you, the client, and to address your problems, concerns, and needs.

More often than not, it is the wealth advisor who is the most effective communicator among the group of experts. He or she is the one who is more cognizant of your overall plan and goals. In almost all cases, your wealth advisor does not possess the greatest legal, accounting or insurance skill. This person assumes the role of a holistic advisor.

A comprehensive wealth advisor begins with identifying your needs, concerns, goals, and desires. It is all about you, the client. As such, the role of your wealth advisor can be summarized as follows:[6]

1. Assist you in creating and growing your wealth.
2. Protect and preserve your accumulated wealth.
3. Direct you in efficiently harvesting your potential wealth.
4. Help you transfer wealth during your lifetime.
5. Advise you on establishing and maintaining a wealth legacy following your death.

Assist You in Creating and Growing Your Wealth

You should expect help in determining your investment strategy, in optimizing your tax efficiency, and in utilizing leverage to grow your wealth.

When it comes to investing, your wealth advisor's most important task is to help you develop and execute your overall investment plan, otherwise known as an **investment policy statement**.[7] This plan is to be used as a road map. It helps you identify your goals and objectives. It allows you to focus and it places in check your emotions and feelings toward investments and wealth building. Emotions, primarily fear or greed, are an investor's worst enemy.

You, therefore, should heed the advice of your wealth advisor and benefit from his/her insight and expertise. You need discipline, a long-time horizon, and level headedness. You need discipline in executing your plan, in realizing that wealth is not built overnight, and in staying the course despite the ups and downs of either the markets or your personal life. In the market, time—a long period of time—is always on your side. I do not use the word *always* lightly, but history reveals the longer you are invested, the more likely you will make money. Be careful not to follow the trends of the day. They come and go, leaving scorched bodies behind. Stay the course in your plan and you will be rewarded. There is no quick road to riches. There are established rules and patterns based on years of historical data. You need to be scientific, calculating, and not swayed by your emotions. Your wealth advisor's job is to prod you and keep you on course.

You pay taxes to support a governmental system that allows you to grow and prosper. That does not mean that you have to hand the government a significant portion of your wealth. Nor does the government expect you to do so. There are legal ways available to you, with the full awareness of the tax collector that you should use to minimize your tax liability. A good wealth advisor, working with an accountant, will help you implement prudent tax plans to allow you to keep a greater portion of your wealth each year by reducing your tax burden.

Throughout the book we have discussed and highlighted ways to help you maximize your investments whether through tax-minimization strategies or through leveraging of existing assets that you have. For example, the purchase of a life insurance policy almost always guarantees you a significant leverage in terms of benefits compared to your premium or cost. You can choose to invest in tax-sheltered vehicles allowing you to invest and shelter your investment gains without being subjected to tax liabilities. Even wealthy individuals borrow money to increase the leverage of their investments and allow them to potentially multiply their investment returns. Borrowing always carries risks. Leveraged borrowing is especially risky because your loss could be many times your initial investment. Err on the side of being conservative.

Protect You and Preserve Your Accumulated Wealth

Once you have accumulated your wealth, if you are like most affluent individuals, your primary goal becomes wealth preservation with moderate growth going forward and an opportunistic eye for exceptional investments, with a only a small slice of your existing wealth.[8] Most wealthy people created their wealth by identifying exceptional opportunities and acting to capture them. That trait rarely fades away for successful entrepreneurs.

Portfolio management and risk management are the two most common tools utilized in protecting and preserving your wealth. Asset allocation, diversification, and tax efficiency are the tools of choice to help protect and moderately grow your investment portfolio. Risk management tools include the purchase of many types of insurance—life, disability, property, health, long-term care, and liability insurance.[9] Your wealth advisor, working with members of your wealth management team, is critical in helping you preserve your assets.

Direct You in Efficiently Harvesting Your Potential Wealth

In the process of acquiring wealth, you need the help and expertise of your wealth advisor, particularly if the major sources of your wealth will be generated from the following:[10]

- *Stock options granted to you by your employer.* You will need advice based on the type of option you hold, whether it is qualified or non-qualified, which affects the tax treatment of these options, and whether your holdings have a large concentration in your company stock and the need to diversify these holdings in a tax-efficient manner.
- *A privately held business that you own and wish to sell to other family members, company employees, or to an outside entity.* In devising a business succession plan, you will need to consider the timing of your transaction, the selection of the purchasers, or recipients of your business, transfer taxes, capital gain taxes, security of the future payments and the proper transfer vehicle. You also need to ensure that the sale produces a sufficient stream of income or a lump sum that would provide for your lifetime support.
- *Growth and appreciation of existing holdings.* If you own real estate, property used in a trade or business, qualified securities, or even some life insurance products, you might be able to delay capital gains taxes when you liquidate these appreciated assets if you properly utilize allowable exchange vehicles. Most people are familiar with 1031 exchanges for property or 1035 exchanges for annuities.
- *Inheritances and gifts.* If you are the recipient of an inheritance or a gift, the Internal Revenue Code allows you to disclaim those rights and transfer the property or asset directly to the secondary beneficiaries. The ability to disclaim must be proactively sought and is not flexible in its election. Your wealth advisor can help you determine whether your family is best served by accepting an inheritance or a gift or by opting to transfer these to the next generation thus helping increase your family's overall wealth.

Help You Transfer Wealth During Your Lifetime

Having guided you in *acquiring* your wealth, your advisor's attention is then redirected toward helping you *distribute* your wealth. You are now faced with choices discussed in detail in Chapter 7 on gifting. These choices include gifting mechanisms; limits and timing of gifts to your spouse, children, and others; ways of maximizing your gifts and reducing your gift- and estate-tax liabilities; and ensuring the privacy of your family affairs and the execution of your wishes during lifetime and at death. When it comes to charitable gifting, most people do so by writing a check. This might be a very tax-inefficient way of gifting and leaving a legacy behind. You need the help of your wealth advisor to determine your charitable gifting strategies that would allow you to maximize the value of your gift while permitting you to potentially avoid paying capital gains on appreciated assets and securing, at the same time, significant tax deductions. More complex strategies might be more appropriate in your case. These could include philanthropic transfers through charitable trusts or family foundations.

The individual that can orchestrate and coordinate your gifting strategy is your wealth advisor working in tandem with your wealth management team—your estate planning lawyer, your CPA, and your insurance agent. It is a complicated task that requires meticulous planning and follow-up and cannot be haphazardly or impulsively thought of and executed.

Advise You on Establishing and Maintaining a Wealth Legacy Following Your Death

Humans are procrastinators, particularly when it comes to issues that evoke fear, are not perceived as urgent in nature, do not provide immediate gratification, or cannot be easily understood. Planning for the aftermath of your death is on top of those issues. Most advisors tend to focus at this stage of wealth management on the probate process and the nonprobate process for nonprobate property. This explains why most people die leaving their estate outright to their heirs.[11] This is the most common form of bequest, even though it might not be the most appropriate.

A comprehensive wealth advisor needs to play a proactive role in communicating ideas, suggestions, and alternatives to simply leaving your assets outright to your heirs. Would it not make more sense to establish a trust that could provide guidance or control, ensure the continuity of asset management, and make available to your heirs the expertise and collective wisdom of your wealth management team? Yes, strategies and concepts can be complicated and confusing. However, your wealth advisor can help you break down complex strategies into simple concepts that can serve your heirs well long after you are gone.

The role of your wealth advisor in devising, managing, and implementing your comprehensive wealth management plan is critical. As a general practitioner, your wealth advisor is instrumental in helping you create and grow your wealth; in guiding you to protect and preserve your accumulated wealth; in advising you on the best strategies to harvest your potential wealth; in assisting you with the most efficient way to distribute wealth during your lifetime; and in helping you to establish and maintain a wealth legacy following your death.

25 Qualities of an Exceptional Wealth Advisor

If you believe that people do business with people and not with companies or institutions, then you agree that it is your wealth advisor that draws you to be a client of a particular company. After all, most full-service Wall Street firms offer largely similar products, except for unique services and products offered usually to ultra-high-net-worth clients. The qualitative difference among firms is ultimately your wealth advisor. This is not to minimize the value that a solid and reputable firm adds to the efforts of your wealth advisor.

Having defined the scope and nature of a holistic wealth advisor's role, what are the 25 qualities and qualifications that you should look for in an exceptional wealth advisor?

1. *Adopts a holistic approach*—You want a wealth advisor who looks at your overall wealth management needs and not merely specialize in one area as he/she will tend, often subconsciously, to gravitate to that area of expertise. You want someone who takes an integrated approach to your needs and is able to articulate all facets of wealth management—investing, wealth growth, wealth preservation, wealth transfer, insurance, estate planning, and debt management.
2. *Plans well*—Has your wealth advisor discussed with you the need to put together an investment policy statement or a plan of action that reflects your goals and how they are to be achieved over time? A plan can help you feel more in control. The more your advisor learns about you—your lifestyle, health, family dynamics, and finances—the more he can help you make informed decisions. There is tremendous value in planning ahead. It gives you the ability to adapt to whatever uncertainties the future presents.
3. *Acts proactively*—Your wealth advisor should take the initiative, on an as-needed basis and between your regularly scheduled meetings, to alert you to the need to take certain actions pertaining to your overall wealth management plan or possibly to reallocate some of your portfolios or positions. In return, you should be responsive, as timing could determine the effectiveness of your advisor's recommendations.
4. *Leads and facilitates*—You want your wealth advisor to be able to properly communicate your needs and desires to your wealth management team—the estate planning and/or tax lawyer, the CPA, the trust officer, the insurance and lending agents, and other professionals whose services might be needed. Your wealth advisor should be a facilitator and should be able to communicate among these experts and take charge in coordinating their efforts on your behalf.

5. *Listens*—Your wealth advisor should listen to you to understand your needs, desires, and fears. Sometimes doing the right thing from a textbook perspective does not mean doing the right thing for you. At times, even if you are unable to properly communicate your concerns, your wealth advisor should have the insight to understand your nuances, hesitations and body language.

6. *Provides solutions*—Your relationship with your wealth advisor should be about providing you with solutions to your needs. "People who invest don't invest for returns alone," says Alan Brown, chief marketing officer of Nuveen Investments, Inc. "They invest because they have children who they want to put through college. There are always strong and powerful human emotions that drive why people put money with us or any other firm."[12] It should not be about pushing products. If there is a need for products, these should be mere tools to meeting your needs.

7. *Holds things in confidence*—You need someone in whom you can confide your innermost concerns and thoughts. You need to be able to share with them your concerns about one of your children, for example, and his/her lack of maturity or responsibility and how to address that issue in your wealth management plan.

8. *Understands your situation*—Your wealth advisor should understand your hopes, fears, goals, and your family dynamics. Your family's best interest is at the very center of all you do at all stages of your wealth management process. Your advisor needs to understand, appreciate and accommodate your family's internal dynamics in helping you devise your overall wealth management plan.

9. *Stays abreast of the industry*—Investment, tax, and estate planning laws, strategies, approaches, and products change or evolve with time. Your wealth advisor, working with your wealth management team, should keep abreast of developments that can affect your overall wealth management plan. Unless your wealth advisor has a curious mind and is willing to invest his time and energy in learning, his advice can be stale with time. This could represent missed opportunities for you. When was the last time your advisor attended a conference, finished reading an industry-related book or publication, or participated in a continuing education program?

10. *Is educated*—Education and titles matter. There are many industry certifications that attest to your advisor's level of expertise and willingness to learn and educate him or herself. Is your advisor a Certified Financial Planner or CFP, a Certified Investment Management Analyst or CIMA®, a Certified Wealth Strategist or CWS™, a Chartered Financial Consultant (ChFC), an estate planning specialist, or a senior investment consultant?

Some of these titles are nationally recognized, others are earned within particular firms.

11. *Is available and accessible*—Is your advisor available to meet when you need to or return your call within a reasonable period of time? He or she should be. Otherwise, look for someone else.

12. *Puts your interests first*—Even though there is a legal difference between "brokers" and "investment advisors" with regard to whose interests they should place first—yours or theirs—no one and no firm will knowingly advocate not doing what is "suitable" for the client. Brokers are executors of the wishes of the clients. They might provide their opinion on a client's request but they do what the clients want and their responsibility to the client does not extend beyond executing orders. "Investment advisors," on the other hand, should always make "suitable" recommendations, but they also have a "fiduciary responsibility" to you, the client.[13] In other words, they have to put your interests ahead of theirs. Setting this legality aside, you should demand that whomever you deal with puts your interests first and foremost.

13. *Contacts you regularly*—In the beginning stage of your relationship with your wealth advisor, the need to be in regular communication is high. Plans are being drawn up and implemented that require regular contact. Past this initial phase of a relationship, you and your advisor should maintain contact with one another on an as-needed basis or, at the very least, once a year. It is important for you to take the initiative and contact your wealth advisor, especially if a development occurs in your life such as a birth, a death, a divorce, retirement or relocation that could have a material impact on your wealth management plan.

14. *Communicates*—Your advisor should possess communication skills that allow you to understand what he is saying. Effective communication, using simple down-to-earth terms, is a must. Frequent communication whether through the mail, over the phone, in face-to-face meetings, and invitations to seminars are characteristics of a good wealth advisor.[14]

15. *Has experience*—Experience counts. Ask your wealth advisor how long he or she has been in the business and what types of companies they have worked for and for how long? You want someone with broad experience and job stability. Hopping around from firm to firm is generally a bad sign, reflecting the inability of that individual to hold a steady job.

16. *Is a team player*—Some advisor teams are made up of an advisor and their assistant. Others are composed of multiple professionals, each specializing in an area of the industry. In either case, what matters is the level and scope of service you are provided and the continuity of meeting your needs should a team member leaves. The industry as a

whole is witnessing the emergence of teams either vertical, where one member is the dominant individual, or horizontal, where members of the team share, often unequally, in the responsibilities and the revenues. Your wealth advisor, whether part of a team or not, should be able to work closely with professionals outside the practice such as attorneys, insurance agents, or tax specialists.

17. *Mirrors your style and approach*—If you like to trade, you might best be served by an advisor who actively trades and makes recommendations of individual stocks or bonds to clients. Realize, however, that this advisor is more of a broker or an investment advisor, rather than a wealth advisor. This style and approach, however, are waning as more advisors are taking a holistic path to financial planning and wealth advising. Nevertheless, it is important to work with an advisor with whom you share a compatible approach.

18. *Caters to a defined client segment*—In order to better serve their clients, some wealth advisors specialize in catering to one or two types of clients. This particular client segmentation could provide exceptional value to clients. For example, some advisors focus on servicing the elderly, business people, physicians, lawyers, executives, and so on. An advisor who focuses on physicians tends to pay particular attention to these clients' concerns and needs—the common inability to focus on wealth management issues, the need to develop asset protection strategies because they tend to be sued frequently, their erratic time schedules and so on. If your advisor specializes in a particular segment of the market that is of relevance to you, take advantage of it, as your advisor is in an exceptional position to help you because of an awareness of your specific needs and concerns.

19. *Is ethical*—All financial firms have and maintain their own code of ethics and require their employees to adhere to both the letter and spirit of these codes. Additionally, most nationally recognized certifications require their recipients to adhere to their own, usually more stringent, ethical code of conduct that spells out their responsibilities and duties toward their clients and outlines the ethical standards that they would have to adhere to in order to qualify to receive and maintain these certifications. For example, a Certified Financial Planner or a Certified Investment Management Analyst (recipients of a CFP or a CIMA designation, respectively) has to adhere to these organizations' own codes of ethics and professional responsibility as a prerequisite to receiving those designations. Ultimately, however, the ethical standards of your wealth advisor become evident in the normal course of your relationship. And, the best of codes of ethics cannot substitute for the internal code of ethics that your advisor chooses to adhere to.

20. *Has a clean record*—Several government and professional regulatory organizations, such as the NASD, your state insurance and securities departments maintain records on the disciplinary history of financial planners and advisors. Ask what organizations your advisor is regulated by and contact these groups to conduct a background check. All registered financial advisors must be able to provide you with a disclosure from called Form ADV Part II, or the state equivalent of that form.[15]

21. *Discloses fees or commissions upfront*—Unless you volunteer your services to a nonprofit organization or a charity, you expect to be properly compensated. The same is to be expected of people providing you with services and products, including your wealth advisor. Like you, providers of either a service or a product expect and need to be compensated. Generally, financial advisors get paid either from fees or commissions. Some advisors are fee-only planners who will bill by the hour or set a flat fee for services rendered, such as devising a financial plan for you. Others collect a percentage of assets under management. By comparison, an advisor or broker working on commission will collect payment for each financial service he provides (such as buying a stock) or product he sells (such as annuities or life insurance). Some advisors generate their income from fees and commissions, depending on the nature of services or products offered. Fees and/or commissions are an issue in the absence of value. If you do not perceive that you are getting your money's worth in terms of services and/or products you are receiving, then fees and/or commissions become an issue. Otherwise, it is the fair price set and paid in the course of a normal transaction. Unquestionably, you have the right to know and agree to the fee or commission that you are expected to pay.

22. *Is discreet*—Your wealth advisor has to be discreet and has to maintain the confidentiality of all that goes on between the two of you. You should expect your business relationship and all the related details to remain confidential.

23. *Is trustworthy*—You have to have trust in your wealth advisor. No matter how talented, well educated, well seasoned your advisor might be, if you do not fully trust that your advisor will always do what is best for you, then you should seek a different advisor. Your ability to trust and have full confidence in your wealth advisor is a quality that should never be compromised.

24. *Shoots straight and admits to making a mistake*—You should respect a wealth advisor that disagrees with you and instills a healthy level of fear in you that puts in check your natural tendency to be greedy. You want an advisor who tells you that you are wrong and points out the negative consequences of an action that you are about to take. There is little value to "yes" advisors. Conversely, you want an advisor that tells

you that he made a mistake or miscalculated a recommendation. That is a sign of a confident advisor who looks after your interests and who deserves your business.

25. *Shows discipline as an investor*—You need a wealth advisor who is disciplined, adheres to the proper principles of investing (the subject of Chapter 2), does not attempt to time the market, and believes in diversification, asset allocation, rebalancing and dollar cost averaging. No one can control the movement or volatility of the market but you can temper both by adhering to and implementing the basic principles of proper investing.

These are most, but not all, of the qualities and qualifications that you should look for in your wealth advisor. If your advisor comes close to possessing these qualities, then you do not have a good advisor, you have a great advisor with exceptional qualities. Do not feel that you are stuck and have to compromise with your current advisor if you are dissatisfied. Demand and seek what you deserve.

Should You Have One or Multiple Wealth Advisors?

When it comes to investing, most individuals, especially affluent ones, tend to have multiple advisors and investment accounts at different firms. Investors do so out of the belief that that they are benefiting from the advice of professionals with varying experiences and different styles who also provide the client with access to their respective firms and their proprietary products. On the surface of it, having access to multiple advisors seems logical and potentially beneficial. In reality, the perceived benefits are outweighed by the following risks and pitfalls:

- *Lack of proper asset allocation*—If you have multiple advisors, how often do you examine the asset allocation of your consolidated portfolio? The common answer is rarely, if ever. In fact, investors tend to hide the fact that they have other advisors, lest they offend one of them. The tendency would be to examine the separate holdings that you have with each advisor without regard to your holdings with the other advisors. Not surprisingly, when reviewing the allocation of their entire investments, many clients are shocked to discover the duplicity and frequent contradictory actions taken by each of their advisors. Clients who conduct these reviews discover that their overall asset allocation has drifted over time and is usually no longer appropriate in meeting their individual objectives.

- *Diversification/concentrations*—If you or your advisors like a certain sector of the market, let us say technology or natural resources, you could end up with highly concentrated positions that adversely affect your consolidated portfolio should the markets turn sour on these sectors. With multiple advisors and, if no one advisor has access to the big picture, you run the risk of ending up with a highly concentrated portfolio that is no longer properly diversified.
- *Tax efficiency*—Unless money managers state that their goal is to manage a tax-efficient portfolio, they will invest and trade to generate an absolute return with little regard to the after-tax performance of their portfolio. Therefore, turnover could be high and mostly made up of short-term capital gains. This, in turn, will generate taxes at ordinary income rates as opposed to the much lower long-term capital gains. Any after-tax gains could be significantly diminished by the inefficient and frequent trading of the money manager. If you have multiple advisors and none of them is coordinating the tax efficiency of your consolidated portfolio, you could end up with a tax inefficient portfolio.

From an investment perspective, having one advisor will insure that someone is structuring the asset allocation of your consolidated investment portfolio; monitoring the asset allocation of your consolidated portfolio; and properly correlating the investments, funds, and managers within your consolidated portfolio.

This discussion relates primarily to the dangers of having multiple investment advisors and accounts at various firms. Imagine what your wealth management plan would look like if you asked multiple wealth advisors to deal with separate pieces of your wealth management plan without coordination. You could potentially end up with an unstructured, overlapping, and most likely a counterproductive plan.

Concluding Remarks

Here is the bottom line. Find yourself one, and only one, wealth advisor who possesses those attributes that make an exceptional wealth advisor. You have been provided in this chapter with a list of 25 of those qualities and qualifications that you should seek in your advisor. Stick to that individual, and move forward. You either have the faith and confidence in that individual's character and qualifications, or you don't! If you don't, keep looking. Ask for referrals from your family, friends, and colleagues who are satisfied with the relationship they have with their advisors. Interview several advisors and select the one person you feel is the most qualified and with whom you feel comfortable and could have a long-term relationship.

Selecting a wealth advisor is one of the most important decisions that you can make in the process of creating, developing and implementing your wealth management plan. It is as important as selecting your primary care physician when it comes to meeting your health care needs. Your wealth advisor is your partner for life. He or she should be qualified to assist you in creating, growing, protecting and preserving your wealth; direct you in harvesting your potential wealth; help you transfer your wealth in the most tax-efficient way during your life and in a manner that fulfills your wishes and satisfies your concerns; and guide you in establishing and maintaining a wealth legacy to provide for your loved ones and those causes that are dear to your heart following your death.

If all of this seems a lot to expect of your wealth advisor, then discuss your expectations and goals and give them the chance to seek outside expert help. If he or she cannot do that much for you, find yourself a wealth advisor that can meet and, preferably, exceed your expectations. Keep in mind that a wealth advisor continues all along to work with your wealth management team—the estate planning attorney, the CPA or accountant, the trust officer, and the insurance specialist. It is not a one-person show, it is a team effort.

Final Comments

What can an author add after living in relative isolation a good portion of a year writing a book, spending years to research its contents, thinking and rethinking concepts and approaches, some of which are complicated even to the experts, attempting to communicate technical jargon into plain English, and yet be able to contribute a meaningful, useful, and human-friendly book? Thank God, I am done! It is time to take a break, go on a vacation (even a short one), and hope that the time and effort spent away from family, friends, and other life's enjoyments have produced a work of value to you, the reader, and contributed, even minimally, to the study of wealth management and, in turn, to the betterment of your quality of life and future financial and wealth security.

My hope is that this book on the basics of wealth management, despite its many pages and sometimes cumbersome charts, data, and analysis, conveys to you seven key messages:

1. *Wealth management is not just about investing.* Investing is only one aspect, and a critical one at that, of wealth management.
2. *Wealth management is not just for the wealthy.* It is for everyone. Whether wealth is measured by how much money you have, what assets you own—liquid or illiquid, investable or noninvestable—or whether you are a white-collar employee, a farmer, a businessman or entrepreneur, a manual laborer, an investor, or a professional such as a lawyer, engineer, or a physician, you need to be aware of the basics of wealth management. Even though some aspects might not apply specifically to your situation, there are still areas of wealth management, irrespective of your age or level of wealth, that are relevant to you and could help you in planning a secure future.
3. *Wealth management's utility and relevance varies from one person to the next.* It depends on your level of wealth, age, stage in life, profession, goals, values, risk tolerance, and time horizon. As a student, you need to manage your limited budget and not get carried away with the irresponsible use of those tempting credit cards that are being offered to you incessantly. As a wage earner, head of household,

a homemaker, a mother, an active member of the working class, in the midst of a thriving career, close to retirement or enjoying the fruits of your hard labor in your retirement, wealth management issues that face you at each stage of your life are different and vary in importance. There is no rule or a one-size-fits-all approach to wealth management.

4. *Wealth management begins with recognizing its need and usefulness.* Aside from adhering to the fundamental ingredients of a successful investment strategy (how your funds, stocks and stock options, bonds, cash and real assets are invested, diversified, and asset allocated), wealth management deals with the following:

- Estate planning issues—at the very least, you need to have a will and a trust.
- Learning to save and manage your debt (the earlier in life, the better).
- Planning for a comfortable retirement, given that the onus of retirement is now shifting from the employer to you the employee.
- Utilizing insurance to protect what you have and mitigate against catastrophic losses. You can also create wealth for your heirs through life insurance.
- Planning your gifting during your life and after your death in such a way that you maximize your gift values and you fulfill your wishes.
- Protecting your hard-earned assets, especially in an age where many lawsuits are frivolous and awards are extravagant.
- Ensuring that you pay your fair share of taxes (and not a penny more). Tax-saving strategies can help you keep more of your earnings and wealth.
- Selecting a wealth management team to help you navigate through the complex maze of issues and constantly shifting legal rules.

5. *Beware of your emotions—primarily fear, greed, and euphoria—as they are counterproductive to a sound investment strategy.* Develop an investment plan or an investment policy statement early in your life, and revisit it at least once a year.

6. *Plan for the unforeseen.* This might relate to your job, health, family dynamics and structure (divorces), and includes mitigating potential future disasters through the use of insurance—health, disability, long-term care, life, property, casualty, auto, and umbrella.

7. *Select a trusted group of experts as your wealth management team.* Do not make the common mistake of having multiple wealth advisors. Select one whom you trust and who understands your needs and goals, who is a qualified and experienced investment advisor, and who can manage the team of wealth management experts that you need—the estate planning lawyer, the trust advisor, the CPA or accountant, and the insurance expert.

To better secure your future and that of your family, become educated and demand more of your advisors. We live in an ever-changing world, and it is virtually impossible to succeed on your own (misplaced self-reliance), in juggling the responsibilities of work, a family life, potential health challenges, and other concerns while trying to single-handedly manage your finances and other wealth management issues.

It is my hope that this book will help you become more aware of the issues pertaining to wealth management and, as a result, inspire you to have the wisdom to seek expert help to enable you to meet your goals of financial security and understand the host of the increasingly complex wealth-related issues. Follow this advice so that you may live comfortably, raise and educate your children, retire with dignity, save early to have sufficient assets to meet the needs of your longer years in retirement, and care for your health and for those whom you love and cherish.

This is not the last book that will address wealth management issues. It is, however, an attempt to identify, in one place and under one title, the basic issues of wealth management, especially in these critical and turbulent times in the financial history of this country. Although the basic framework of wealth management will not change any time in the foreseeable future, many specifics and details will. Wealth management rules are dictated, to a large extent, by the continually changing state and federal laws that will invariably have a direct effect on your future wealth management plans. In turbulent times, as we have witnessed over the past two years or so, the need for a well-seasoned, confident, experienced and stable wealth advisor is even more pertinent. Your wealth advisor should help you navigate, along with the wealth management team that you have put together, through these stressful and tumultuous times. Rash mistakes in times of utter fear can cost you dearly for years to come.

If you have enjoyed and benefited from reading this book, pass it along to someone you care about. Better yet, keep it as a reference and a guide. And, next time you are invited to a friend's house for dinner, forget the bottle of wine or the cholesterol-laden chocolate cake! Gift them a copy of this book and help them build a more secure future from learning about the basics of wealth management.

Notes

Preface

1. "Americans are Getting Poorer, Says Fed Data," *Financial Times*, 7 March 2008, p. 1.
2. James Altucher, "Pick Stocks, Buy Houses, Don't Worry," *Financial Times*, 14 August 2007, p. 6.
3. Capgemini/Merrill Lynch, *World Wealth Report*, 2004, 2005, and 2006; *Learn About the Affluent,* CEG Worldwide LLC, p. 1.2; Russ Alan Prince and Hannah Shaw Grove; *Inside the Family Office Managing the Fortunes of the Exceptionally Wealthy*, 2004.
4. Daniel Thomas, "World's Rich Shrug off Credit Crunch and Swell to 8 Million," *Financial Times*, 21 April 2008, p. 6; based on the 2008 wealth report compiled by Citi Private Bank and Knight Frank.
5. Ibid.
6. "Interview with Robert Kiyosaki," author of *Rich Dad, Poor Dad*, by Charles Goyette, in *Local Icon*, 2007, p. 26.
7. Census Bureau, Investment News quoted in *By the Numbers*, 24 March 2008.
8. Russ Alan Prince and Richard J. Flynn. "Creating a Family Office Practice," *Financial Advisor Magazine*, 21 February 2008.
9. *Learn About the Affluent*, CEG Worldwide LLC, p. 1.1.
10. Russ Alan Prince and David A. Geracioti. *Cultivating the Middle-Class Millionaire, 2005* quoted in *The Future of the Business: Industry Trends and Advisor Responses*, CEG Worldwide LLC.
11. Ibid.
12. Ibid.
13. Merrill Lynch Investment Managers, 2001; quoted in the CEG Worldwide study.
14. More than 4 out of 10 clients with investable assets between $2.0 million and $6.0 million have, on average, three or more advisors. Source: Russ Alan Prince and David A. Geracioti. *Cultivating the Middle-Class Millionaire, 2005*.
15. Ibid.

16. Russ Alan Prince and Brett Van Bortel *The Millionaire's Advisor: High-Touch, High-Profit Relationship Strategies of Advisors to the Wealth*. New York: Institutional Investor, 2003; analyzed by CEG Worldwide.
17. *Learn About the Affluent*, CEG Worldwide LLC, p. 131.
18. Prince and Geracioti.
19. Ibid.
20. *Learn About the Affluent*, CEG Worldwide LLC.

Author's Note

1. "Daily Market Barometer," CSG Analyst Group, 10 October 2008.
2. "Bear," *By the Numbers*, Michael A. Higley (publisher), 13 October 2008.
3. John Authers, Chris Giles, and Neil Hume, "Market Crash Shakes World," *Financial Times*, 12 October 2008, p. 1.
4. "Decades," *By the Numbers*, Michael A. Higley (publisher), 13 October 2008.
5. Neil McLeisch, Head of European Credit Strategy, "GWMG Capital Markets Conference Call Recap," 10 October 2008.
6. James Politi and Grishna Guha, "Households Face 'Perfect Storm'," *Financial Times*, 10 October 2008, p. 6.
7. Chrystia Freeland, "US Facing Four Consequences of Lost Pensions," *Financial Times*, 13 October 2008, p. 4.
8. "Companies Cut Dividends by $22.5B," *Tomorrow's Headlines*, Dow Jones & Company, 3 October 2008, p. 3.
9. Russ Wiles, "Hard Times Making Retirement Harder," *Arizona Republic*, 5 October 2008, p. A6.
10. "Weekly Market Recap," *Market Insight Series*, 13 October 2008, p. 1.
11. "Bush Confirms Equity Buys, Moves to Stabilize Markets," *Dow Jones Tomorrow's News Today*, 14 October 2008, p. 1.
12. Ibid.
13. Pete Seeley, "This is the Real Thing," *Outlook*, 14 October 2008, p. 2.
14. John Authers, "The Short View," *Financial Times*, 15 October 2008, p. 17.
15. *Coping with the Bulls, Bears and Beyond*. Claymore Securities, Inc., 1 October 2008.

Chapter 1: Wealth Management: The Cornerstone of Your Future Security

1. *Practicing the Best Practices*. www.djnewswires.com, October 26, 2007.
2. Ibid.

3. Cannon Financial Institute has identified a similar, yet somewhat different set of wealth management issues. These include: investment issues, insurance issues, liability issues, qualified retirement plan/IRA issues, stock option issues, business succession plan issues, durable power of attorney issues, gifting to children/descendent issues, charitable gifting during life issues, titling of asset issues, executor/trustee issues, distribution of wealth at death issues, and charitable inclinations at death issues. Phil Buchannan, *13 Wealth Management Issues.* Audio S*eries;* www.cannonfinancial.com; accessed on 11 October 2008. With over 40 years of experience, Cannon Financial Institute is recognized as one of the leading providers of practical and relevant training for the financial services industry.
4. *Wealth Management*, www.cascade-inc.com; accessed on 13 March 2008.
5. Ibid.
6. Hannah Shaw Grove and Russ Allan Prince, "Private Wealth Management," *Financial Advisor*, April 2006, p. 48.

Chapter 2: The 15 Ingredients of a Successful Investment Strategy

1. **Disclaimer**: The information presented in this chapter is not intended to be a financial forecast of future events, a guarantee of future results, nor investment advice. This chapter—in fact, this entire book—may contain views and strategies that may not be suitable for all investors or individuals. Past performance is no guarantee of future results. Results may vary differ with changing market conditions.
2. The source data on the return series for the major asset classes can be found in Jerome Sigel, *Stocks for the Long Run*, 3rd edition. (Burr Ridge, IL: Irwin Professional Publishing, 2002.)
3. Ibid. The total returns after inflation on the broadest index of stocks available at the time. (Stocks-Real-Total Return Index: 1801–2006).
4. Ibid. The total returns on an index on U.S. government bonds after inflation. (Bonds-Real-Total Return Index: 1801–2006).
5. Ibid. Total returns on U.S. Treasury Bills after inflation. (Bills-Real-Accumulative Index: 1801–2006).
6. Ibid. This represents the value of one U.S. dollar of gold bullion after inflation. (Bills-Real-Accumulative Index: 1801–2006).
7. Ibid. This represents the purchasing power of one U.S. dollar (Money: 1801–2006).
8. Ibbotson Associates, Inc. *Large Capitalization Stock Returns* (reproduced in: *The Seven Deadly Sins of Investing*).

9. Even though stocks have historically outperformed bonds over the long term, over shorter periods, results can differ. In 1990 and 2002, for example, bonds actually outperformed stocks.

10. Dirk Hofschire, "2000s: A 'Lost Decade' for U.S. Stocks?," *Fidelity Investment*, July 31, 2008, pp. 1–3.

11. Anthony B. Davidow, *Asset Allocation and Manager Selection* (New York: Morgan Stanley, May 2007), p. 1.

12. "The Benefits of Diversification," Steven L. Mintz, Dana Dakin, and Thomas Willison. *Beyond Wall Street: The Art of Investing.* (Hoboken, NJ: John Wiley & Sons, 1998), p. 3.

13. Anthony B. Davidow, *Asset Allocation and Manager Selection*, p. 3.

14. *Diversification: A Look at Correlation* (New York: Investment Consulting Services, Morgan Stanley, November 1999), p. 3.

15. "Stay Invested...Think Diversification," Nuveen Investments, 14 February 2008.

16. *Act Like an Institution: Alternative Strategies*, Phoenix Investments, November 2007, p. 8.

17. "Correlated Markets Erode Diversification," *Tomorrow's News Today*, 28 February 2008, p. 4.

18. Ibid.

19. Shirley Abraham. *Did We Learn our Lesson During the Bear Market?* JP Morgan Fleming Asset Management, January 2004, p. 2.

20. *Portfolio Architect*, Morgan Stanley Funds, October 2004, p. 9. Please refer to source for all applicable disclaimers.

21. *Act Like an Institution: Alternative Strategies*, Phoenix Investment Partners, November 2007, p. 12.

22. **Hedge funds** are private investment vehicles restricted to certain qualified private and public institutional investors; **funds of funds** are a professionally managed portfolio of individual hedge funds or other alternative investments, potentially offering diversification across managers, strategies, styles and/or sectors; **managed futures** are commodity pools managed by professional Commodity Training Advisors (CTAs), that typically invest in futures, interbank currency forwards, options on futures and forwards; **private equity** is private direct investment in companies through single manager or fund of funds limited partnerships. These investments focus on long-term performance objectives; **real estate** is private investment in real estate through a passive investment vehicle (excluding exchange traded REITs); **real assets** is a sector-based private investments in individual ventures or commodities (including precious metals, oil and gas exploration, and timer properties); **exchange funds** are private placement vehicles enabling holders of concentrated single-stock positions to exchange

those stocks for a diversified portfolio. *Overview of Alternative Investments.* Morgan Stanley, July 2007, p. 4.

23. Ibid., p. 6.

24. *Act Like an Institution,* p. 11.

25. Ibid., p. 11.

26. "Introduction and Executive Summary," *Jones Private Equity Funds-of-Funds State of the Market.* www.fis.dowjones.com; accessed on 18 August 2008, pp. 6–9.

27. *2007 Yale Annual Report; 2007 Harvard Management Company Annual John Harvard Letter.*

28. *Phoenix Diversifier Pholio.* Phoenix Investment Partners, December 2007, p. 2. This more recent study shows that between 2006 and 2007, Yale University's exposure to alternatives increased to 70 percent while Harvard endowment's exposure to alternatives increased to 62 percent based on the *2007 Yale Endowment Annual Report* and the *2007 Harvard Management Company Annual John Harvard letter.*

29. *Portfolio Risk Management: Beta Aware Investing and the Role of Alternative Asset Classes and Investments in Client Portfolios.* Morgan Stanley, December 2007, p. 7.

30. Schroders Individual Investor Survey, "By the Numbers," *Investment News,* 23 July 2007.

31. Van Kampen Investments, "Van Kampen International Growth Fund Offers Clients a World of Possibilities," *The Beacon,* Summer 2007, p. 3.

32. *By the Numbers.* 1 October 2007: "Wall Street Journal and S&P." (*By the Numbers* is a one-page subscription-only private weekly publication that publishes bits of interesting data from various publications.)

33. Van Kampen Investments, "Van Kampen International Growth Fund Offers Clients a World of Possibilities," *The Beacon,* Summer 2007, p. 6; *World of Opportunity in International Funds, Changes in Advisor Usage in International Products, FRC, 2007.*

34. Pete Seeley, "Asset Allocation: Simple Points to Consider," *Income Outlook,* The MSIM Institute, Morgan Stanley, November 2006.

35. "Taking Advantage of Opportunities in Uncertain Economic Times," *The American College Connections,* March 2008, p. 1.

36. *Wall Street Journal* quoted in "By the Numbers," 31 March 2008.

37. Russ Wiles. "Foreign Investing Surges: Weak Dollar Sparked Rise in Trend," *Arizona Republic,* 28 October 2007, p. D 1.

38. *International ADR Strategy,* JP Morgan Asset Management, 1 Q 2007, p. 2.

39. Savita Iyer, "Over There: Advisors are Looking Overseas," *Investment Advisor,* August 2006, p. 78.

40. *Guide to the Markets*, JP Morgan Asset Management, 1Q 2008, p. 42.

41. Anthony Davidow. *The Road to Financial Success*. Consulting Services Group, Morgan Stanley, May 2007, p. 4.

42. As of 2008, only 153 of the 500 largest global companies are based in the United States. "Global 500–2008," www.cnnmoney.com; accessed on October 11, 2008.

43. "Overseas Investing Made Easy," *Tomorrow's News Today*, 17 January 2007, p. 4.

44. In engineering, 10 out of the 10 largest companies in the world are non-U.S. companies; in electronics, 9 out of the 10 largest are non-U.S., in auto manufacturing, 8 out of the largest are non-U.S., and in banking, 7 out of the 10 largest are non-U.S. "A New Look at International Investing," *Issues of interest*. Van Kampen Investments, August 2007, p. 3.

45. "International Stocks: Achieving Effective Diversification," *The Experienced Investor Series*, Neuberger Berman, February 2007.

46. Stefano Cavaglia, Christopher Brightman, and Michael Aked. "The Increasing Importance of Industry Factors," *Financial Analysts Journal*, September/October 2000.

47. "Overseas Investing Made Easy," *Tomorrow's News Today*, 17 January 2007, p. 4.

48. Jeremy Siegel, "The Future for Investors," Presentation to the Investment Management Consultants Association, Spring 2007, Phoenix, AZ.

49. Joshua Kennon, "Dollar Cost Averaging," www.about.com; accessed on 18 February 2008.

50. Maurice Suhre, "Dollar Cost and Value Averaging," *The Investment FAQ*, 11 December 1992.

51. John Waggoner, "Dollar-Cost Averaging's Not All It's Cracked Up to Be," *USA Today*, 13 July 2006.

52. Walter Updegrave, "Don't Buy into Dollar-Cost Averaging," CNN-Money.com, 5 February 2008.

53. Jack Piazza, "Rebalancing Your Portfolio," www.seninvest.com; accessed on 19 February 2008.

54. "Beginners' Guide to Asset Allocation, Diversification, and Rebalancing," U.S. Securities and Exchange Commission, www.sec.gov; accessed on 19 February 2008.

55. "Rebalance Portfolios More Frequently in Secular Bear Markets and Less Frequently in Bull Markets to Enhance Returns," www.CrestmontResearch.com.

56. *The Importance of Automatic Portfolio Rebalancing*. UBS, Global Asset Management, 2003.

57. *Build Your Future on Our Strengths*, www.munder.com; accessed on 11 October 2008.

58. In another study, the average annualized pension plan return was 12.9 percent, compared to 13.1 percent for the average stock fund, and 5.3 percent for the average equity fund investor between 1984 and 2000. Dalbar, Inc. and John C. Bogle; www.investmentctr.com and www.mercer.com/ic; accessed on 11 October 2008.

59. "What Is Your Biggest Investment Mistake?," *Arizona Republic*, 1 July 2007, p. D 7.

60. *By the Numbers*, 10 September 2007.

61. *The Seven Deadly Sins of Investing*, unpublished presentation by an unidentified author distributed during a seminar for investment advisors, 2007.

62. *Portfolio Architect*, Morgan Stanley Funds, 2004, p. 5.

63. Anthony B. Davidow. *The Road to Financial Success*. Morgan Stanley, May 2007, p. 2.

64. Ibid.

65. Merrill Lynch Investment Strategy quoted in *Arizona Republic*, 26 November 2006, p. D 6. The S&P 500 is used as an indicator of a diversified domestic portfolio.

66. S&P 500 Composite Index, with dividends reinvested. Market high and low dates based on the Dow Industrial Average. Past results are not predictive of future results.

67. "The Perils of Market Timing," *American Funds*, 2008.

68. BTN Research, quoted in *By the Numbers*, 31 March 2008.

69. Bloomberg and Morgan Stanley Investment Advisors, Inc. The stock market is represented by the S&P 500 Index.

70. BTN Research, quoted in *By the Numbers*, 1 October 2007.

71. *Market Update: Tracking the Correction*. Morgan Stanley Research, 5 August 2007, p. 3.

72. *Investment Strategy and Asset Allocation Commentary*. Morgan Stanley, 21 May 2007.

73. *The American President—Election Year Implications*. Morgan Stanley Research North America, 17 January 2008, p. 6.

74. Ibid.

75. Steve Shreve, "Five Investing Pitfalls to Avoid," www.investors.com; accessed on 26 February 2008.

76. *David Darst Investment Strategy and Asset Allocation Commentary*. Morgan Stanley, 30 July 2007, p. 4.

77. Shirley Abraham. *Did We Learn Our Lesson During the Bear Market? There is More than Just Performance*. JP Morgan Fleming Asset Management, January 2004, p. 8.

78. Ibid., p. 11.

79. Ibid., p. 16.

80. Ibid., p. 26.

81. Ibid., p. 31.

82. "The Nice Thing about Volatility," *Tomorrow's News Today*, 25 January 2008, p. 5.

83. Chris McKhann, "Introducing the VIX Options," *Investopedia*; accessed on 8 February 2008.

84. "The Nice Thing about Volatility," p. 5.

85. *Guide to the Markets*. JP Morgan Asset Management, 1 Q 2008, p. 41.

86. U.S. Department of Labor quoted in *By the Numbers*, 25 February 2008.

87. Mellon Analytical Solutions and Ibbotson quoted in *Build Your Future on Our Strengths*. Munder Capital, August 2007, p. 2.

88. "The Mathematics of Investing," www.ameriprise.com; accessed on 25 February 2008.

89. Ibid.

90. Russ Wiles, "Clues Found in PBGC's Asset Allocation Policy," *Arizona Republic*, 24 February 2008, p. D 7.

91. "Ending Value of $100,000 Invested in Three Combinations of Taxable and Tax-Deferred Accounts," *Tax Burden*. MSIM, Morgan Stanley, December 2003. The data assume reinvestment of all income and do not account for taxes or transaction fees.

92. "International REITs—A Great Diversification Opportunity," www.investorsolutions.com; accessed on 26 February 2008.

93. "Small Reward for Money-Market Instruments," *Tomorrow's News Today*, 11 February 2008, p. 4.

94. www.isda.org; accessed on 3 March 2008.

95. www.finpipe.com; accessed on 3 March 2008.

96. "Derivatives as an Investment," www.finance.cch.com; accessed on 26 February 2008.

97. "Derivatives Time Bomb," www.investopedia.com; accessed on 3 March 2008.

98. *Act Like an Institution: Alternative Strategies*. Phoenix Investment Partners, November 2007, p. 21.

99. Pete Seeley. *Evaluating Alternatives to Conventional Stocks and Bonds*. The MSIM Institute, November 2007, p. 4.

100. Frank Armstrong. "The Best Investment You Will Ever Make," www.investorsolutions.com; accessed on 26 February 2008.

101. Investment Company Institute, March 2008.

102. An abbreviated, yet informative, guide on investment vehicles is Standard & Poor's *Guide to Money & Investing* by Virginia B. Morris and Kenneth M. Morris (New York: Lightbulb Press, 2007).

103. Robert J. Gordon. "Target Date Funds: Panacea or Hallucinogen," www.investorsolutions.com; accessed on 26 February 2008.

104. *The Importance of Understanding Equity Indexes*; www.iShares.com.

105. Virginia B. Morris and Kenneth M. Morris. "Constructing an Index," *S&P's Guide to Money & Investing* (New York: Lightbulb Press, 2007), p. 96.

106. *The Importance of Understanding Equity Indexes*; www.iShares.com.

107. "Index Funds Are a Smart Bet," www.sound-investing.com; accessed on 26 February 2008.

108. Ana Maria Martinetti-Katz. "Stripping the ETF," www.investorsolutions. com; accessed on 26 February 2008.

109. "ETFs Target Individual Investors," *Tomorrow's News Today*, 2 October 2007, p. 5.

110. "Active ETFs May Not Be Hit Overnight," *Tomorrow's News Today*, 5 March 2008, p. 4.

111. FT Reporters. "Surge in Volume of Exchange Traded Funds, *The Financial Times*, 1 June 2007, p. 22.

112. "Frequently Asked Questions about Unit Investment Trusts," www.ici. org; accessed on 2 March 2008.

113. "Managed Account Innovation," *Registered Rep.*, August 2006, p. 60.

114. Ibid.

115. A number of sources, including my own observations, were used for this section. Some of these sources include: "Common Investor Mistakes," *Financial Success*, August 2007, p. 3; "Investing Pitfalls," www. sound-investing.com; accessed on 26 February 2008; Ken Shreve, "Five Investing Pitfalls to Avoid, According to Investor's Business Daily," www.investors.com; accessed on 26 February 2008; and "5 Common Investment Mistakes," www.fineweb.com; accessed on 19 February 2008.

116. Ken Shreve, "Five Investing Pitfalls to Avoid, According to Investor's Business Daily," www.investors.com; accessed on 26 February 2008.

117. Ibid.

Chapter 3: Why Everyone Needs an Estate Plan

1. *Control Your Wealth: A Guide to Growing, Protecting and Transitioning Your Estate*. Morgan Stanley Trust, Jersey City, NJ, October 2001, p. 3.

2. *Why Need a Will*, Morgan Stanley Dean Witter Trust, Jersey City, NJ, October 1998, pp. 2–3.

3. Expenses include attorney's fees, executor's commissions, appraiser's fees, and court costs.

4. *Control Your Wealth: A Guide to Growing, Protecting and Transitioning Your Estate*. Morgan Stanley Trust, Jersey City, NJ, October 2001, p. 9.

5. *How to Keep Money in the Family—Planning to Minimize Estate Taxes and Maximize Family Protection*. Morgan Stanley Dean Witter Trust, Jersey City, NJ, July 2000, p. 17.

6. *MFS Heritage Planning News*. MFS Investments, Spring 2005, p. 2.

7. Chapter 6 will discuss in detail the uses and benefits of life insurance in the wealth management process.

8. This section is based on: *How to Keep Money in the Family*. Morgan Stanley Dean Witter Trust, Jersey City, NJ, July 2000, pp. 21–22.

9. The proceeds of your life insurance policy will be part of your estate unless you place the life insurance policy inside of an irrevocable life insurance trust (ILIT).

10. This information is based on an illustration provided by a major life insurance policy prepared on 8 August 2007.

Chapter 4: Learn to Save and Properly Manage Your Debt

1. Neale S. Godfrey, quoted in "Birds, Bees, Bucks: Parents, Lessons for Your Kids, Life," *Arizona Republic*, 30 September 2007, p. D 5.

2. "U.S. Consumer Bankruptcy Filings Up 40%," *Tomorrow's News Today*, 3 January 2008, p. 3.

3. Shira Boss, "Save, Save, Don't Splurge on a Piggy Bank, a Tin Can Will Do," *New York Times*, 1 September 2007, p. B 5.

4. Ibid.

5. Eileen Powell, "10% May Not Feather Your Nest," *Arizona Republic*, 8 July 2007, p. D 2.

6. Insurance Information Institute; www.iii.org; accessed on 8 August 2007.

7. "Consumer Credit Increased $12.2 Billion," *Tomorrow's News Today*, 5 October 2007, p. 2.

8. Christine Dugas, "Credit-Card Debtors Lose Traditional Refuge from Higher Interest," *USA Today,* reprinted in the *Arizona Republic*, 9 September 2007, p. D 7.

9. Ibid.

10. Ibid.

11. Ibid.

12. Federal Reserve, cited in *By the Numbers*, 27 August 2007.

13. Federal Reserve, cited in *By the Numbers*, 24 March 2008.

14. Federal Reserve, cited in *By the Numbers*, 27 August 2007.

15. AARP, cited in *By the Numbers*, 18 June 2007.

16. Prudential Financial, cited in the *Arizona Republic*, 28 October 2007, p. D 7.

17. Employee Benefit Research Institute, quoted in *By the Numbers*, September 2007.
18. Paul B. Brown. "The Cost of Living with Debt," *New York Times*, 1 September 2007, p. B 5.
19. Ibid.
20. The College Board, *Trends in Student Aid 2005*; fidelity.investments@ fmr.com; accessed on 10 August 2006.
21. Sandra Block, "Plan the Road to College," *USA Today*, reprinted in the *Arizona Republic*, 4 February 2007, p. 6.
22. ICI and College Savings Plan Network, December 2006; www.fidelity.com; accessed on 30 August 2006.
23. *By the Numbers*, 10 December 2007.
24. www.statefarm.com; accessed on 5 December 2007.
25. Eileen Alt Powell, "10% May Not Feather Your Nest," *Arizona Republic*, 8 July 2007, p. D 2.
26. Ibid.
27. Department of Labor cited in *By the Numbers*, July 2007.
28. *Hard-Frozen Defined Benefit Plans: Findings for 2003-2004 and Preliminary Findings for* 2005. Pension Benefit Guaranty Corporation, August 2008; www. pbgc.com; accessed on 12 October 2008.
29. IRS Publication 590 at www.irs.gov. See also Chapter 5 for additional information.
30. *Time to Stock Up in Retirement*, T. Rowe Price, Second Quarter 2005, p. 6.
31. Fidelity Research Institute, quoted in *By the Numbers*, July 2007.
32. *Newsweek,* cited in *By the Numbers*, 10 December 2007.
33. Chapter 5 will address in greater detail the issue of how to plan for retirement.
34. "America Tops 11 Countries in Retirement Savings—AXA's Global Retirement Scope Survey Reveal Americans Lead in Retirement Savings but Lag in Pension Security." Released on January 23, 2007; www.axa-equitable.com; accessed on 11 October 2007.
35. *2006 World Wealth Report Briefing*. Capgemini Consulting prepared for Morgan Stanley Global Wealth Management, 5 September 2006, p. 14.
36. *Giving USA*. 2007. Glenview, IL: Giving USA Foundation, 2008. In 2007, charitable giving in the United States increased to an estimated $306.39 billion, exceeding $300 billion for the first time in history, according to *Giving USA 2008*; www.givingusa.org; accessed on 11 October 2008.
37. "Boomers May Leave Heirs Little," *Tomorrow's News Today*, 5 December 2007, p. 5.
38. www.investopedia.com; accessed on 5 December 2007.

39. Calculations in this section are based on a Morgan Stanley publication titled, *How Much Do You Really Know About Retirement?* September 2007.
40. "What is the Latte Factor?" Source: Unknown. Seminar handout.
41. See Chapter 2 to understand the positive effect of dollar cost averaging on an investment account.
42. "Tax Deferral Can Mean More Money in Retirement," *American Legacy*, April 2006, p. 8.
43. **Disclaimer**: Investment in these plans is not FDIC-insured, nor are they deposits of or guaranteed by a bank or any other entity, so an individual may lose money. Review the applicable Program Disclosure Statements, which contain more information on investment options, risk factors, fees and expenses and possible tax consequences. Investors should read the Program Disclosure Statements carefully before investing.
44. **Disclaimer:** The writings herein and throughout the chapter and the book are written for informational and educational purposes only. They are not intended or written to be used, and they cannot be used by any taxpayer, for the purpose of avoiding penalties that may be imposed on the taxpayer under U.S. federal tax laws. Each taxpayer should seek advice based on the taxpayer's particular circumstances from an independent tax advisor.
45. Sandra Block, "Plan the Road to College," *USA TODAY*, reprinted in the *Arizona Republic*, 4 February 2007, p. 6.
46. "Educational Savings Plans and Loans," www.iii.com; Insurance Information Institute; accessed on 7 August 2007.
47. Ibid.
48. "Funding Your Child's College Education," www.statefarm.com; accessed on 5 December 2007.
49. "529 College Plan Choices Are All Over the Map," *USA Today*, 8 July 2002.
50. "Another Look at Section 529 Plans," *Financial Success*, July/August 2007, p. 3.
51. Qualified expenses include tuition, fees, books, supplies, room and board.
52. Russ Wiles. "College Plan May Offer Tax Break," *AZCentral.com*, 24 June 2007.
53. Chris Stack. "Understanding 529 Income, Gift & Estate Tax Benefits & Maximizing Their Value," Savingforcollege.com.
54. Ibid.
55. Contribution limits are based on the cost of higher education rather than family income; www.statefarm.com; accessed on 5 December 2007.

56. Ibid.
57. Ibid.
58. Sandra Block, "Plan the Road to College," *USA Today*, reprinted in the *Arizona Republic*, 4 February 2007, p. 6.
59. *Dream. Build. Achieve*, Higher Education 529 Fund, Van Kampen Investments, August 2004.
60. www.statefarm.com; accessed on 5 December 2007.
61. Ibid.
62. "New Legislation Makes 529 College Savings Plans Even More Attractive," OppenheimerFunds, 9 May 2008.
63. *Redefine Retirement: Your Retirement Plan Guide*. Nationwide, June 2007, p. 9.
64. "Finding Money to Save," *Financial Success*, May/June 2007.
65. *Tax Planning: 2007 and Beyond*. Morgan Stanley, December 2007.
66. www.statefarm.com; accessed on 5 December 2007.
67. "Enter the Tax Man," *Registered Rep.*, August 2006, p. 99.
68. Ibid.
69. "Using the Roth IRA to Save for College," www.fairmark.com; accessed on 10 December 2007.
70. *2008 IRA and Tax Planning Reference Guide*. OppenheimerFunds, January 30, 2008, p. 1.
71. "Spousal IRAs," www.smartmoney.com; accessed on 11 December 2007.
72. If you are buying these bonds for others, be mindful of the gifting limitations. Consult your tax advisor.
73. "How Savings Accounts Compare," *Arizona Republic*, 27 August 2006, p. D 5.
74. "Why Borrowing Is More Expensive than Saving," www.advisor.fidelity.com; accessed on 25 October 2007.
75. The results are based on a 7 percent rate of return with earnings compounded, and do not reflect the actual performance of any particular product or interest rate of any particular loan. The effect of taxes, fees, and expenses is not shown.
76. This loan assumes an 8.5 percent interest rate, which is the highest rate on a PLUS (Parent Loan for Undergraduate Education) loan that you, the parent, can take out for educational purposes.
77. www.fidelity.investments@fmr.com; accessed on 30 August 2007.
78. Andrew Johnson. "Scholarships, Loans Repay the Effort It Takes to Get Them," *The Arizona Republic*, 27 August 2006, p. D 4.
79. "What Is More Important?" *Financial Success*, July/August 2007.
80. These figures are for 2004 for households with individuals age 65 and older. Source: *An Update on Private Pensions*, August 2006.

81. "A Mortgage and Your Retirement," *Financial Success*, May/June 2007.
82. Ibid.
83. "The Cost of Living with Debt," *New York Times*, 1 September 2007, p. B 5.
84. Consult with your tax advisor on this and all tax-related issues.
85. *Market Insight Series*, JP Morgan Asset Management, 12 May 2008.
86. "The Cost of Living with Debt," *New York Times*, 1 September 2007, p. B 5.
87. Kristin Vorce. "How to Manage Store Credit Cards," reprinted in the *Arizona Republic*, 18 November 2007, p. D 7.
88. Christine Dugas. "Home Equity Loans Quickly Drying Up," *USA Today*, 9 September, 2007.
89. John Johnston, "Birds, Bees, Bucks: Parents, Lessons for your Kids, Life," *Arizona Republic*, 30 September 2007, p. D 5.
90. Ibid.
91. "Tips to Help College Students Manage their Money," www.iii.org; accessed on 7 September 2007.
92. Ibid.
93. Jilian Mincer, "Don't Forget Credit Score in Credit Crunch," *Dow Jones News Plus*, 21 September 2007.
94. Ibid.
95. Russ Wiles, "Knowledge of Financing Falls Short," *Arizona Republic*, May 11, 2008; accessed on 12 October 2008.
96. This section is based on Jilian Mincer's article, noted above.
97. Ibid.
98. Ibid.
99. Ibid.
100. David Horowitz, "Fighting Back Against ID Theft," *The Costco Connection*, January 2008, p. 13.
101. "Consumer Fraud and Identity Theft," www.iii.org [Insurance Information Institute]; accessed on 5 September 2007.
102. Ibid.
103. "Credit Risks for Young People," *The Costco Connection*, September 2007, p. 71.
104. Based on "New Hiring Law Spurs ID-Theft Fears," *Arizona Republic*, 19 August 2007, p. A 6.
105. Horowitz, p. 13.
106. "Household Net Worth Up 2.1%," *Tomorrow's News Today*, 17 September 2007, p. 3.
107. Russ Wiles, "Bailout's Success Riding on Housing Market," *Arizona Republic*, 5 October 2008, pp. 1 and 6.
108. "Real Estate, Gross and Net," *By the Numbers*, 26 November 2007.

Chapter 5: How to Plan for a Comfortable Retirement

1. http://www.agewave.com/media_files/demography.html.
2. IRS Publication 590 at www.irs.gov.
3. Thomas Rowley, "How to Be a Chief Retirement Officer" *Advisor Insights*, 2005, p. 131.
4. Rowley, p. 97.
5. John Waggoner, "4 Stages of Life to Begin Retirement Planning," *USA Today*; reprinted in the *Arizona Republic*, 7 August 2005.
6. Harris Interactive. *America Speaks Out on Retirement: 2007 Investor Research*.
7. *2004 Survey of Recent Retirees*, Prudential Financial, March 2004.
8. David Horowitz, *The Costco Connection*, August 2007, p. 11.
9. Employee Benefit Research Institute and Mathew Greenwald & Associates, Inc., *2006 Retirement Confidence Survey*.
10. "Entrepreneurship and the New Retiree," *The Financial Insider*, Volume XXVI, Number IV, p. 6.
11. CNNMoney.com, cited in *By The Numbers*, 6 August, 2007.
12. *By The Numbers*, 23 July 28, 2007.
13. Glenn Ruffenach and Kelly Greene, *The Wall Street Journal Complete Retirement Guidebook* (New York: Three Rivers Press 2007), pp. 120–122.
14. Ibid., p. 121. The Employee Benefit Research Institute found that 55 percent of retirees spent 100 percent or more in retirement while Aon Consulting and Georgia State University have found that the average retiree measured by an income of about $60,000 needs about 75 percent of that income after retiring.
15. Ibid., p. 122.
16. "*What Can You Expect from Social Security*," *OppenheimerFunds*, 27 February 2008, p. 2.
17. "Observer," *Journal of Financial Planning*, August 2006.
18. *Tax Rule for Retirement Distributions*, MFS Investment Management, December 2007.
19. *The Wall Street Journal Complete Retirement Guidebook*, p. 191.
20. Two great Web sites to estimate your life expectancy are: www.livingto100.com and www.eons.com—the eons.com will ask you to answer a list of questions before your life expectancy is calculated and even recommends easy steps to take to increase your life expectancy. The process takes no more than 10 minutes and is very informative.
21. *Time to Stock Up in Retirement*, T. Rowe Price, Second Quarter 2005, p. 4.
22. 2008 Guide to Social Security, 36th Edition. Louisville, KY; Mercer LLC, November 2007, p. 19.

23. "Savings Needed to Fund Health Insurance and Health Care Expenses in Retirement," Employee Benefit Research Institute Brief Issue Brief #295, July 2006; www.ebri.org; accessed on 12 October 2008.

24. Eight out of 10 of the 78 million baby boomers say that their retirement involves some kind of work, whether part-time or full-time. They plan to work past age 65 and many plan to work into their 70s. "Savings, Pensions and Work," www.aarp.org; accessed on 12 October 2008.

25. 79 percent of baby boomers expect to continue working far beyond the traditional retirement age. Anthony B. Davidow, *The New Retirement Age,* Morgan Stanley, Consulting Services Group, July 2007, p. 2.

26. Rowley, p. 89.

27. "Historical Poverty Tables—People," U.S. Census Bureau; www.census.gov; accessed on 12 October 2008.

28. "Sources of Retirement Income," U.S. Bureau of Labor Statistics www. bls.gov; accessed on 12 October 2008. 29. "Don't Underestimate the Value of Social Security Benefits," *Financial Success*, September/ October 2007, p. 4.

29. Ibid.

30. Ruffenach and Greene, p. 189.

31. The discussion in this section is based on Chapter 10, "Social Security and Medicare," in Glenn Ruffenach and Kelly Greene, *The Wall Street Journal Complete Retirement Guidebook* (New York: Three Rivers Press 2007), pp. 189-207.

32. 2008 Guide to Social Security, 36th Edition. Louisville, KY: Mercer LLC, November 2007. Benefit examples for workers with maximum earnings.

33. Consult your tax advisor on all tax related issues. For a hypothetical calculation and a demonstration of this benefit, see the *Complete Retirement Guidebook*, pp. 193–195.

34. Calculations by James Mahoney and Peter Carlson of Prudential Retirement reproduced in the *Complete Retirement Guidebook*, p. 195.

35. "Entrepreneurship and the New Retiree," *The Financial Insider*, Volume XXVI, Number IV, p. 6.

36. On April 12, 2000, President Bill Clinton signed into law the Senior Citizens' Freedom to Work Act of 2000. This legislation, made retroactive to January 1, 2000, repealed an earnings limitation on Social Security benefits for individuals ages 65 to 69.

37. *Complete Retirement Guidebook*, p. 198. To see current limits, go to www.irs.gov.

38. Social Security Administration cited in *By the Numbers*, 31 March 2008.

39. In a survey commissioned by U.S. Trust and entitled, "What the Wealthy Think: U.S. Trust Survey of Affluent Americans," June 2006, p. 11, 48% of those surveyed said that they were more concerned that Social Security will run out.

40. www.ssa.gov/history quoted in *What Can You Expect from Social Security*, OppenheimerFunds, 27 February 2008, p. 2.
41. Office of Management and Budget, cited in *By the Numbers*, 6 August 2007.
42. "The Changing Times of Social Security...," MetLife Brochure, July 2007.
43. David C. John, "Misleading the Public: How the Social Security Trust Fund Really Works," *Executive Memorandum*. The Heritage Foundation, September 2, 2004.
44. David Walker, "America Risks the Fate of the Roman Empire," *Financial Times*, 22 August 2007, p. 9.
45. "Treasury Spurs Social Security Talk," *Tomorrow's News Today*, 24 September 2007, p. 3.
46. www.ssa.gov/history, cited in *What Can You Expect from Social Security*, OppenheimerFunds, 27 February 2008, p. 2.
47. *By the Numbers*, 31 March 2008.
48. *Complete Retirement Guidebook*, p. 3.
49. Ibid., pp. 166–167.
50. *Tax Planning for Businesses Quickfinder Handbook*, 2005 edition (Fort Worth, TX: Quickfinder Handbooks), pp. 6–18.
51. *A Complete Library of Essential Financial Concepts* (Denver: Cannon Financial Institute, Kettley Publishing Company, 2005), p. 373.
52. Russ Wiles, "Financial Advice Now Comes with the Job," *The Arizona Republic*, 13 May 2007, p. D 2.
53. *By the Numbers*, 30 July 2007.
54. Wiles, "Financial Advice Now Comes with the Job," p. D 2.
55. Sandra Block, "Look before Rolling Over 401(k) Money," *USA Today*, reprinted in the *Arizona Republic*, 12 December 2006, p. D. 6.
56. *The Financial Advisor's 2007 Pocket Reference Guide*, Magic Financial Publications, p. 71.
57. For descriptions of these plans review: *The Financial Advisor's 2007 Pocket Reference Guide* and Cannon Financial Institute's *A Complete Library of Essential Financial Concepts*.
58. Ruffenach and Greene, p. 175.
59. *The Financial Advisor's 2007 Pocket Reference Guide*, p. 64.
60. Russ Wiles, "IRAs Remain Solid, But Underused, Investment," *Arizona Republic*, 29 January 2006, p. D 4.
61. *A Complete Library of Essential Financial Concepts*, p. 321.
62. *The Financial Advisor's 2007 Pocket Reference Guide*, p. 64.
63. Russ Wiles, "U.S. Loosens Rules on Roth IRAs," *Arizona Republic*, 1 April 2007, p. D 6.
64. Principal Financial Group cited in *By the Numbers*, August 2007.
65. "Observer," *Journal of Financial Planning*, April 2007.

66. Please review the earlier discussion in this chapter dealing with the impact of income from working on your Social Security benefits.

67. www.iii.org/individuals/annuities/basics; Insurance Information Institute; accessed on 12 October 2008.

68. "Who Should Buy Variable Annuities?" www.smartmoney.com; accessed on 12 October 2008.

69. Russ Wiles, "New State Law Shields Insurance, Annuities," *Arizona Republic*, 1 June 2004.

70. www.assetprotectionbook; accessed on 8 October 2008.

71. "Who Should Buy Variable Annuities?" www.smartmoney.com; accessed on 12 October 2008.

72. "What's Wrong with Variable Annuities," www.smartmoney.com/retirement/investing/, 5 August 2005.

73. Not all annuities guarantee income for life. Immediate annuities and those with lifetime income riders guarantee income for life.

74. An excellent source on this topic is John Hancock's publication, *10 Common IRA Mistakes,* Boston, MA: John Hancock Funds, LLC, January 2007. The discussion in this section is largely based on this publication.

75. Ruffenach and Greene, p. 175.

76. Adam and Ryan inherit $250,000 each and neither needs the money now. Adam takes full distribution immediately and pays $87,500 in taxes leaving him with $162,500. Over a 30-year period, assuming an annual return of 8 percent and with all gains being taxed the year they were earned at an effective rate of 20 percent, Adam's funds grow to $1,044,966. Ryan, on the other hand, decides to stretch the inherited IRA, pays taxes on the required minimum distributions (RMD), invests the RMD proceeds at the same 8 percent growth rate. Thirty years later, Ryan will have $871,863 in after-tax RMD proceeds and would still have $1,058,560 in the beneficiary IRA for a total of $1,930,423. This demonstrates the benefits of IRA stretching which allows for tax-deferred growth and delays as much as possible paying taxes on portions of the inherited IRA. *10 Common IRA Mistakes*, p. 6.

77. "Beneficiary Planning," http://advisor.fidelity.com; accessed on 10 August 2006.

78. Consult with your CPA or tax attorney on all tax-related issues.

79. John Hancock Retirement Plan Services, cited in *By the Numbers*, August 2007.

80. MFS Investment Management, cited in *By the Numbers*, September 2007.

81. Russ Wiles, "Pension Act May Be Boost for 401(k)s," *Arizona Republic*, 17 September 2006, p. D 6.

82. Refer to the discussion on asset allocation.

83. If you had $1 million invested 100 percent in the S&P 500 at the beginning of 1973 and you withdrew an inflation-adjusted $70,000 at the beginning of each year beginning in 1973, you would have run out of

money in 17 years. If, by comparison, you began your inflation-adjusted $70,000 a year at the beginning of 1982, you would have accumulated, after your annual withdrawals, $10.1 million by the end of 2006. This is largely due to the performance of the S&P 500 at the time of each withdrawal phase. This example highlights the importance of timing of withdrawals for retirees. These hypothetical calculations ignore the impact of taxes on the account, which are due upon withdrawal and is for illustrative purposes only. BTN Research, quoted in *By the Numbers*, 10 September 2007.

84. John Nersesian, "Consistency Matters," *New Frontier*, Nuveen Investments, 2 Q 2007, p. 3.

85. Zvi Bodie, "Wise Pension Strategy Up until Retirement," *Financial Times*, 7 April 10, 2008, p. 6.

Chapter 6: Why Insurance Is a Must in Your Wealth Management Plan

1. *American Families at Risk,* LIMRA (Life Insurance and Market Research Association) International, September 2007.

2. Ibid.

3. Ibid.

4. Ibid.

5. Ibid.

6. Hillary Chura, "Disability, the Insurance that Is Often Sadly Overlooked," *New York Times*, 30 June 2007, p. B 7.

7. Ibid.

8. Ibid.

9. Glenn Ruffenach and Kelly Greene, "Long-Term Care Strategies," *The Wall Street Journal Complete Retirement Guidebook*, p. 210.

10. "How Can I Insure Against Loss of Income," www.iii.org/individuals/disability/lossofincome/; accessed on 5 September 2007.

11. "Aging Costs," *Arizona Republic*, 28 January 2007, p. D 6.

12. "Aging Costs," p. D 6.

13. "Should I Buy Long-Term Care Insurance?" www.iii.org; accessed on 7 September 2007.

14. www.longtermcare.genworth.com; accessed on 17 September 2007.

15. "Aging Costs," p. D 6.

16. Insurance Information Institute, www.iii.org; accessed on 7 August 2007.

17. If you earn, for example, $30,000 a year or possess few if any assets, you may be hard pressed to find an insurance policy that would issue you a large life insurance policy with, say, $5 million in a death benefit. Most insurance companies need to have justification, credible reasons, and a financial statement to issue policies for $1 million or above.

18. "What Are the Types of Term Insurance Policies?" www.iii.org; accessed on 5 September 2007.
19. "What Are the Principal Types of Life Insurance?" www.iii.org; accessed on 5 September 2007.
20. *American Families at Risk.* Life Insurance Awareness Month, LIMRA International, September 2007.
21. "What Are the Principal Types of Life Insurance?"
22. "What Are the Different Types of Permanent Policies?"
23. "Insurance Planning," *2007 Pocket Reference Guide*, p. 25.
24. Chura, p. B 7.
25. www.iii.org/individuals/disability/; accessed on 5 September 2007.
26. Russ Wiles. "5 Financial Facts that could be New to You," *Arizona Republic*, 1 July 2007, p. D 7.
27. Chura, p. B 7.
28. Ibid.
29. www.axaonline.com; accessed on 10 November 2006.
30. www.iii.org/individuals/disability/; accessed on 5 September 2007.
31. Ibid.
32. Chura, p. B 7.
33. "Will I Need Long-Term Care?" www.iii.org/individuals/longtermcare/; accessed on 7 September 2007.
34. "How Much Does Long-Term Care Cost?" www.iii.org/individuals/longtermcare/; accessed on 7 September 2007.
35. "Long-Term Care Premiums on Rise," *Tomorrow's News Today*, 25 September 2007, p. 4.
36. You should inquire about your eligibility with the specialized government agency.
37. Hal Gaisford, personal interview, Genworth Financial, 17 September 2007.
38. "Should I Buy Long-Term Care Insurance?" www.iii.org/individuals/longtermcare/; accessed on 7 September 2007.
39. *The Financial Advisor's 2007 Pocket Reference Guide*, p. 30.
40. *Success Connections.* Genworth Life, October 2006, p. 1.
41. "What's the Best Age to Buy Long-Term Care Insurance?" www.iii.org; accessed on 7 August 2007.
42. "Aging Costs," p. D 6.
43. U.S. Department of Commerce and Bureau of Labor Statistics cited in: www.iii.org; accessed on 7 August 2007.
44. *The Financial Advisor's 2007 Pocket Reference Guide*, p. 30.
45. Glenn Thrush, "Clinton Plan: Require All to Sign Up for Insurance," *Newsday* reprinted in the *Arizona Republic*, 16 September 2007, p. A 4.
46. In 2007, health care costs represented 16 percent of U.S. gross domestic product, the highest level in the developed world. Francesco Guerrera,

"Intel Alert on U.S. 'Achilles Heel'," *Financial Times*, 28 September 2007, p. 19.

47. Robert Knight, "U.S. to Spend More on Health Benefits," *Financial Times*, 11 September 2007, p. 7.

48. Russ Wiles, "Who Needs Insurance?" *Arizona Republic*, 6 November 2005, p. D 1.

49. *The Financial Advisor's 2007 Pocket Reference Guide*, pp. 28–29.

50. "How Much Life Insurance Do I Need?" www.iii.org; accessed on 5 September 2007.

51. This is based on a quote from an actual illustration generated by a reputable U.S.-based life insurance company on 17 September 2007.

52. If the cumulative premiums paid during the first seven years (seven-year test) at any time exceed the total of the net level premiums for the same period then a policy becomes a Modified Endowment Contract. For example, if your annual premium is $1,000 a year and on year four, your total premiums exceeded $4,000, then your contract will become a Modified Endowment Contract. *A Complete Library of Essential Financial Concepts*, p. 230.

53. Policies classified as Modified Endowment Contracts (MEC), may be subject to tax when a loan or withdrawal is made, and a federal tax penalty of 10 percent may also apply if the loan or withdrawal is taken prior to age $59^{1}/_{2}$.

54. A buy-sell arrangement is an agreement in which one party agrees to buy, and the other agrees to sell, business interest in the case of disability, retirement or death.

55. Roy M. Adams, *21st Century Estate Planning: Practical Applications* (New York: Cannon Financial Institute, 2005), p. 330.

56. *Planning Strategies at a Glance*, John Hancock Life Insurance, May 2007, p. 17.

57. *Nationwide Long-Term Care Rider*, Nationwide Insurance, 2005, p. 7.

58. Steve J. Moore, Highland Capital Brokerage, e-mail sent on October 7, 2008.

59. You will receive long-term care benefits if your doctor certifies that: (a) you have a cognitive impairment including Alzheimer's or dementia; or (b) you are unable to perform two or more of the activities of daily living for a period of 90 days. These daily activities include: bathing, continence, dressing, eating, toileting, and transferring (moving into or out of a bed, chair or wheelchair). *Nationwide Long-Term Care Rider*, 2005, p. 6.

60. Ibid., p. 5.

61. **Disclaimer:** This information is provided for educational purposes. The information cannot be used or relied upon for the purpose of avoiding IRS penalties. The information is not intended to provide tax, accounting

or legal advice. As with all matters of a tax or a legal nature, you should consult your own tax or legal counsel for advice.

62. Steve J. Moore, Highland Capital Brokerage, interview, October 7, 2008 and November 25, 2008. On January 1, 2009, the IRS has adopted new mortality tables requiring life insurance companies to extend coverage beyond age 100. This effectively would make life insurance policy proceeds income-tax free beyond the old age limit of 100.

63. As with all tax-related issues, consult a tax qualified advisor to determine the adverse tax consequences, if any, resulting from a life policy continuing beyond age 100.

64. Outstanding loans will reduce the death benefit proceeds received by your beneficiaries and, both loans and withdrawals also reduce your policy's cash value and may be subject to fees and charges. Depending upon the performance of the investment choices within a variable universal life insurance policy, the account value for loans and withdrawals may be worth more or less than the original amount invested in the policy.

65. *The Tax Treatment of Life Insurance*, Hartford Insurance, 2006, p. 3.

66. Ibid.

67. Christopher R. Jarvis, David B. Mandell, Celia R. Clark, and Glenn M. Terrones. "Avoiding the 70% Retirement Plan Tax Trap," *Wealth Protection MD* (El Segundo, CA: Guardian Publishing LLC, 2004), p. 319.

68. Annuities do not receive a "stepped up basis" upon death, making them a much less attractive wealth transfer vehicle.

69. "American Families at Risk," LIMRA, Life Insurance Awareness Month, September 2007; www.limra.com; accessed on 12 October 2008.

70. "How Much Life Insurance Do I Need?" www.iii.org; accessed on 5 September 2007.

71. Ibid.

72. "Should I Buy Life Insurance on My Child's Life?" www.iii.org; accessed on 7 September 2007.

73. "Good Time to Get, Change Life Insurance," *Tomorrow's News Today*, Dow Jones, 13 June 2006, p. 4.

74. Russ Wiles, "Are You Paying Too Much? Let's Check," *Arizona Republic*, 8 July 2007, p. D 2.

75. Mark A. Teitelbaum, "Trust Owned Life Insurance: Is It An Accident Waiting to Happen?" *National Underwriter*, 17 May 2004, p. 41.

76. "American Families at Risk."

Chapter 7: How to Plan Your Gifting and Maximize Its Value

1. www.irs.gov; accessed on 11 October 2007.
2. *A Complete Library of Essential Financial Concepts*, p. 572.

3. www.360financialilliteracy.org; accessed on 11 October 2007.
4. Ibid.
5. Ibid.
6. **Disclaimer:** The information, discussion, and analysis in this chapter are intended to educate and better inform you about the basic provisions of the federal gift tax laws. This chapter is designed to help you take the most advantage of planning and maximizing your gifting strategies. The information herein is not a substitute for legal or accounting advice. There are numerous exceptions and conditions to some of the concepts discussed. Changes are continual in federal gift and estate tax laws and future changes cannot be predicted.
7. The general rule is that any gift is a taxable gift. However, the IRS allows for many exceptions to this rule. These exceptions are discussed in detail in this chapter. One of those exceptions is "gifts to a political organization for its use." www.irs.gov; accessed on 11 October 2007.
8. Adams, *21st Century Estate Planning*, p. 206.
9. "Transfers to Non-Citizen Spouses," *A Complete Library of Essential Financial Concepts*, Cannon Financial Institute, Kettley Publishing Company, 2005, p. 664.
10. Julius H. Giarmarco, "Estate Planning for Non-Citizen Spouses"; www.disinherit-irs.com; accessed on 8 October 2008, p. 1.
11. Adams, p. 206.
12. Ibid.
13. Adams, pp. 50–51.
14. Your taxable estate is your gross estate less allowable deductions. The allowable deductions include funeral expenses paid out of your estate, debts that you owed at the time of death, and the marital deduction (the value of your property that passes from your estate to your surviving spouse). www.irs.gov; accessed on 11 October 2007.
15. *The Financial Advisor's 2007 Reference Guide*, p. 17.
16. Adams, p. 36.
17. "Special Needs Trust," *A Complete Library of Essential Financial Concepts*, Cannon Financial Institute, Kettley Publishing Company, 2005, p. 615.
18. David B. Caruso. "Helmsley's Bequest to Dog Not So Unusual," *Arizona Republic*, 2 September 2007, p. A 17.
19. *Giving USA*, 2007. Glenview, IL: Giving USA Foundation, 2008.
20. "Charitable Giving Factoids," *Financial Advisor*, September 2007, p. 90.
21. Adams, p. 52.
22. *How to Keep Money in the Family*, Morgan Stanley Dean Witter Trust, Jersey City, New Jersey, July 2000, p. 15.
23. *A Complete Library of Essential Financial Concepts*, Cannon Financial Institute, Kettley Publishing Company, 2005, p. 606.

24. This annual exclusion amount was indexed for inflation after 1998 and, as a result, is $12,000 for 2006–2008. Adams, p. 46.
25. Adams, p. 168.
26. www.ctj.org; accessed on 11 October 2007.
27. *A Complete Library of Essential Financial Concepts*, Cannon Financial Institute, Kettley Publishing Company, 2005, p. 607, and Roy, p. 48.
28. Roy, p. 48.
29. *A Complete Library of Essential Financial Concepts*, Cannon Financial Institute, Kettley Publishing Company, 2005, p. 607.
30. Ibid. p. 563.
31. *The Financial Advisor's 2007 Reference Guide*, p. 17.
32. Some states impose also their own GST, and starting in 2004, the GST exemption is the same amount as the applicable exclusion amount for estate tax purposes. www.360financialliteracy.org; accessed on 11 October 2007.
33. The scenario is based on an actual client case.
34. Adams, p. 94.
35. Ibid., p. 169.
36. Ibid., p. 168.

Chapter 8: Asset Protection Strategies

1. **Disclaimer:** The information contained in this chapter is for general use, and while it is believed that all information is reliable and accurate, it is important to remember individual situations may be entirely different. The information provided is not written or intended as tax, legal, or financial advice and may not be relied on for purposes of avoiding any federal tax penalties. Individuals are encouraged to seek advice from their own tax, legal, or financial advisors. Neither the information presented nor any opinion expressed constitutes a representation by the author or a solicitation of the purchase or sale of any securities.
2. www.rjmintz.com/new-deep-pockets/; accessed on 12 October 2008.
3. "Litigation Trend—The Ability to Pay," The Asset Protection Law Center, www.rjmintz.com/ability-to-pay; accessed on 13 August 2007.
4. "The Litigation Explosion," The Asset Protection Law Center, www.rjmintz.com/ability-to-pay; accessed on 13 August 2007.
5. Ibid.
6. Jarvis, Mandell, Clark and Terrones, p. 37.
7. "Litigation Trend," The Asset Protection Law Center, www.rjmintz.com, accessed on 13 August 2007.

8. Ibid.
9. Ibid.
10. Ibid.
11. *Asset Protection Strategies: An Integral Part of Planning for Affluent Clients*, Nuveen Investments, November 2005, pp. 1–2.
12. Ibid. p. 3.
13. www.rjmintz.com/avoid-business-parternships.html; accessed on 13 August 2007.
14. Ibid.
15. Ibid.
16. Gabriel K. Heiser, "General Principles of Asset Protection," www.library.findlaw.com; accessed on 25 August 2005.
17. Jarvis et. al., p. 40.
18. "Asset Protection at a Glance," *The Financial Insider*, 2006, Volume XXVI, Number III, p. 8.
19. Ibid., p. 8.
20. In Arizona, for example, a new law passed in 2004, increasing the value of protection extended to home equity from $100,000 to $150,000. The same law also shielded the entire cash value of life insurance policies and annuity contracts from creditors if the owner or the beneficiaries are sued. Russ Wiles, "New State Law Shields Insurance, Annuities," *Arizona Republic*, 1 June 2004. Although the life insurance and annuity laws were subsequently modified, they still enjoy a favorable asset protection status.
21. You may look up your specific state's homestead exemption limits on www.homesteadexemption.org.
22. Ann Couch, CPA, Presentation titled, "Asset Protection for Medical Professionals," Scottsdale, Arizona, 2 November 2005.
23. Heiser, p. 2.
24. *Asset Protection Strategies: An Integral Part of Planning for Affluent Clients*, Nuveen Investments, November 2005, p. 5.
25. Ibid., p. 4.
26. Please note that the purchase of a home insurance policy does not cover you automatically against certain losses such as flooding, wind, rainfall, or other potential causes of loss. Your coverage is determined by the terms of the policy. You cannot assume that you are covered for any and all losses. This is a critical step in properly protecting one of your largest assets—your home. Read your policy carefully and amend it to provide you with the coverage that you seek.
27. Jarvis et. al., p. 67.
28. For a more detailed discussion on the subject of insurance, please review Chapter 6.

29. Jarvis et. al., p. 72.
30. www.rjmintz.com/life-insurance-trust; accessed on 13 August 2007.
31. Russ Wiles, "New State Law Shields Insurance, Annuities."
32. Bill Hogan, "Ken Lay's Nest Egg," 2 February 2002, www.motherjones. com/news/feature/2002/02/enron_insure.html.
33. John C. Vryhof. Personal interview. Phoenix, AZ, October 7, 2008.
34. This discussion is based on Jarvis, et. al., pp. 73–74.
35. Russ Wiles, "Preserve Wealth from Calamity," *Arizona Republic*, 14 October 2007, p. D 2.
36. www.rjmintz.com; accessed on 13 August 2007.
37. Ibid.
38. www.rjmintz.com/appch8.html; accessed on 13 August 2007.
39. For a more comprehensive discussion of the benefits of life insurance, including the irrevocable life insurance trust, please refer to Chapter 6.
40. www.rjmintz.com/appch8.html; accessed on 13 August 2007.
41. Heiser et. al., p. 3.
42. Jarvis et. al., p. 85.
43. Ibid., p. 85.
44. Mindy Fetterman, "Get Smart as You Plan to Bequeath Assets," *USA Today,* reprinted in *The Arizona Republic*, 26 August 2007, p. D 2.
45. *Asset Protection Strategies: An Integral Part of Planning for Affluent Clients*, p. 8.
46. McCabe O'Donnell, *The Estate Planner*, Phoenix, Arizona, January/February 2007, p. 4.
47. *Asset Protection Strategies: An Integral Part of Planning for Affluent Clients*, p. 9.
48. This section is based on an article by K. Gabriel Heiser, "General Principles of Asset Protection," www.library.findlaw.com; accessed on 25 August 2005.
49. Nick Ravo, "The Offshore Trust: A Shield Against Certain Swords," *New York Times,* 20 July 1997; and untitled article in the *Wall Street Journal*, 14 October 2003, p. D 1.
50. Tom Duncan, JD, "Individual Asset Protection Strategies," private presentation, Scottsdale, Arizona, 10 October 2006.
51. Jarvis et. al., p. 77.
52. In a recent case, the court set aside the protections of an LLC when the debtor was the sole or 100 percent owner of the interests of the LLC. Lawyers are no longer recommending single-owner LLCs and FLPs out of fear that this precedent might weaken the asset protection features of these vehicles. Jarvis et. al., p. 103.
53. Jarvis et. al., pp. 75–82.
54. Ibid., p. 78.
55. In Arizona, for example, up to $150,000 of a home's equity is protected, compared to unlimited protection for annuities, cash value life

insurance policies, retirement plans and IRAs. John C. Vryhof, JD, in a presentation entitled, "Asset Protection Strategies for Medical Professionals," Scottsdale, Arizona, 2 November 2005.

56. Ibid.

57. Note your state's regulated restrictions, if any, on asset protection limitations on your home equity, cash value life insurance, and annuities.

Chapter 9: Taxes and Tax-Saving Strategies

1. **Disclaimer**: The information, discussion, and analysis in this chapter are intended to educate and better inform you about types of taxes and tax-saving strategies. This chapter is designed to help you incorporate tax-saving strategies in your wealth management plan, as it is a critical component. The information herein is not a substitute for legal, tax, or accounting advice.

2. "America's Tax Freedom Day Arrives April 30 in 2007, Two Days Later than 2006," www.taxfoundation.org; accessed on 30 December 2007.

3. "History: Taxation Levels," www.wikipedia.org; accessed on 28 December 2007.

4. Ibid.

5. "History of the U.S. Tax System," U.S. Department of the Treasury, www.treas.gov; accessed on 28 December 2007.

6. Ibid.

7. Ibid.

8. Ibid.

9. Ibid.

10. Ibid.

11. John W. Ervin. *Major Tax Planning*. (Los Angeles: M. Bender, 1966), p. 1.

12. Adams. *21st Century Estate Planning*, p. 1.

13. *Historical Tables*: Budget of the United States Government Fiscal Year 2009; www.gpoaccess.gov; accessed on 12 October 2008.

14. Ibid.

15. www.investopedia.com; accessed on 30 December 2007.

16. "Top 1% Pay Greater Dollar Amount in Income Taxes to Federal Government than Bottom 90%," www.taxfoundation.org; accessed on 30 December 2007.

17. Ibid.

18. "Taxation," www.encarta-msn.com; accessed on 31 December 2007.

19. Ibid.

20. *Policy Brief*. Organization for Economic Co-operation and Development (OECD), October 2007, p. 3.

21. www.enarta.msn.com; accessed on 31 December 2007.

22. Rebecca Berlin. "What Are Payroll Taxes?" www.alllaw.com; accessed on 30 December 2007.

23. "Taxation."

24. www.wikipedia.org; accessed on 28 December 2007.

25. "Taxation."

26. *The Financial Advisor's 2007 Pocket Reference Guide*, p. 84.

27. *Tax Planning: 2007 and Beyond*, Morgan Stanley, November 2007, p. 2.

28. "Taxes on Capital Gains," www.aol.money.com; accessed on 31 December 2007.

29. *The Financial Advisor's 2007 Pocket Reference Guide*, p. 88.

30. Lisa Gray with Richard Joyner. *Alternative Minimum Tax: Its Impact on Investment Policy*, Investment Management Consultants' Association (IMCA), 2003, p. 4.

31. Ibid.

32. "House Passes AMT Relief," *Tomorrow's Headlines*. Dow Jones & Company, October 3, 2008, p. 2.

33. Kayleen Gordon, accountant, unpublished memorandum, December 2007.

34. A comprehensive discussion on gifting and estate taxes may be found in Chapter 7.

35. "Taxation."

36. Ibid.

37. For more information, you can long on www.taxadmin.org.

38. "Age for 'Kiddie Tax' Raised Again," *Financial Success*, January/February 2008, p. 2.

39. Paul B. Brown. "Honest, All Types Cheat on Taxes," *New York Times*, 15 April 2006.

40. Ibid.

41. "Taxation."

42. Ibid.

43. www.taxfoundation.org; accessed on 30 December 2007.

44. Ibbotson Associates, 1 March 2001. This calculation is based on a $10,000 investment in large company stocks, assuming a 28 percent marginal tax rate.

45. Howard Scott. "Getting the Most from Your After-Tax Dollars," *The Costco Connection*, February 2006, p. 15.

46. Lisa Gray with Richard Joyner, *Alternative Minimum Tax: Its Impact on Investment Policy*, IMCA, 2003, p. 9.

47. Center for Disease Control and the IRS, cited in *By the Numbers*, 10 September 2007.

48. *What the Wealthy Think: U.S. Trust Survey of Affluent Americans*, U.S. Trust, June 2006, p. 19.

49. AXA Financial cited in *By the Numbers*, September 2007.

50. Karen Hube. "A Boomer's Guide to Taxes," *Barron's*, 12 February 2007.

51. Ibid.

52. "Strategies for Wealthy Investors," www.advisor.fidelity.com; accessed on 25 October 2007.

53. If a donor dies within the five-year period, a portion of the transferred amount will be included in the donor's estate for estate tax purposes.

54. To qualify for the 0 percent capital gain rate, the minor child's income has to be $1,800 or less. For 2008, a minor child is defined as one who is 19 and younger or under 24 and, still a full-time student dependent on the parents. *Tax Planning: 2007 and Beyond*, Morgan Stanley, November 2007.

55. Ibid.

56. Ibid.

57. Ibid.

58. "Tax Planning for Major Life Events," *Financial Success*, January/February 2008, p. 3.

59. Jordan E. Goodman, "Taxes: How Do I Pay the Least Amount?" www.moneyanswers.com; accessed on 28 December 2007.

60. Russ Wiles, "It's Time to Get Real with Finances in 2008," *Arizona Republic*, 6 January 2008, p. D 5.

61. "Common Tax Credits," www.finance.yahoo.com; accessed on 13 January 2008.

62. Ann Couch, CPA. Personal interview. Scottsdale, AZ, October 9, 2008.

63. *The Financial Advisor's 2007 Pocket Reference Guide*, pp. 89–90.

64. Ann Couch, CPA. Personal interview. Scottsdale, AZ, October 9, 2008.

65. "Common Tax Credits," www.finance.yahoo.com; accessed on 13 January 2008.

66. State specific tax credits exist as well. For example, for the 2007 tax year, Arizona provided a dollar-for-dollar tax credit for contributions, up to $400 per married couple filing jointly and $200 per single filer, to support public schools; $1,000 for a married couple filing jointly or $500 for a single filer to support private school tuition; and $400 per married couple filing jointly or half of that for a single filer to support designated nonprofits and receive the "working poor tax credit." http://www.revenue.state.az.us/. Additionally, filers may also receive a federal tax deduction for these contributions. In other words, when you contribute to a designated nonprofit, say $500, you will receive your contribution back from the State of Arizona in the form of a tax credit and you may be able to get a tax deduction on your federal taxes.

67. Bill Bischoff, "Three Year-End Tax Strategies for 2007," www.smartmoney.com; accessed on 11 December 2007.

68. The Rehmann Group, "Tax Minimization Services," www.rehmann.com; accessed on 28 December 2007.
69. Kevin McCormally, "The 13 Most Overlooked Tax Deductions," www.kiplinger.com; December 2007.
70. Ibid.
71. For a comprehensive study on long-term tax strategies, refer to: *How to Pay Zero Taxes, 2005: Your Guide to Every Tax Break the IRS Allows* by Jeff A. Schnepper or William Perez, "Tax Planning: U.S.—Deductions & Credits," www.about.com.
72. Sandra Block, "Look Before Rolling Over 401(k) Money," *USA Today*, reprinted in the *Arizona Republic*, 10 December 2006, p. D 6.
73. George D. Lambert, "Rolling Over Company Stock: A Decision to Think Twice About," www.investopedia.com; 23 June 2005.
74. *Employer Stock Distributions and Net Unrealized Appreciation*, Morgan Stanley, April 2007, pp. 3–4.
75. Ibid., p. 3.
76. Russ Wiles, "401(k) Key to Obscure Tax Break," *Arizona Republic*, 28 May 2007, p. D 3.
77. *Tax Planning: 2007 and Beyond*, Morgan Stanley, November 2007.
78. Ibid.
79. "Bypassing the Capital Gains Tax with Charitable Remainder Trusts," www.assetlawyer.com; accessed on 28 December 2007.
80. Howard Scott, "Getting the Most from Your After-Tax Dollars," *The Costco Connection*, February 2006, p. 15.
81. *The Financial Advisor's 2007 Pocket Reference Guide*, p. 88.
82. www.finance.yahoo.com; accessed on 9 October 2008.
83. Scott, p. 15.
84. Ibid.
85. Ibid.
86. Ibid.
87. Brown, "Honest, All Types Cheat on Taxes."
88. "Minimizing Taxes," *Professional Planning Services for You & Your Family*, Sagemark Consulting, March 2003, p. 3.

Chapter 10: The Role and Qualities of an Exceptional Wealth Advisor

1. *RainMaker: Strategic Partnering with High-End Attorneys and CPAs To Create a Pipeline of Affluent Client Referrals—Keynote Summary*, Van Kampen Consulting, 2005, p. 2. According to the Financial Industry Regulatory Authority (FINRA), the largest nongovernment regulator for

all securities firms doing business in the United States, there are over 5,000 brokerage firms, about 171,000 branch offices and more than 672,000 registered securities representatives; www.finra.org.

2. "Stock Market Crash of 1987," www.money-zine.com; accessed on 18 August 2008.

3. Nick Murray. *The New Financial Advisor*, 2001, p. 2.

4. Reem Heakal, "What Was the Glass-Steagall Act?" 16 July 2003, www.investopedia.com

5. Adams, *21st Century Estate*, p. 718.

6. Ibid, pp. 718–719.

7. For a comprehensive discussion on investing, please review the chapter in the book titled *The 15 Ingredients of a Successful Investment Strategy*.

8. Interview with the author conducted with an ultra high-net worth client, 14 October 2007.

9. Please refer to Chapter 8 for a comprehensive review and a step-by-step plan to help you protect your wealth.

10. Adams, pp. 723–724.

11. Adams, p. 726.

12. *New Frontiers*, Nuveen Investments, 2Q 2006, p. 2.

13. Ruffenach and Greene, *The Wall Street Journal Complete Retirement Guidebook*, pp. 111–113.

14. Susan Hirshman, "Lessons from the Best: How Successful Wealth Managers Got That Way," *Investment Advisor*, August 2006, pp. 67–68.

15. You can use these Web sites to check on your advisor: www.nasaa.org (North American Securities Administrators Association); www.naic.org (National Association of Insurance Commissioners); www.nasd.com (National Association of Securities Dealers); www.finra.org (Financial Industry Regulatory Authority); and www.sec.gov (Securities and Exchange Commission).

About the Author

Bishara A. Bahbah, PhD, is a senior consultant at a major Wall Street firm. He is a Certified Wealth Management Analyst (CIMA®), a Certified Wealth Strategist (CWS™), and an international wealth specialist, as well as an estate planning consultant and a wealth advisor. Dr. Bahbah received his master's and PhD degrees from Harvard University's Graduate School of Arts and Sciences, on a full scholarship. He received his bachelor's degree from Brigham Young University in International Relations and graduated as a valedictorian nominee. He holds an advanced certificate in fund raising and management from George Washington University and attended classes at the University of Pennsylvania's Wharton School of Business and the University of Chicago's School of Business.

His career began as an editor-in-chief of a daily newspaper in Jerusalem. He then taught at Brigham Young University, where he was a visiting and subsequently an adjunct professor. He moved to Washington, D.C., in the 1980s, where he headed a nonprofit organization, became the editor-in-chief of a monthly magazine, and was one of the founders and the first director of a public policy think tank. In 1991, he was appointed as the associate director of Harvard's Institute for Social and Economic Policy in the Middle East and taught public policy at Harvard's Kennedy School of Government. He was recruited by the Estee Lauder family and became president and CEO of a privately held corporation, Television Development Partners.

His accomplishments have earned him the privilege of being listed since the late 1990s in *Who's Who in the World, Who's Who in the Media and Communications*, and *Who's Who in America*. In 1992, he was selected by Brigham Young University as one of ten alumni who were honored that year.

As a prolific author, his first book was published in 1986 by St. Martin's Press in New York. He has contributed chapters to several published books. He is currently a guest editorial writer for the *Arizona Republic*. His articles have appeared in numerous other publications, including: *The International Encyclopedia of Communications*, the *Journal of Communication*, the *World & I*, the *Chicago Tribune,* and the *Salt Lake Tribune*.

Dr. Bahbah has appeared on numerous radio and television shows, including: CNN News, C-Span, Fox News, Al-Jazeera Television, Canadian

Broadcasting Corporation (CBC) Newsworld TV, McNeil-Lehrer NewsHour, National Public Radio (NPR), Voice of America, ABC Radio Network, and Pacifica Radio Network. He has been interviewed and quoted by *Newsweek*, the *Wall Street Journal, UPI*, the *Jerusalem Post*, the *Los Angeles Times*, and *Defense & Diplomacy*.

Dr. Bahbah has spoken at a host of world-renowned institutions, including: The World Economic Forum, The World Affairs Council, The World Economic Development Congress, UNESCO, Columbia University, Georgetown University, The Brookings Institution, the U.S. State Department's Foreign Service Institute, the University of Southern California in Los Angeles (UCLA), and the U.S. Air Force Academy.

Besides research, writing, and public speaking, Dr. Bahbah is one of the founders and the former chairman of a children's charity. He serves on numerous boards of directors that promote humanitarian work, education, and tolerance.

He is the proud father of four children—Leila, As'ad, Jubran, and Remzi. His most important, yet most difficult, mission is to help nurture them into productive and responsible citizens.

Index